THE STRANGLED CRY

BY THE SAME AUTHOR

The Coming Struggle for Power
The Menace of Fascism
The Nature of Capitalist Crisis
The Theory and Practice of Socialism
What are we to do?
A Programme for Progress
A Faith to Fight for
Post D
Contemporary Capitalism
The End of Empire

The Strangled Cry
and other unparliamentary papers

JOHN STRACHEY

WILLIAM SLOANE ASSOCIATES
NEW YORK

D
415
.S75
1942

909.82
S894s

LIBRARY
FLORIDA STATE UNIVERSITY
TALLAHASSEE, FLORIDA

Copyright © 1962 by John Strachey

Two chapters of this book are reprinted from Mr Strachey's book,
Digging for Mrs Miller, copyright © 1941 by Random House, Inc.,
with their permission.

First Ops is reprinted by permission of *The New Yorker*
and is copyright © 1942 by The New Yorker Magazine, Inc.

All rights reserved
Printed in Great Britain

Library of Congress Catalog Card Number 62-16885

Contents

Preface

These papers are "unparliamentary" in the sense that they are, perhaps, too outspoken for a politician safely to have written. They are also "unparliamentary" in the sense that they have little direct connection with my duties as a British Member of Parliament.

They consist of those of my occasional writings which, as it seems to me, are worth republishing. I must thank the Editors of *Encounter*, of the *New Yorker*, the British Broadcasting Corporation, *The New Statesman and Nation*, and *Universities and Left Review* for permission to reprint. Three of the papers in Part II, Troopship, Digging for Mrs Miller and The Big Bomb appeared originally between covers but are now out of print. I thank Penguin Books, Victor Gollancz and Random House for permission to republish.

JOHN STRACHEY

Part I

The Strangled Cry

The Strangled Cry

A LITERATURE is neither the worse nor the better for being reactionary: that depends on what it is reacting against.

In this case, however, the reaction cuts deep. For the literature to be discussed is not only, and in the end not even principally, a reaction against the values of present-day Communism; it is also a reaction against five hundred years of rationalism and empiricism; against, in short, the enlightenment. That is its scandal, and its power.

The literature has exercised, and exercises, an immense influence. From one point of view it *is* the social and political literature of our day. It is voluminous; it appears in a score of languages; it ranges from books which on the surface have no connection with public affairs to works of overt political polemics. Indeed it has by now so formed the intellectual climate of the West that many people may regard the subject as closed. But to do so is still to suppose that what is at issue is merely a reaction against Communism. In fact what is at stake goes far deeper than that. I have chosen only four authors, and five books, as examples. So drastic a procedure may serve to emphasise those aspects of the literature with which alone I am competent to deal. Since I am by trade a politician those are its specifically political aspects.

Such an approach involves a paradox at the outset. For this is an anti-political literature: it turns away from the public towards the private life. How then can it be said to have specifically political features? But the rejection of politics is itself a political programme. To despair is also to act.

I. Europe

In the spring of 1941, I was serving as the Adjutant, or maid-of-all-work, of No. 87 Fighter Squadron of the Royal Air Force, at that time stationed near Bath. One day a pilot opened the door of the Mess and said, with disinterest, 'Someone to see the Adjutant.' There entered the rumpled, battle-dressed figure of Private Koestler of the Pioneer Corps, surely one of the oddest men ever to dig a British latrine.

He was a member of that unpardonably brilliant Hungarian emigration which has peopled the universities, the publishing houses, the laboratories, and the authors' societies of the West. Why this particular little country should have become, as it were, radioactive and have thrown off these stimulating, if irritant, human particles is unknown. But it did so. For what Europe as a whole is to the world, namely something small, intelligent, aggravating, and indispensable, Central Europe is to Europe. In turn, what Central Europe is to Europe, Hungary is to Central Europe: and finally, perhaps, what Hungary is to Central Europe, Arthur Koestler is to Hungary.

Since his emigration, Koestler has wandered round the world, trailing an aura of novels, equations, amours, alcohol, and quarrels. On the second time round, and after abandoning it on the first round in deep disgust, he has apparently re-settled in England. But he has not done so, we may be sure, because he has a high opinion of that country. It will be rather because he may have come to feel that just as Churchill characterised democracy as the 'worst system of government in the world, except the others' so England is the worst country in the world to live in, except the others.

In the spring of 1941, Koestler's reputation, already considerable, had just been made world-wide by the publication of *Darkness at Noon*. It will also be recalled that the situation of Britain was at that time unrelaxed. We met as humble members of the armed forces of the only considerable power which was still withstanding Hitler, who was then in uneasy alliance with Russia. Although *Darkness at Noon* had been published some months before, I had only just read it. It might have been supposed that I should have been, at that time, in a receptive mood for the main anti-Communist manifesto of the day. (In some respects the book is a manifesto rather than a novel.) But it was not so; I still had strong inhibitions to reading this kind of book about Russia.

'Even if I had read such books, I should not have believed them. I should probably have put them down without finishing them. I would have known that, in the war between Capitalism and Communism, books are weapons, and like all serviceable weapons, loaded . . . the fever with which I decided to read my first anti-Communist book. I mean fever quite literally; and furtiveness as if I was committing an unpardonable sin, as I was. For the fact that I had voluntarily opened the book could mean only one thing: I had begun to doubt.' (*Whittaker Chambers*)

There was an element of all that in it, even a year after a break with Communism. However, in the ample leisure which is such a feature of life in the armed services in war-time, during the long hours of sitting in the Adjutant's office at the airfield from which 87 Squadron operated, I had nerved myself to read the book. Though I had not liked it, it had made a stunning impression. At that time only one thing about the book mattered: was it true? Were things in Russia really like this?

But eighteen years do strange things to a book. To re-read *Darkness at Noon* today is to appreciate the seismic change in all our points of view. Nobody can today be in the least interested in whether the book is true or not: of course it is true. The murders, the tortures, the confessions, the starvation, all happened. Khrushchev has described them more authoritatively than Koestler. When it was published about twenty years ago, the book caused riots in Paris, broke friendships, split families, and was denounced by many people who were by no means Communists. Today no one is likely to feel particularly strongly about it. As an accusation the book has become beside the point. If it is to survive it must be for other qualities.

What then is left of Koestler's book, now that its main assertion has become a commonplace? A good deal is left as a matter of fact. This was the first book to begin to reveal the far-reaching consequences upon the mind and spirit of the West of the rejection of Communism. It revealed that Communism could not be rejected without re-emphasising just those aspects of life which had been least emphasised, and not only by Communism. And that might mean calling in question the whole rationalist tradition. The values which the book began to preach were subversive of much more than Communism. For these reasons the things which are left in it even now, when its main assertion is undisputed, are still highly important.

In the first place the book re-affirms defiantly those values which cluster round personal relations. There is, for example, the incident of 'Little Loewy'. Koestler here portrays a kind of Communist, half-vagabond half-saint, to be found in the Communist parties of the nineteen-twenties and thirties. These men and women really did give their lives, often with great simplicity, for Communism. Koestler makes 'Little Loewy' a gentle, intelligent hunchback from south Germany, who has had to fly his country after a theft of arms. He drifts about in France and Belgium, harried by the police, shunted backwards and forwards over the border, and rejected by the local Communist parties because he has had to get out of Germany without his party papers. (And then there is the incident of catching the cats, which readers of the book will hardly forget.) In the end, Loewy establishes himself in a Belgian port. He promptly starts a Communist party branch amongst the dockers and because he has a warm, selfless nature, makes it an outstanding success.

It is now the period of the Abyssinian War. It is the task of all Communist parties of Western Europe to boycott and blockade the Fascist aggressor, especially in respect of his most essential supply, namely oil. Little Loewy's dockers organise solidly against the handling of 'black' petrol destined for Italy. Then Rubashov, Koestler's composite Trotsky-Bukharin hero, is sent to Belgium to prepare them for the fact that five Russian tankers are approaching their port loaded with petrol for the Fascists. If now, he must inform them, Russia were to stop supplying, other countries would 'greedily spring into the breach'. Such a substitution 'would only hamper the development of Russian industry'. In short the blockade and boycott must be raised for the Russian petrol. The dockers' branch is split and destroyed. All that Little Loewy has accomplished is ruined. So he hangs himself.

'What are you telling me this for?' Rubashov asks, when Little Loewy tells him his life story. 'Because it is instructive,' Loewy answers. 'Because it is a typical example. . . . For years the best of us have been crushed in that way.' And that is true. Stalinism passed across the naked bodies of all that was best—and it was very good—in the Communist movement. It either physically wrecked or intellectually and morally degraded just those potential and actual saints of which any church militant has so absolute a need. They were like wild flowers growing in the wasteland of the national Communist parties. They gave that sharp impression of beauty-set-in-desolation that one sometimes got, in the war decade, from the willow herb as it waved upon the bomb sites in London. Some of them were destroyed dramatically like Little Loewy in Koestler's book. Others were merely dried up from within. They gradually became automata who had so many times overridden, in their perfect obedience, every natural instinct in them that they had ceased to be human beings at all: all were destroyed.

Koestler does not fail to ask why Communism thus stamped upon almost every spontaneous and natural expression of human personality. Why, in particular, did it destroy, or distort out of recognition, the very best and most attractive of its own, thus doing its cause enormous damage? It cannot have done so for the fun of the thing. There must have been a necessity which forced Communism to push the regimentation of its supporters (which, of course, every creed and every government must impose in some degree) to unprecedented lengths. The answer is simple. All this was done that Russia, the first socialist society in history, might be preserved. The humanity of all the best of the Communists was trampled out of them, in the supposed interests of the safety and preservation of Russia. Nor did this seem to the men and women involved to be an unworthy cause for which to be destroyed. Right through the period Russia remained the promised land of the revolution. Every detail of what was happening there—or of what was supposed to be happening there— every success and every officially admitted setback (for they knew no others) was the impassioned concern of the faithful. Koestler perfectly conveys this attitude to Russia in his description of how Little Loewy's Belgian dock workers question Rubashov about Russian conditions:

'They enquired about the development of production in the

light metal industry, like children asking the exact size of the grapes of Canaan.'

To such men and women the argument that literally everything was justified for the preservation of Russia, as the bastion of world socialism, appealed with compulsive force. For the sake of this, all the nightmarish qualities of the Stalinist period seemed indispensable to a truly believing Communist. *Darkness at Noon* does full justice to this argument. In general it is a formidable characteristic of this literature, that it puts the Communists' own case a great deal better than they have ever succeeded in putting it for themselves. There is no shirking of the ultimate issues at stake. These writers know, not merely with their minds but with their whole beings, the full force of the Communist world view, and they do not hesitate to express it.

In *Darkness at Noon* Gletkin, Rubashov's second interrogator, is the spokesman of Communist doctrine as it was in the nineteen-thirties. The Gletkin passages are the core of the book. They express adequately (and in 1940 this was new) the real Communist justification for what Stalin was doing. Gletkin induces Rubashov to sign his confession with this same argument that everything without exception must be sacrificed for the maintenance and security of 'the bastion':

' "You know what is at stake here," Gletkin went on. "For the first time in history, a revolution has not only conquered power but also kept it. We have made our country a bastion of the new era. It covers a sixth of the world and contains a tenth of the world's population."

' "The leader of the Party," Gletkin's voice went on, "had the wider perspective and more tenacious tactics. He realised that everything depended on surviving the period of world reaction and keeping the bastion. He had realised that it might last ten, perhaps twenty, perhaps fifty years, until the world was ripe for a fresh wave of revolution. Until then we stand alone. Until then we have only one duty: not to perish."

' ". . . Not to perish," sounded Gletkin's voice. "The bulwark must be held, at any price and with any sacrifice. The leader of the Party recognised this principle with unrivalled clear-sighted-ness, and has consistently applied it. The policy of the International had to be subordinated to our national policy. Whoever did not understand this necessity had to be destroyed. Whole sets of our best functionaries in Europe had to be physically liquidated. We did not recoil from crushing our own organisations abroad when the interests of the Bastion required it. We did not recoil from co-operation with the police of reactionary countries in order to suppress revolutionary movements which came at the wrong moment. We did not recoil from betraying our friends and compromising with our enemies in order to preserve the Bastion. That was the task which history had given us, the representatives of the victorious revolution. The short-sighted, the aesthetes, the moralists did not understand. But the leader of the Revolution understood that all depended on one thing: to be the better stayer." '

For a Communist in the nineteen-thirties who was seized of that argument, the local or temporary state of things in Russia seemed a matter of secondary importance. In front of everybody's eyes the Marxist prognosis of the development of a latter-day capitalism was apparently fulfilling itself. Outside Russia, it *was* becoming more and more impossible to use anything like the whole of the productive apparatus; unemployment *was* consequently becoming endemic; the misery of the wage-earners and peasants *was* ever-increasing; the violence, hysteria, and general irrationality of the governing classes of the main capitalisms *was* mounting; attempts at gradualist reform by social democratic methods *had* failed; finally, Fascism was being established not only in such peripheral countries as Italy and Spain, but also, and decisively, in Germany, one of the major, advanced capitalisms. It was above all this apparition of evil incarnate in the form of Fascism which gave the Communist argument power. For that argument taught that Fascism was no accidental catastrophe but the logical and inevitable consequence of 'capitalism-in-decay'. Nazi Germany, with its psychopathic propensity for both internal violence and external aggression, was seen as the exemplar which each and every capitalist society must soon imitate if such societies were left in existence. Fascism, the argument continued, was not the product of this or that national characteristic or circum-

B

stance, but was the form which all latter-day capitalisms must sooner rather than later assume. In general the capitalist world gave a convincing impression of having fallen into a pit of abomination from which there was no way out. How much did even the ugliest features of the new socialist society matter if it gave even the possibility of the re-building of civilisation upon a viable basis?

As a matter of fact Gletkin's arguments appealed very strongly, when once they were understood, to non-Communists also. I knew one man of first-rate powers, but without previous acquaintance with Communist doctrine, who as late as the nineteen-forties was definitely influenced in a *pro-Communist* direction by reading *Darkness at Noon*.

'But what *is* the answer to Gletkin?' he used to say. And the truth is that at that time there was no conclusive answer to Gletkin. If capitalist society had continued its many-sided decline into economic, social, cultural, and every other kind of decadence, then there would have been no proof that even Stalinist methods were unjustified in order to preserve a way out for mankind. All that could be said was that one was not prepared to accept those methods: to lie, cheat, murder, and in our case in Britain to betray one's country to Hitler, because there was no conclusive answer to an argument.

But now, of course, history itself has answered Gletkin, and has done so in two equally unexpected ways. In the first place, the apparently predestined curve of capitalist development has abruptly turned upwards again. The major capitalisms have unmistakably taken on a new lease of life. True they have had to undergo considerable changes in their social and economic structures in order to stage this revival. But it has been found that the job can apparently be done by means of measures which, relative to revolution, are very mild. By strengthening trade unionism here, by social security there, by government support for farm prices in the other place, and by a little Keynesian (or crypto-Keynesian) management all round (by, in short, the application of a now fairly well-tried list of household remedies), a new version of the old system can be made to work, not perfectly indeed, but surprisingly well, considering how human institutions do work. Fifteen years after the end of the Second World War, there are still no signs of the reappearance of those unmistakable symptoms of social decline which stigmatised capitalism twenty-five years ago. To allege that the American or the British wage-earners are now sinking into ever-increasing misery is merely funny. To deny the effectiveness, so far at least, of the democratic process in the key countries of the developed West today, is merely perverse. No one but a blind fanatic can possibly say that such societies as America, Britain, North-West Europe, or Japan, are today in obvious decline and offer no way of carrying on human civilisation.

Thus history's verdict on Russian Communism in its Stalinist form is not that all its outrages were too wicked to be borne; it is simply that they were unnecessary. It did not turn out to be the case that humanity had no other way out than this. Humanity is not confronted with the choice of going Communist or destroying civilisation. There are, it seems, a plurality of ways forward for human society, at the different stages of its development which have currently been reached in various parts of the world. Certainly Stalinist Communism is one of these ways; but it is neither the only nor an attractive way. No well-balanced man or woman is today likely to give it that absolute allegiance which it demands, and which it could often command a quarter of a century ago.

But that is only one side of history's answer to Gletkin. Its other answer has been given by the character of Russia's own development. And this is the more subtle answer. For it is not that Stalin's methods have led to disaster. On the contrary, the bastion has been preserved all right. What we now experience are the consequences not of the failure but of the success of Stalinist policy. Russian conditions have not become more nightmarish: they have become much better—and much more ordinary. The bastion, in the very process of being preserved, has become, simply, another country in the process of industrialisation. True, her industrialisation has been rapid. But it is even a myth that it has been uniquely rapid. It has been more rapid than Britain's but less rapid than Japan's, for instance. It is true that the peoples of all other countries as well as Russia went through, or are going through, agonies of one kind or another during the process of primary industrialisation. Russia's tortures during the Stalinist period can now be seen as merely one version of those agonies. But the fatal truth is that the end result, namely industrialised Russia as she emerges, turns out to be familiar. The Russia of the nineteen-sixties is no longer a torture-chamber: it is a fine country in many respects. It has some notable advantages over other industrialised countries: its economy appears to be more stable and to have a more sustained rate of growth; it has less difficulty in devoting a really adequate proportion of its national income to longer-term objectives such as higher education, instead of to television sets and motor cars. These may well prove to be formidable advantages. If we in the non-Communist part of the world do not pull our social socks up we shall have some very unpleasant surprises. Today, however, there is little danger of these Russian advantages being overlooked. On the contrary, after nearly half a century wasted in a denial that we had anything to learn from the Russian system, we are now in danger of being unnecessarily overawed by its achievements. For Russian society has notable disadvantages also. It still lacks many of the most elementary civil liberties and has not developed even a rudimentary democratic control over its government. Again, in external affairs Russia behaves very much like all other powerful countries. The suppression of the Hungarian revolution was perhaps no worse than other such suppressions by other imperial powers; but only the wilfully blind can suppose it to have been any better. The fact is that the torture-chambers were filled, the springs of objective truth defiled and the socialist vision debased, and all in order to carry through the process of primary industrialisation in just about the time (forty years) which it usually takes nowadays.

Koestler, in the well-known 'photograph passage', described the glory of the socialist vision of the founding fathers of the revolution:

'A picture appeared in his mind's eye, a big photograph in a wooden frame: the delegates to the first congress of the Party. They sat at a long wooden table, some with their elbows propped on it, others with their hands on their knees; bearded and earnest, they gazed into the photographer's lens. Above each head was a small circle, enclosing a number corresponding to a name printed underneath. All were solemn, only the old man who was presiding had a sly and amused look in his slit Tartar eyes. Rubashov sat second to his right, with his pince-nez on his nose. No. 1 sat somewhere at the lower end of the table, four-square and heavy. They looked like the meeting of a provincial town council, and were preparing the greatest revolution in human history. They were at that time a handful of men of an entirely new species: militant philosophers. They were as familiar with the prisons in the towns of Europe as commercial travellers with the hotels. They dreamed of power with the object of abolishing power; of ruling over the people to wean them from the habit of being ruled'.

What has the resultant great power, which behaves in so familiar a way, have to do with all that? Stalinism degraded that socialist vision of a truly human society, which really was—and is—'the hope of the world': and it did so merely in order to create one more modern, industrialised nation-state.

The means have been terrible, the result commonplace.

Twenty years ago both sides of this extraordinary double twist in historical development were still hidden. Both worlds were still in apparently mortal crisis. Everyone who understood still felt that they had to make a desperate choice between the horrible world of Stalin and what Chambers was to call, as late as 1950, 'the unsaveable society' of capitalism-in-decay. It is this which accounts for the characteristic shrillness of the literature of reaction. There is something hysterical, for example, about *Darkness at Noon*: everything is pushed not only as far, but a little farther, than it will go. But perhaps the book is none the worse for that: these were hysterical events in an hysterical period. The men who wrote these books regarded them as agonised, half-strangled outcries against an advancing, and almost certainly invincible tyranny. Their very manuscripts had, in many cases, to be smuggled out of reach of the agents of this or that dictatorship. Or their authors felt themselves to be, and often were, in danger of persecution or assassination.

In Koestler's case it was not the Russian dictatorship from which he was in physical danger, but the advancing Nazis. The book was written partly in Paris, and partly in a French concentration camp, in 1939 and 1940, and the manuscript had to be smuggled out by his devoted translator and collaborator, Daphne Hardy. The desperation in these books is not put on: it is justified by the times and by the predicaments of their authors. Moreover, what force the literature gains from the fact that it has been written by men who worked and fought in the great struggles of our time: by men who collided with events and were shattered by them, and then somehow or other, and to some extent, put themselves together again. 'Only a participant can be a profound observer,' said Trotsky. Of course we can hardly expect balanced, judicial verdicts from such men. Their own pasts stand in the way of that. 'His whole past was sore, and festered at every touch,' Koestler wrote, nominally of Rubashov. But at any rate their books are not chronicles of what they said to their mistresses and of what their mistresses said to them, a subject of more limited interest than is often supposed.

I recollect asking Koestler at that meeting in 1941 what he had meant by his title, *Darkness at Noon*. My mind was still so numb that the simple obvious meaning of an eclipse of human reason, just when the enlightenment should have reached its noontide, in the coming to power of the first government to be consciously based upon rationalism, had wholly escaped me. Far more remarkable, it had escaped the author himself. Koestler told me that the title had actually been thought of by Daphne Hardy and that he didn't quite know what it meant but that it seemed to have the right ring to it. Such are the clairvoyant powers of the unconscious of an author of high talent at a turning-point in history.

Darkness at Noon is the starting-point of the literature of reaction. The book reaches but does not develop what was to become the main theme of that literature, namely the retreat from rationalism. It is still mainly concerned with the intellectual and moral catastrophe to which Communism has led. For no one would have thought of the retreat from rationalism if they had not been stunned by the Communist catastrophe. But already the two themes are interlocked. A few minutes before his execution, Rubashov is made to reflect as follows:

'Rubashov stared through the bars of the window at the patch of blue above the machine-gun tower. Looking back over his past, it seemed to him now that for forty years he had been running amuck—the running amuck of pure reason. Perhaps it did not suit man to be completely freed from old bonds, from the steadying brakes of "Thou shalt not" and "Thou mayst not", and to be allowed to tear along straight towards the goal.

'What had he once written in his diary? "We have thrown overboard all conventions, our sole guiding principle is that of consequent logica; we are sailing without ethical ballast. . . ."

'Perhaps the heart of the evil lay there. Perhaps it did not suit mankind to sail without ballast. And perhaps reason alone was a defective compass, which led one on such a winding, twisted course that the goal finally disappeared in the mist. . . .

'Perhaps now would come the time of great darkness.'

Koestler was to develop the critique of contemporary rationalism in many of his subsequent books. But the theme may be pursued in the works of other writers also.

II. England

Arthur Koestler, if you meet him in the street, is Central Europe. George Orwell, walking down the road, was England—not, of course, the England of convention, of John Bull: just the contrary. He was one of the least bluff or hearty men who ever lived. He was another England: subtle, retired, but very sharp. He was the England of the major eccentrics, the major satirists. Lean and long of body, cadaverous, ravaged in face, with shining quixotic eyes, you might easily have taken him for one more English idealist crank. And so he nearly was. But in the end he became, for good and ill, far more than that. He was a major writer, and by means of his pen, he became one of the most effective men of his generation.

Animal Farm was his masterpiece. The contrast between it and

Darkness at Noon could hardly be greater. At first glance, you might think that Orwell's little book hardly merited serious consideration in the context of world tragedy. *Animal Farm* is called on the title page 'A Fairy Story'; and so it is. (I met some children the other day who were greatly enjoying it without the slightest idea of what it was about; they were enjoying it not otherwise than generations of children have enjoyed *Gulliver*.) The farm which the animals capture by their revolution is a real English farm, in real English country. The book is downright pretty! How can one compare this elegant fancy with the unrelenting *reportage* of *Darkness at Noon*? And yet a dismissal of Orwell would be hasty.

The most famous passage in the book touches a theme which was to preoccupy Orwell for the rest of his life. After the revolution the animals had written up the seven commandments of 'Animalism' upon the barn wall. The sixth was '*No animal shall kill any other animal*', and the seventh was '*All animals are equal*'. As time goes on, the animals notice, or half-notice, that some of these commandments don't look quite the same. For instance, after purges have begun the sixth commandment reads 'No animal shall kill any other animal without cause'. The words '*without cause*' had not been noticed before. Finally, the animals find that all the commandments have disappeared except the last, and that this now reads '*All animals are equal, but some animals are more equal than others*'.

Thus the subject which, together with physical torture, was to make Orwell hag-ridden for the rest of his life, had appeared. This is the theme of the falsification of the past. Orwell was obsessed with the conviction that in the last resort it was forgery, even more than violence, which could destroy human reason. Of course it must be forgery upon what the Communists call 'a world-historical scale'. But already, in 1945, when *Animal Farm* was published, Orwell had before him the elimination of Trotsky, the second figure of the Russian Revolution, from the historical record, almost as if he had never existed. Orwell was here reaching for what was to become his final conviction, namely that Communist rationalism, which sought to be rationalism pushed to its utmost conclusion, abruptly turned into its opposite of total irrationalism. He had had the hair-raising thought that an all-powerful government might have power over the past as well as over the present. If so, he was to show, human consciousness might be made to diverge permanently from objective reality into a land of subjective nightmare.

There is a sort of catch or trap set somewhere in the character of Orwell's type of Englishman. On the surface everything is easy and charming. The great English satirists write fables and fairy stories and the children love them. How can their fond countrymen compare such books with the furious polemics of continental political controversy? But look a little below the surface. A cold repugnance and despair is hidden in the pretty pages. After all the charm of Lilliput we encounter the Yahoos:

'. . . at three in the afternoon I got safe to my house at Rother-hithe. My wife and children received me with great surprise and joy, because they concluded me certainly dead; but I must freely confess the sight of them filled me only with hatred, disgust, and contempt . . . when I began to consider that by copulating with one of the Yahoo species I had become a parent of more, it struck me with the utmost shame, confusion, and horror. As soon as I entered the house my wife took me in her arms and kissed me; at which having not been used to the touch of that odious animal for so many years, I fell into a swoon for almost an hour.'

The great repugnance was in Orwell too. And before his death it was to find overt expression.

Orwell's second major political work was less perfect than *Animal Farm* just because it was so much more overt. Nevertheless *Nineteen Eighty-Four* is a formidable book and it has been immensely influential. Orwell lent his powerful, detailed, concrete imagination to the task of describing a nightmare, in order, if possible, which he very much doubted, to avert it. The result is the most intolerable of all the pessimistic, inverted, Utopias. The condition of England in *Nineteen Eighty-Four* has become, down to the minutest detail, everything which Orwell most abominated and which most terrified him.

The main theme of the book is thought-control in general and control over the past in particular. In this field the particularity of Orwell's imagination is remarkable. At the first level, thought-control is exercised by two-way television sets in every room, by means of which the 'Thought Police' can see and listen to, as well as, if they like, be seen by, every citizen at any time, day or night. At the next level the government is introducing a new language called 'Newspeak', the object of which is nothing less than to make it impossible to express thoughts unwelcome to the authorities. The substitution of 'Newspeak' for 'Oldspeak' (or present-day English) is designed to effect nothing less than the destruction of human reason by linguistic means. I do not know if any of the contemporary school of linguistic philosophers have made a study of Orwell in this respect. To the layman his *tour de force* of imagination is extremely effective, producing a genuine realisation of the extent to which, precisely, 'language, truth, and logic' are interdependent. A prime object of Newspeak is so drastically to cut down the vocabulary that the expression of heretical ideas, and with a few simple exceptions, ideas at all, becomes impossible.

'All words grouping themselves round the concepts of liberty and equality, for instance, were contained in the single word 'Crimethink', while all words grouping themselves round the concept of objectivity and rationalism were contained in the single word 'Oldthink'.'

The book has a detailed and learned linguistic Appendix on the problems presented by this enterprise. This Appendix is in many respects much more alarming than the melodrama of the latter part of the book. Moreover, more than the acquisition of the new language is required for the governors themselves, the members of the Inner Party. They must be provided with a philosophy. This need is met by *doublethink*, a philosophy based on a version of extreme subjectivism—indeed it is solipsism—which enables its practitioners sincerely to believe a proposition at one level and its opposite at a deeper level.

The horror of all this is focused for Winston Smith, Orwell's hero, in the party's procedure and apparatus for altering the past. When, for example, there is a 'diplomatic revolution', and Oceania, the dictatorship of which England (now called Airstrip One) is a part, changes sides in the permanent world war which is being waged, so that she is now fighting, say, Eurasia and is allied with Eastasia, the party at once blots out all record of the fact that up till then she has been fighting Eastasia and been allied to Eurasia. Any verbal allusion to or hint of the change is punished by instant death. Every file copy of every newspaper is suitably re-written and re-printed. Every record of every speech is amended. (Winston Smith is professionally employed by the Ministry of Truth on this quite skilled re-write job.) All other records are systematically destroyed by being dropped into great furnaces, down the 'memory holes' with which the Ministry is equipped. The same procedure is used when there is occasion to shoot leading members of the Inner Party; a new incriminating past, amply documented from contemporary records, is manufactured for them, and all record of their actual past is eliminated. Smith is especially fascinated and terrified by this past-control procedure. In the end, under torture, his 'Gletkin' (O'Brien) explains to him that to a man more adequately educated in *doublethink* than he is, the past really is altered. For all records, and in a little while all consciousness, of the old past are destroyed, and records and consciousness of a new past are provided. Therefore, as reality is wholly subjective, there is no problem. The party has power over the past also.

In *Nineteen Eighty-Four* the party has not yet achieved its objective of moulding human nature in a wholly suitable way. Members of the Outer Party are still subject to regrettable lapses, and a tense struggle by all means, from education, spying, torture, and shooting, has to be waged to keep them in line. Above all, personal private life has to be eliminated to the maximum possible extent.

Winston Smith, though in his thoughts alone, has begun to deviate. He knows that such deviations, even if they remain forever unspoken, must lead to his death under torture; but he cannot, or will not, wholly control his thoughts. His downfall is simple and natural. The girls of the Outer Party are subjected to an intensely puritanical education, designed to make them incapable of any pleasure in the sexual act. Marital intercourse is permitted, but only so long as it is joyless. It is known as 'our weekly party duty'; but all other sexual intercourse is punishable by death. Smith has noticed a girl who seems a particularly strident and horrible example of the 'party norm'. She screams particularly loudly in the 'hate periods', volunteers for even more of the party work than is necessary, and appears odiously athletic, puritanical, and conformist. To his dismay this girl seems to be eyeing him. Has she sensed his deviations? He keeps running across her, too often for it to be chance. She is probably an agent of the Thought Police. He thinks he is done for. Then she slips a scrap of paper into his hand. He cannot at once look at it.

'Whatever was written on the paper, it must have some kind of political meaning. So far as he could see there were two possibilities. One, much the more likely, was that the girl was an agent of the Thought Police, just as he had feared. He did not know why the Thought Police should choose to deliver their messages in such a fashion, but perhaps they had their reasons. The thing that was written on the paper might be a threat, a summons, an order to commit suicide, a trap of some description. But there was another, wilder possibility that kept raising its head, though he tried vainly to suppress it. This was, that the message did not come from the Thought Police at all, but from some kind of underground organisation.'

At the first safe moment, be unrolls the screwed-up paper. On it are written the three words:

I LOVE YOU

The rest of the book is largely concerned with the resultant love-affair between Smith and Julia, and the innate subversiveness of love is well displayed. Here is a private passion, uncontrolled and unregulated by the party, a passion strong enough to make people act independently and spontaneously. No wonder the party sees the necessity of stamping it out.

Julia turns out to be by no means a romantic revolutionary, nor yet an intellectual. She just wants some hearty sex, normally mingled with tender emotion. Somehow she has preserved her power of natural joy against the conditioning of the party. She has secretly copulated with quite a few Outer Party members already. She simply wants Winston Smith as her man. But it is precisely this assertion of the human norm which must lead, Orwell demonstrates (he never asserts), to revolt against the party norm. Winston and Julia begin, with infinite difficulty and circumspection, to create a secret private life for themselves. The preservation of Julia's sexual normality has led her to regard the whole party ideology as tosh. This is already intolerable because, though in Julia it does not even prompt her to any kind of action, yet in an intellectual like Winston Smith it leads directly to dreams of revolt.

So far *Nineteen Eighty-Four* is magnificently achieved. But from the moment when Winston and Julia are, inevitably, caught and their interrogation and torture begins, the book deteriorates. It is not, to be sure, that Orwell's powers of imagination fail. On the contrary, the fanatical ingenuity with which both intellectual and physical tortures are described cannot be exaggerated. But the fact is that the subject of physical torture, though it was clearly another of his obsessions, was not one with which Orwell was equipped to deal. He had never been tortured, any more than most of the rest of us have been. And those who have no personal experience of this matter may be presumed to know nothing whatever about it.

Be that as it may, Orwell's preoccupation with torture and terror gives his book the agonised and frenzied note—the note of the strangled cry—which characterises this literature as a whole. In Orwell's case alone the cause of his frenzy is largely subjective. Both Koestler and Pasternak's actual manuscripts had to be smuggled away from authorities disposed to suppress them. Their authors were in danger of their lives from those authorities. Chambers also wrote his book in an atmosphere of seething melodrama, of papers hidden in pumpkins, of the Communist underground, of FBI agents and the Hiss case. Orwell wrote *Nineteen Eighty-Four* in the relative stability of post-war Britain. What gives it its frenzy is probably that it is the work of a dying man: for when Orwell wrote it he was already in an advanced stage of tuberculosis.

The practical influence of *Nineteen Eighty-Four* (and it was appreciable) was, in Britain, reactionary in the narrow political sense of that term. Many of those who for one reason or another felt that their interests were threatened by the British Labour Government, which was in its period of office when the book was published, managed to persuade themselves that the British brand of democratic socialism was taking the country along the road to *Nineteen Eighty-Four*. That almost pedantically libertarian government (which, for instance, made it possible, for the first time in British history for a subject to sue the government) was solemnly arraigned as intending, or at any rate tending, to take us all into the Orwellian nightmare. But of course authors cannot be held responsible for the wilder distortions of their meaning which some readers will inevitably make. In fact it has been the fairly thorough overhaul of the British system, mainly (though by no means exclusively) carried out by the Labour Government, which has given a vigorous new lease of life to British democratic and libertarian institutions. This is an example of the tendency of this whole literature to damage the very forces which, by maintaining a tolerable social balance, can avert all that these writers so desperately, and so justly, fear.

On the central issue posed in these pages, namely the issue of the contemporary retreat from rationalism as a whole, *Nineteen Eighty-Four* is significant in another way. The European, the American, and even perhaps the Russian, authors whose works we are discussing, all consider, we shall find, that Communism is the culmination of the rationalist tradition. In this sense they consider that Communism *is* rationalism in its contemporary form. Hence when they depict what they consider to be the ghastly consequences of Communism and cry for its repudiation, they must perforce repudiate rationalism also. And to a varying degree this is what each of them does. Koestler considers that reason has run amuck: that now it must be limited by the 'Oceanic sense', which is his name for mystical experience. Chambers forthrightly declares that there is no alternative to Communism except an acceptance of the supernatural: that no one who does not accept one form or other of supernaturalism has really broken with Communism. Pasternak's message is, it is true, far more subtle. Nevertheless he devotes his masterpiece to showing

how little those sides of life which, he considers, can alone
be dealt with rationally, matter as compared with those deeper
elements in the human condition which can only be handled by
superrational methods.

Orwell, the Englishman, alone implies an opposite view. In
Nineteen Eighty-Four Communism itself, now indistinguishable
from Fascism, is depicted as patently irrational. It has lost almost
all touch with objective reality and pursues psychopathic social
objectives. Moreover, Orwell is here, of course, merely extra-
polating into the year 1984 those tendencies of Communism
which, he considered, were only too apparent in 1949. The
lesson of his book is *not* that the catastrophe which Communism
has suffered proves that reason carried to its logical conclusion
leads to horror; that consequently we must retreat from reason
into some form of mysticism or supernaturalism. On the contrary, what Orwell is saying is that the catastrophe of our times
occurred precisely because the Communists (and, of course, still
more the Fascists) deserted reason. He is saying that the Communists, without being aware of it, have lost touch with reality:
that their doctrine has become, precisely, a mysticism, an
authoritarian revelation.

Orwell nowhere argues all this. He nowhere makes it clear that
he is denouncing both Fascism and Communism from a rational
standpoint. It would not have occurred to him to do any such
thing. His rationalism is of the rough-and-ready, highly empirical,
English kind. He is undidactic, untheoretical. But nowhere,
equally, does he suggest the alternative of mysticism or supernaturalism. Indeed his whole satire, in both books, is directed to
demonstrating that once criticism has been suppressed, a society
must inevitably come to depend upon authority, revelation, and
mystery. His whole message is epigrammatically contained in his
famous aphorism that the original proposition that '*all animals
are equal*' will, in the absence of freedom to dissent, inevitably
receive the addendum '*but some animals are more equal than others*'.
In other words, without the liberty of prophesying, the subtleties
of the dialectic will degenerate into the obscenities of *doublethink*.
For him it is not that the Communists have discredited reason by
pushing it to its logical conclusion. On the contrary, it is that
they have betrayed reason by abandoning its living empirical

methodology for an unchanging revelation. His whole satire was an exposure of the consequences of pathological unreason. Therefore, though he did not say anything, or perhaps even think anything, about it, his books are at bottom a defence, all the more unquestioning for being tacit, of the assumptions of traditional English empiricism.

If Orwell had been a more systematic thinker he might perhaps have fused his brilliant linguistic insights with his general political outlook to form a social philosophy of a particularly concrete and applied character. He might have sorted out for us the question of why and how reason may at a certain point tumble over into 'rationalism', in the narrow, rigid, and dogmatic sense of that word: into a kind of 'rationalism' which is fully as authoritarian as the tenets of a revealed religion. He might have given social empiricism a firmer basis, and at the same time shown us how to do justice to those personal, aesthetic, and religious values about which we can as yet say so little—except that we can all now see that their neglect is fatal. I do not know whether, if he had lived, Orwell might have attempted something of the sort. This at least is the direction in which his work pointed.

The remainder of my essay is devoted to an American and a Russian who, in very different ways, have struggled with these issues.

III. America

Koestler's and Orwell's books were fictional in form but factual in content. Whittaker Chambers' autobiography, *Witness*, is factual in form but is often considered to be fictional in content. This accusation is not, however, in my opinion well-founded. Mr Chambers is a witness of truth: of truth as he sees it: of *his* truth. 'That is my truth,' said Zarathustra, 'now tell me yours.'

Again, Koestler and Orwell are two fastidious craftsmen in words, Chambers is a writer possessing major powers, but also capable of dreadful failures: of failures in taste, for example, so grave that many of his passages have the opposite effect from that intended. For this and other reasons, *Witness* is, in its own way, fully as intolerable a book as *Nineteen Eighty-Four*. Moreover it is no fantasy about imaginary events of the future but an *ex parte* account of the most disastrous political trial in the history of America; of a trial which almost ruined American liberalism for a whole decade. As such it evoked (and evokes) a passionate resistance which no work of fiction could encounter. Indeed I have hardly met an American liberal who was not outraged by the mere suggestion that this was a major work which it was impossible to ignore. Those few who do not regard it as too vile to read, point out the extraordinary atmosphere of lurid melodrama which pervades it: they excoriate its rhetoric, its bombast, its hysteria, and its sentimentality. Above all they dismiss it as the work of that most odious of men, an informer.

But melodrama, rhetoric, bombast, and sentimentality are by no means fatal defects in a book. If they were we should have to exclude from the canon half the major works of English literature from the Elizabethans to Dickens. If there is enough else in a book these defects have always been forgiven, as the near inevitable failures of a man who was at least attempting to scale the heights. Let us come at once to the final accusation, that anyhow this is the work of an informer, to be denounced on that score alone. For the very fact that it is the work of an informer is, in truth, one of the main reasons for placing *Witness* amongst the formative books of our time.

The question of whether or not an informer must be for ever a moral Ishmael has poignancy in contemporary America. For the McCarthyite persecutions (mild as they were by twentieth-century standards) were bad enough to fix a horror of informing in the minds of all those American liberals, and they were very numerous, who had passed, to a greater or lesser degree, through the Communist experience. Men and women who have had no sympathy for Communism for many years are still outraged by those who, under the pressure of the Committee for Un-American Activities, informed on their friends, thus often ruining their careers. The refusal to inform was, and still is, their test of decency. Their especial hatred is reserved for Chambers who, by initiating the Hiss case, both ruined many lives and played an important part in American liberalism's ejection from office and power. Chambers is well aware of the consequences to himself of what he has done. He has several passages on informing which

C

exhibit both the force and melodrama of his writing. One of them reads:

'There is in men a very deep-rooted instinct that they may not inform against those whose kindness and affection they had shared, at whose tables they have eaten and under whose roofs they have slept, whose wives and children they have known as friends—and that regardless of who those others are or of what crimes they have committed. It is an absolute prohibition. It is written in no book, but it is more binding than any code that exists. If of necessity a man must violate that prohibition, and it is part of the tragedy of history that, for the greater good, men sometimes must, the man who violates it must do so in the full consciousness that there is a penalty. That penalty is a kind of death, most deadly if a man must go on living. It is not violent. It is not even a deepening shadow. It is a simple loss of something as when a filter removes all colour from the light. I felt its foretouch. It was soon to be on me.'

It is an agonising issue. On the one hand there can be no doubt that the consequences of Chambers' denunciations were disastrous for the political and social life of America. For the effects of such denunciations were to spread far beyond the eradication of Communists from the actual government service, into a witch-hunt conducted against everyone holding radical opinions even if they occupied entirely non-governmental positions. It was imperative to fight the witch-hunters. And those American liberals who courageously refused to give the names of men and women in private life who were suspected of sympathy with Communism, or who had been, or even perhaps still were, Communists, were fully justified.

But what Chambers felt that he had to do was something different. He was concerned with men who were in high positions in the actual administrative apparatus of the government. He considered it his duty to inform, first privately, and then, when no attention was paid to that, publicly, upon these men. Was he or was he not right to do so? What was at stake was not really the supposed necessity of stopping the transmission of government secrets. Anyone who has had access to Cabinet papers knows that it is only an exaggeration to say that, except in periods of actual war, there are no such things as government secrets. It was much more a question of the unforeseeable consequences of leaving in policy-forming positions men whose motives and purposes—all the more formidable when they are quite free from considerations of personal gain—were to serve not their own government but another government. The answer even to this second question is not necessarily obvious, however. Looking back we may conclude that it would not have made all that difference if Hiss, White, and the others had remained in the American government service. The influence of Communism in America (once appreciable) was in such rapid decline that they would probably have been impotent. Any residual harm they might have done in American policy-making would probably have been much less extensive than was the damage to the fabric of American society which the consequences, direct and indirect, of their removal were to cause.

What is really at issue is not the impossible task of weighing the terrible and known consequences of Chambers speaking out against the unknown but possibly unimportant consequences of his silence. In the final analysis, what is at issue is the necessity of a society, like an individual, to face reality. And the conspiratorial aspects of Communism were part of social reality during the decades in question. They were not the only, nor the most important, aspects of Communism. But they existed, and exist. Moreover, in the America of the third and fourth decades of this century, they were sufficiently real to make it inevitable that someone, be it Chambers or another, should make them explicit and public.

American society, however, was unprepared for the revelation of the existence of a real, though not very large or powerful, conspiracy within it. At first this horribly unwelcome, and to many people grotesque, revelation was simply rejected. Chambers had the utmost difficulty in establishing his facts. When he did establish them, when he was believed, an avalanche of fear, anger, hatred, and revenge was unloosed. Ridden by the politicians of the Right, as the one way in which American liberalism could be broken, this avalanche of reaction rolled on until it reached its loathsome climax in the person of Senator McCarthy. When at last it was over, it was seen to have done enormous damage, not so much to the concrete political and economic achievements of the New Deal—these have survived well on the whole—but to the vigour, freedom, and boldness of American thought and culture.

Such were the consequences of the unpreparedness of American society to deal with the terrifying apparition within it of the conspiratorial aspects of Communism. Chambers cannot be held to have been more than a trigger-mechanism. He did what he had to do. In the confusion and misapprehensions of social reality from which not he alone, but almost everyone else also, suffered, he had to inform. The individual cannot take upon himself to judge whether a particular piece of a conspiracy, of which he happens to have knowledge, is sufficiently significant for his government to deal with drastically and publicly. A wise and self-confident government may conclude that the dropping of a few men from a few committees and the unexpectedly early retirement from government service of a few others, is all that is needed: that to do more than this will do much more harm than good. But that must be the government's responsibility. The individual must supply it with the facts. Only men and women who have never taken Communism seriously, however closely they may have been associated with it, can doubt that it is the duty of an ex-Communist to inform his government of activities, such as espionage, or the penetration of its armed forces or administrative apparatus, by party members, or by anyone working under party direction. The failure of many American liberals, however amiable, to comprehend this fact of contemporary political life is a symptom of their failure to comprehend what have been the tragic necessities of the first half of our century. Perhaps they will not be the necessities of the second half: but precisely in order that they may not be it is indispensable to comprehend them. And Chambers, for all the repulsion of his book, can do more than any other American writer to enable them to do so.

Both the American and the British intellectual 'establishments' may dismiss the idea that they have anything to learn either from Chambers' book or, for that matter, from any further discussion of the Communist issue, such as this essay attempts. The British intellectual establishment, with few exceptions, never did take Communism seriously. The corresponding American circles once did so, but now regard the whole question as closed. In one sense no doubt it is. No well-balanced thinker is likely to accept the seamless robe of Marxism-Leninism again. The objective evidence against doing so is too strong. But it will go hardly with the West if its intellectuals now sink back into a smug disregard of either the Communist faith or the Communist fact. Unless we feel in ourselves the relentless, but potentially fruitful, tension between Communist values and our own we shall make little sense of the contemporary world. To fail to take Communism with the utmost seriousness is still almost as disastrous a mistake as to take Communism hysterically, as Chambers did and still does. The one misappreciation leads headlong to the other. It is true that Communism as a faith (though not as a national power) is now in evident decline: but those who complacently write it off will receive unpleasant surprises. There is still enough dynamic in Communism—and, of course, more than enough sheer power in Russia and China—for that. And when these unpleasant surprises come, those who have refused to take Communism seriously will be sure to rush to the other extreme and take it hysterically. Communism is not, as all Communists, and many anti-Communists, supposed in the first half of the century, the *only* thing that matters. But woe betide the lazy philistines who think that Communism does not now matter at all, or that the moral and intellectual dilemmas which it poses are not real and agonising. For even this waning faith could prove irresistible if it were met by a wholly faithless generation: by a generation whose sole silly ambition was to get rich quick.

To put the matter bluntly, *Witness* is an American book about the life and death issues of our day, which is not superficial. It is not superficial because almost alone of fully articulate Americans, Chambers has had a Marxist training. And whatever else a Marxist training may do to a man—and it often ruins him—it is a sovereign remedy for superficiality. It is, no doubt, one of the many irritating characteristics of all those who have been, to any considerable degree, through the Communist experience that they, at heart, consider that all those who have not are in some degree superficial. Perhaps it may be possible to forgive this intellectual arrogance when it is recalled how much damage of other kinds that experience usually inflicts upon them. But the characteristic is there.

Chambers' book, however, is the proof that there has been another America: a tragic America, opposite in almost every respect from the glossy, unthinking America of appearances: an America of terrible and searing conflicts, an America which makes our little Britain seem still a haven of tranquillity. It will be by facing and then transcending those conflicts of their own immediate past that Americans of the second half of the century will be able to avoid their repetition. For this purpose, Chambers' book is of primary importance. It is important precisely because it and its author have had such disastrous effects. For this immensely gifted man was fated to make mistakes in judgment so terrible that in both his Communist, and then in his anti-Communist, periods he has done fearful harm. To understand how all that happened: to see how this man of some genius both suffered and inflicted these disasters, is imperative. For we have to live with the fruits of what he and his generation did and suffered.

First of all we may dispose summarily of the issue which inevitably preoccupied the readers of the book when it originally appeared, almost to the exclusion of all other issues. This was the issue of the guilt or innocence of Mr Alger Hiss and the others accused of conspiracy and espionage by Chambers. Eight years later everyone can see that, just as in the case of Koestler's indictment of Stalinism, there can be no doubt of the general correctness of the accusations. Precisely what these particular accused men did or did not do may remain to some extent in doubt. But that Communist Party members behaved in this way, as a duty, only the wilfully ignorant can now deny. They would have been intolerably bad Communists, indeed they would not have been Communists at all, if they had not. This issue out of the way, we should examine *Witness* simply as a major document of our time.

In this book also the Communist case is much better put than its own protagonists have ever managed to do. In a short chapter called *The Outrage and Hope of the World* Chambers splendidly conveys what Communism meant to those who received its message during the first half of the twentieth century. Chambers writes that men in the West are moved to Communism by 'just two challenges, the problem of war and the problem of economic crisis', and that 'both crises are aspects of a greater crisis of history for which Communism offers a plausible explanation and which it promises to end'.

'. . . his decision to become a Communist seems to the man who makes it as a choice between a world that is dying and a world that is coming to birth, as an effort to save by political surgery whatever is sound in the foredoomed body of a civilisation which nothing less drastic can save—a civilisation foredoomed first of all by its reluctance to face the fact that the crisis exists or to face it with the force and clarity necessary to overcome it.

Thus the Communist Party presents itself as the one organisa-tion of the will to survive the crisis in a civilisation where that will is elsewhere divided, wavering, or absent. It is in the name of that will to survive the crisis, which is not theoretical but closes in from all sides, that the Communists first justified the use of terror and tyranny, which are repugnant to most men by nature and which the whole tradition of the West specifically repudiates.

It is in the name of that will to survive that Communism turns to the working class as a source of unspoiled energy which may salvage the crumbling of the West. For the revolution is never stronger than the failure of civilisation. Communism is never stronger than the failure of other faiths.'

It is clear that this still seemed an extremely powerful argument to Chambers, writing in 1950 or 1951. Today, ten years later, we notice at once that it is no longer fully applicable. One of the two challenges, that of economic crisis, is for the present at least not there any longer. The other challenge, that of war, is. But it has changed its character: there is no longer any high probability of war between 'rival capitalist powers'. The threat which pre-occupies us is of war between the Capitalist and Communist worlds. Hence the adoption of Communism cannot any longer appear to a man as the effort to transcend war by means of international revolutionary action. On the contrary, to adopt Communism today is merely to change sides in a threatened conflict.

It is a strength of Chambers' book that, like the other writers of this literature, he does justice to the intense idealism, mixed in the most extraordinary way with the basest passions, which pervaded the Communist movement of his time. For instance he writes of a Communist veteran with whom he came in contact: 'In her worked the revolutionary will to overcome ignorance and prejudice in the name of militant compassion and intelligent human unity.' Even more strikingly he speaks of 'the appeal of Communism . . . whenever it coincides with humanity and compassion, especially when the outside world denies them'. He illustrates this with an account of the effects of his own treatment (obligatory, as he notes, for a Communist) of the Chambers' negro maid, Edith Murray, in Baltimore:

'To those who wonder what the appeal of Communism is, this episode may be worth pondering upon. . . . When Edith Murray first sat down to table with us—and we were the first white people who had ever asked her to sit at the same table with them—she showed fear, then embarrassment. I will not presume to say what her final feeling was. In any case, what we had to give her was not a place at our table. What we had to give her was something that belonged to her by right, but which had been taken from her, and which we were merely giving back. It was her human dignity. Thus, by insisting on acting as Communists must, we found ourselves unwittingly acting as Christians should. I submit that that cuts to the heart of one aspect of the Communist appeal.'

Some years afterwards at the second Hiss trial, Edith Murray, summoned to identify Chambers, was the only person willing to say, not merely that what Chambers said was true, but that 'he was a good man'.

It is all the stranger than in spite of these passages, and of much other evidence of his clear appreciation of the positive sides of Communism, Chambers should repeatedly assert that Communism is 'absolutely evil'. This is no doubt part of the whole mystical or metaphysical position which Chambers has adopted, and which we must consider. But at the level of simple common sense, could self-contradiction be more complete? A dozen times he writes that Communism always was, is now, and always will be, 'absolutely evil': and a dozen times he explains with wonderful eloquence that Communism often coincided with humanity and compassion and made Communists behave as Christians should. The un-metaphysical mind can make nothing of this. The tragedy of Communism lies precisely in the fact that it had the most glorious aspirations of any political movement in history. That is why Communism is still worthy of the most serious and searching criticism. It is barely worth while to spend time and trouble in denouncing the abominations of Fascism any longer. But we must continue to subject Communism to strict appraisal. For it fell from the highest pinnacles of human aspiration. It was not, is not, and will never be 'absolutely evil'; for that very reason Communism must be adjudged the graver matter by far. 'Lilies that fester smell far worse than weeds.'

If Chambers cannot assess the ethics of Communism without self-contradiction, he also disastrously misjudges the resilience and flexibility of the non-Communist society in which he lives. Writing in the early fifties he was still convinced that Communism was almost certain to defeat the West: and he implies strongly that the only hope for the survival of the West is world war at an early date. The West is 'the unsaveable society'. 'We have joined the losing side,' he tells his wife when he breaks with the Communists. 'The world economic and military crisis closes in from every side.' He is still convinced that as far as this world is concerned the Communists alone really know what they are about: that they can only be opposed in a mood of metaphysical defiance and despair, because, though almost certain to triumph, they are absolutely evil. Above all it is disastrous even to attempt to modify and reform Western society on New Deal or social democratic lines, because this plays into the hands of the Communists.

Could political folly go farther? The exact opposite of almost every one of the above propositions has proved correct. How *could* a man of Chambers' immense political learning and ability make such fantastic errors? How little intellectual ability and knowledge count, as against emotional stability, for the purpose of reaching wise political decisions! For no doubt it was Chambers' emotional instability which led him to misread history just as grossly after he had left the Communist Party as before.

At any rate, any fool can now see that far from it proving impossible to make our Western economies work by means of rather limited reforms, it has turned out to be comparatively easy to do so. And as to war, the survival of the West (and the East for that matter) rests precisely in staving off a third world war by every prudent means. Again, Communism, though the official doctrine of two of the most powerful states in the world, is obviously a waning force, less and less capable of inspiring the minds and hearts of men. As such it is virtually extinct in Eastern Europe, and steadily relaxing its hold in Russia. It is still really alive only in China and in a section (but only a section) of the revolutionary intelligentsia of the undeveloped world. In such a situation the one immediate danger for the West would be a failure to carry through and carry on the continuing process of the modification of their economic structures, which has so far given such remarkably favourable results. (The longer term danger would no doubt be a failure to find a satisfying faith by which the people of an affluent society may live. This is indeed an acute danger, and here a study of Chambers' book, with all its inconsistencies, can be immensely valuable.)

Chambers was doomed seriously to damage the one force, reforming American liberalism, which could falsify his prophecies of catastrophe. Fortunately, by the time of the Hiss case, the New Deal had done its essential work. The three indispensable modifications of the American economy had taken place. Mass Trade Unionism had been firmly established. The farmers had been compulsorily cartelised and subsidised under statute. The traditions of meeting the onset of depression with higher, instead of lower, government expenditure, and with lower, instead of higher, taxation, had been established (in practice although not overtly). Accordingly, the crisis ceased 'to close in from every side'. Humanly enough Chambers simply did not notice.

The central contention of Chambers' book has still to be considered. Chambers is at heart concerned with none of the things which have been so far discussed. They are important to him, but incidental to his main purpose, which is to assert that the catastrophe of Communism is merely a part of the catastrophe of the rational, empirical approach to the universe as a whole: that there is no alternative to Communism except a belief in one or other form of supernaturalism.

Chambers repeatedly makes this assertion; for example, he thus describes his conversion from Communism:

'What I had been fell from me like dirty rags. The rags that fell from me were not only Communism. What fell was the whole web of the materialist modern mind—the luminous shroud which it has spun about the spirit of man, paralysing in the name of rationalism the instinct of his soul for God, denying in the name of knowledge the reality of the soul and its birthright in that mystery on which mere knowledge falters and shatters at every step. If I had rejected only Communism, I would have rejected only one political expression of the modern mind, the most logical because the most brutal in enforcing the myth of man's material per-fectibility, the most persuasive because the least hypocritical in announcing its purpose and forcibly removing the obstacles to it.'

The book is full of such passages. For example: '. . . man's occasional lapses from God end inevitably in intolerable shallow-ness of thought combined with incalculable mischief in action.' Or again, we are told that the conflict between 'the two great camps of men—those who reject and those who worship God—becomes irrepressible. Those camps are not only outside, but also within nations. The most conspicuously menacing form of that rejection is Communism. But there are other forms of the same rejection, which in any case Communism did not originate, but merely adopted and adapted. . . . For if my story is worth telling, it is because I rejected in turn each of the characteristic endings of life in our time—the revolutionary ending and the success ending. I chose a third ending.' (Chambers makes it clear that he means a religious ending.)

These passages make *Witness* the most explicit example of the literature which we are examining. It will be better to postpone comment until the evidence of a Russian witness also has been heard. But let us note one characteristic of Chambers' testimony. For him the lack of a religious sense (of which lack Communism is merely, he writes, a manifestation) leads to 'intolerable shallow-ness of thought' and, through that, to 'incalculable mischief in action'. And he implies that this shallowness of thought and mischief in action are characteristic of the two 'endings of life in our time—the revolutionary ending and the success ending'.

The negative aspect of this conclusion at least is profoundly important. It is the most important single truth of our time that neither the revolutionary ideal nor the personal-success ideal will suffice. The revolutionary ideal is seen to be necessary and good at certain times and places where intolerable and otherwise im-movable institutional obstacles stand in the way of elementary social justice and decency. But when that is manifestly no longer the case, the revolutionary ideal becomes simply irrelevant. At such times and places it becomes grotesque to ask men not only to die, but to lie and forge and spy and deceive, for the sake of an irrelevance. Nevertheless it is precisely at such times and places that the emptiness of the alternative ideal of personal success—usually in its simplest form of personal self-enrichment—stands revealed. As Chambers, quoting Dante, puts it, those 'that were neither for God nor Satan, but were for themselves', will never make a world worth living in. Chambers is a thousand times right in his pessimistic rejection of both these contemporary ideals. It is because of this that his book should be studied above all perhaps by his fellow countrymen: when they have faced its dilemmas they will have faced the contemporary world.

There remains the question of whether Chambers is right also in his positive assertion that the sole remaining ideal is the relig-ious. And what specifically does he mean by the religious ideal, or 'ending' as he calls it? Chambers did not, like so many ex-Communists, enter the Roman Catholic Church and accept the full panoply of religious dogma. Instead he turned to the Society of Friends, the least dogmatic, and the least superstitious, of all organised religious bodies.

IV. Russia

The culminating expression of the literature under discussion has come out of Russia itself. In Pasternak's *Dr Zhivago* we hear

again the characteristic strangled cry. How could it be otherwise
when the work could not be published in its own country, the
manuscript was probably in danger, and the book had to be
smuggled abroad in equivocal circumstances?

The apparition of this Russian novel of the classical tradition,
escaping from the Soviet Union of the nineteen-fifties, has made
an extraordinary impression upon the world. Not that this has
been an advantage; on the contrary, the passions, prejudices, and
vulgar propaganda which these events have aroused in the West
have done nothing but harm to the book. They have obscured the
message which it sought to send to us, and confused judgment
upon its merits.

For that matter it is none of my business to discuss the book's
literary quality: it has been over-discussed already. As to that an
opinion may be quoted rather than asserted. Mr Edmund
Wilson, perhaps the most authoritative critic now using the
English language, has written: '*Dr Zhivago* will, I believe, come
to stand as one of the great events in man's literary and moral
history.'

One could hardly put it higher than that! But it would be hasty
to conclude that Wilson is necessarily wrong. Such a book has a
hundred aspects, with many of which these pages have no concern.
Indeed, *Dr Zhivago* contains relatively little overt criticism either
of rationalism in general or Communism in particular. It is a
positive book; it is an assertion, almost a celebration. 'In it,'
Wilson writes: 'positive values—Christianity and love and art—
are presented with such overwhelming power that the barbarities
against which they must assert themselves seem lacking in long-
range importance.' The trinity of values is broadly conceived. It is
not only love, in the sense of the passion of a man and woman for
each other, but the whole skein of personal relations, which is
celebrated. It is a mysterious, unnamed something, the creativeness of which is fleetingly revealed in art, rather than art itself,
which is extolled. And it is religion, in the form of the Christianity
of the Greek Orthodox Church, but yet religion as an historical
phenomenon, which is worshipped. There is bitter criticism of
twentieth-century values, Communist and Capitalist alike, in all
this; but it emerges only incidentally, and, so to say, unavoidably.
It emerges because twentieth-century thought and feeling have

disastrously disregarded the things which Pasternak believed to be above all important. It is not his fault if his assertion becomes a condemnation.

In one of its aspects *Zhivago* is a simple love story, as straightforward and tragic as *Romeo and Juliet* or *Anna Karenina*. As in a million other such stories, the hero and heroine, Yury and Lara, meet, love, are parted, suffer, come together again, and are finally destroyed by remorseless fate. What has this sort of thing to do with the reaction against a rationalistic view of the world? Yury and Lara could have loved and lost anywhere, at any time. At the heart of the conflict which racks them is a private situation; it is simply that they are each married to other people, whom both of them also love; in this respect their tragedy could have happened in Bayswater as easily as in Siberia.

Nevertheless, the love story in *Zhivago* is, from the Russian Government's—and most other governments'—point of view, profoundly subversive. It is subversive in the sense that Julia's love of Winston Smith was subversive. Of course no one would have worried if Pasternak had just told us that some character of his called Yury was in love with another character called Lara. Such statements are fully permissible even on the standards of the Union of Soviet Writers. But Pasternak has done a great deal more than that. He has somehow conveyed to us the force of their love: he has shown its intolerant power in action. And that was not easily to be forgiven him, for he has asserted that this relationship is in some respects more important than anything else: more important perhaps—and here was his blasphemy—than 'the revolution' itself. This part of the book is a hymn to 'weeping anarchic Aphrodite'. The political, or rather anti-political, impact of the book will be lost unless the force of the love story is recalled.

At the climax of the book, Lara and Yury become acutely threatened by the revolution. In a desperate purge before the introduction of the NEP, the local Communist authorities are rounding up everybody who might be expected to be non-conformists, whether in fact they are or not, all people with questionable pasts, ex-bourgeois and the like. Lara, because her

husband (though he has been a famous Red Commissar) has by
now been himself purged and is on the run, and Yury because
he is so far from being a Communist, are in particular danger.
Knowing it is really no good—in order to take advantage of their
remaining days in their own way, in order to use them up 'saying
good-bye to life'—they go to hide in an abandoned, half-ruined
house in the Siberian countryside. It is deep winter. They are
together there with Lara's little girl for less than three weeks. At
this point two of the book's main themes, namely the exaltation
of physical creation by love, and of aesthetic creation by, in this
case, poetry, come together and fuse. Wilson has written that this
chapter is 'like nothing else in the whole of fiction'. They feel
ecstasy in being together in isolation. The fearfully hard manual
work they have to do to survive in the abandoned house in the
Siberian winter is sanctified.

'In the rush of some task or other their hands would meet and
join and then they set down whatever they were carrying, weak
and giddy, all thoughts driven from their heads. And the moments
went by until it was late and, horrified, they both remembered
that Katya had been left on her own much too long or that the
horse was unwatered and unfed, and rushed off, conscience-
stricken, to make up for lost time and make good what they had
left undone.'

(It must be recalled that we are hearing Pasternak's voice muffled
and confused by translation.* For example, Wilson writes that
the Russian of this last sentence is far richer—'the minutes ran
into hours'. One may sympathise with the translators in their
almost insuperable task but one may also mourn this immense
impoverishment of language. The impact of the work in Russian
must be of a different order of magnitude.)

And now Yury's other passion, his passion for aesthetic
creation, takes possession of him with a grip more ferocious even
than his passion for Lara. He sits alone far into the night writing
poetry in a way more absorbed than ever before or after. In all
this ecstasy, desperation, and grinding physical work by day,

* See Manya Harari, *Encounter*, May, 1959, and Edmund Wilson's reply,
Encounter, June, 1959.

'his greatest torment was his impatience for the night, his longing so to express his anguish that others should weep'.

The themes intersect. The writer's instinct to communicate so 'that others should weep' takes priority. There follows a consummate description of the poetic process itself. For an instant, in the beleaguered house, the flame of creation in both its forms has towered up. We are made to feel that such a force must be omnipotent: that its action though 'no stronger than a flower' will indeed 'raise the wreckful siege of battering days'. Then Yury, disturbed by a strange sound, looks out of the window:

'He was dazzled by the white flame playing on the shadowless, moonlit snow, and could at first see nothing. Then the long, whimpering, deep-bellied baying sounded again, muffled by the distance, and he noticed four long shadows, no thicker than pencil strokes, on the edge of the snow-field just beyond the gully.

The wolves stood in a row, their heads raised and their muzzles pointing towards the house, baying at the moon or at its silver reflection on the windows.'

All we can say is that those four pencil strokes have now been indelibly drawn upon the sheet of world literature. The miracle of black ink has had its might. In one of the ways that is possible, immortality, which, Pasternak writes, is 'only a stronger word for life', has asserted itself against death and corruption.

But in the world of things the wolves immediately close in. In Pasternak's scrupulously unextenuating narrative, Yury and Lara are parted, separately crushed and degraded, and their dead bodies thrown upon the garbage heap. Yury gets back to Moscow only to go to seed, 'gradually losing his knowledge and skill as a doctor and a writer', to die pointlessly of a worn-out heart muscle in a broken-down Moscow tram. Lara's fate is worse. After the most subtle agonies that Pasternak can devise for her, she is still 'a casually beautiful woman', still capable of rising to the heights of poetic and emotional imagination. She gets back to Moscow in time to attend Yury's funeral. She is invited by Yury's half-brother, who is a high Communist functionary, but who has appreciated him, to help edit the poems he has left. Then

Pasternak makes one of his few violent (although still oblique) comments upon the régime. He kills his marvellous heroine, exquisite and strong, on whom he has lavished his creative powers, in two dreadful, icy, off-hand sentences:

'One day Lara went out and did not come back. She must have been arrested in the street, as so often happened in those days, and she died or vanished somewhere, forgotten as a nameless number on a list which later was mislaid, in one of the innumerable mixed or women's concentration camps in the north.'

This relentless picture of the degradation and destruction of Yury and Lara's kind of people by war and revolution raises the issue of whether or not the Yurys and Laras were, after all, feeble sentimentalists—were, to use the inimitable English schoolboy's expression, 'dripping wet'. This indeed is what the Russian literary officials reiterate.

There are, surely, two things to say about that. In the first place it is perfectly true that men possessed of the highest creative powers are unusually vulnerable. A man simply cannot have it both ways: if he possesses the immensely heightened sensibilities of a poet, he cannot be as hard as nails at the same time. It is quite true that Yury was 'too soft' to survive intact the First World War, the two revolutions, the famine, and the three years' civil war. If he had not been he could not possibly have been the incarnation of the creative process. No one can give birth while clad in armour.

On the other hand, for us in the West to accuse Yury of being 'a weakling' is to make ourselves ridiculous. Are we pretending that we possess the physical toughness to go through a tenth of what Yury went through before he cracked? After all, he was a thoroughly efficient doctor who served in the First World War, was wounded, took part in local administration during the February Revolution, went back to his hospital job in Moscow, stuck to it through the October Revolution when most of his colleagues refused to go on working, survived two Moscow winters of famine, had typhus, got his family out to Siberia, survived two years in the Siberian *tayga* as the medical officer of the Partisans, and walked back to Moscow through the starving countryside.

D

Are we then to rise sternly from our desks in our centrally-heated rooms and accuse him of weakness?

The really staggering thing is how a Yury can have survived as long as he did. And of course when we ask that question we are really asking the question of how Pasternak survived. We do not know enough of the facts to be able to answer, but we may be sure that his survival could not have been accomplished without both an immense initial vitality and without extraordinary resilience, skill, and flexibility. Of the initial vitality I can, as it happens, bear witness.

I met Pasternak at a Writers Congress in Paris some twenty-five years ago. I knew no more of him than that he was a famous Russian poet, and I could not really communicate with him across the language barrier. But I have never forgotten the sense of incomparable aliveness in the man. He was possessed with immortality—in his sense of 'only a stronger word for life'. Of his survival through the darkest times of all in the nineteen-thirties little is, I think, known. There is one anecdote. In one of the very worst years an English visitor to Moscow is said to have somehow got hold of his telephone number and rung him up. Pasternak replied: 'Oh, but my dear fellow, didn't you know? I died some years ago.' All we can say is that by some extraordinary grace, this most vulnerable and most provocative of the creative minds of Russia lived on right through it all, into the nineteen-sixties; and just before he died sent us his genius.

'Personal relations for ever and ever,' as E. M. Forster extolled them: even personal relations raised to the point of passionate love, are far indeed from being Pasternak's be-all and end-all. We saw that at the very climax of his passion, it was not for Lara that Yury could hardly contain his impatience for the night: it was for his desk! One of the things which Pasternak's whole book extols as an ultimate value in life is aesthetic creation. This whole aspect of his book is highly relevant to our theme.

Pasternak makes only one or two overt statements on the subject of aesthetics for instance:—

'I have always thought that art is not a category, not a realm in which there are innumerable concepts and varied phenomena,

but that, on the contrary, it is something concentrated, strictly
limited. It is a principle which comes into every work of art, a
force applied to it and a truth worked out in it. And I have never
seen it as a form but rather as a hidden, secret part of content.
All this is as clear to me as daylight. I feel it in every bone of my
body, but it's terribly difficult to express or to define it. . . .'

'A work of art can appeal to us in all sorts of ways—by its
theme, subject, situations, characters. But above all it appeals to
us by the presence in it of art. One is much more shaken by the
presence of art in *Crime and Punishment* than by Raskolnikov's
crime. . . .'

'There is no plurality in art. Primitive art, the art of Egypt,
Greece, our own—it is all, I think, one and the same art throughout, an art which remains itself through thousands of years. You
can call it an idea, a statement about life, so all-embracing that it
can't be split up into separate words; and if there is so much as a
particle of it in any work which includes other things as well,
it outweighs all the other ingredients in significance and turns
out to be the essence, the heart and soul of the work.'

Pasternak does not know, any more than anyone else does, what
this 'it' is. But at the crisis of the book he comes nearer to giving
an insight into the process of aesthetic creation than perhaps
anyone else has succeeded in doing. In a passage which has
already become famous he describes how Yury felt (just before
he saw the wolves) when he really got going that night in the
beleaguered house:

'After two or three stanzas and several images by which he was
himself astonished, his work took possession of him and he experienced the approach of what is called inspiration. At such
moments the correlation of the forces controlling the artist is,
as it were, stood on its head. The ascendancy is no longer with the
artist or the state of mind which he is trying to express, but
with language, his instrument of expression. Language, the home
and dwelling of beauty and meaning, itself begins to think and
speak for man and turns wholly into music, not in the sense of
outward, audible sounds, but by virtue of the power and momentum of its inward flow. Then, like the current of a mighty river

polishing stones and turning wheels by its very movement the flow of speech creates in passing, by the force of its own laws, rhyme and rhythm and countless other forms and formations, still more important and until now undiscovered, unconsidered, and unnamed.

'At such moments Yury felt that the main part of his work was not being done by him but by something which was above him and controlling him; the thought and poetry of the world as it was at that moment and as it would be in the future. He was controlled by the next step it was to take in the order of its historical development; and he felt himself to be only the pretext and the pivot setting it in motion.'

It will be seen that the process of inspiration is quite unmystically described. There is nothing supernatural 'above him and control-ling him': it is 'the thought and poetry of the world as it was at that moment and as it would be in the future'. He *was* 'the next step it was to take in the order of its historical development'. Again, it is interesting to notice that this passage is not only highly dialectical but echoes a specifically Marxist concept. Just as Marx said that the Hegelian dialectic was standing on its head and that he had turned it right side up, so Pasternak says that in the most intense moments of creation, the correlation of forces controlling the artist is stood on its head: language, the mere instrument of expression, becomes the originating force, and makes the poet its instrument. Pasternak, steeped in Hegelianism at Marburg under Professor Cohen was, whether he liked it or not, the co-heir of Marx in this whole way of thinking.

There are not many other passages in the book which discuss aesthetic creation. But there are a hundred which exemplify it. The book is saturated with nature poetry, and it ends, uniquely, in a series of poems. These are almost inaccessible to us in translation, but we can faintly glimpse their indispensability to the text. In this specifically aesthetic aspect of the book, Pasternak is surely saying the same thing as he is saying in his love story. He is saying that if you think that either personal relations or aesthetic creation are all very well in their way, but that just now you haven't time for such frills; that you're too busy waging the class war, or making money, or winning national wars, or running

an empire, and things of that sort, well so be it. Only at the end
of the day you will make the unpleasant discovery that life is not
worth living. No one knows why—at any rate no one can put
it into so many words—but these things are aspects of the point
and purpose of life. Take them away and nothing is left.

For Pasternak, physical creation through love and aesthetic
creation through art are subsumed in the religious conception of
the resurrection. Scattered through the book, yet an integral
part of it, are a whole series of passages which if they were
brought together would give us Pasternak's cosmology, or his
theology if one prefers to call it so. Indeed art, love, and religion
are for Pasternak barely separable concepts. 'Art,' he writes, 'has
two constant, unending preoccupations: it is always meditating
upon death and it is always thereby creating life.' Thus the whole
book is in many respects an uninterrupted meditation upon death
and resurrection. Love is the resurrection of the body. Art is the
resurrection of the spirit. The agonies and disasters of his characters, their moments of glory and creation, are all, in one of their
aspects, incidents in a parable of death and resurrection.

This is for Pasternak the central aspect of religion. But he
describes also a whole religious view of history, or, as it can
equally well be called, an historical view of religion. At the very
beginning of the book Yury's uncle Kolya, who is his main
intellectual influence, explains his religious position:

'As I was saying, one must be true to Christ. I'll explain. What
you don't understand is that it is possible to be an atheist, it is
possible not to know if God exists or why he should, and yet
to believe that man does not live in a state of nature but in
history, and that history as we know it now began with Christ,
it was founded by Him on the Gospels. Now what is history?
Its beginning is that of the centuries of systematic work devoted
to the solution of the enigma of death, so that death itself may
eventually be overcome. That is why people write symphonies,
and why they discover mathematical infinity and electro-magnetic
waves. Now, you can't advance in this direction without a certain
upsurge of spirit. You can't make such discoveries without
spiritual equipment, and for this, everything necessary has been

given us in the Gospels. What is it? Firstly the love of one's neighbour—the supreme form of living energy. Once it fills the heart of man it has to overflow and spend itself. And secondly, the two concepts which are the main part of the make-up of modern man—without them he is inconceivable—the ideas of free personality and of life regarded as sacrifice. Mind you, all this is still quite new.'

At the start then, love and art, and for that matter science, are tied up in a bundle labelled religion. (In this passage it is labelled 'The Christian Religion', which will sound rather parochial to many an Indian, Chinese, or Japanese reader.) Pasternak believed, so far as I can see, in a completely unsupernatural religion— if that is not a contradiction in terms. The atheist, Uncle Kolya says, can be a perfectly good Christian, if he recognises that the Gospels made the basic ethical discovery upon which everything else hangs. Pasternak's religion, while saturated with the poetry, the ritual, the forms of communication, of the Greek Orthodox Church, which he loved, seems to be at bottom an ethical doctrine, unmystical, untranscendental.

This impression is confirmed by what Uncle Kolya goes on to say. Christianity to him is essentially an enlargement, an intensification of man's consciousness. He goes so far as to declare that before Christianity there was 'no history'. This seems to be a sort of religious equivalent to Engels' view that everything so far has been social pre-history: that human history proper will only begin with socialism, when man makes his 'leap from the kingdom of necessity to the kingdom of freedom'. Uncle Kolya says that the classical world was all

'blood and beastliness and cruelty and pock-marked Caligulas untroubled by the suspicion that any man who enslaved others is inevitably second-rate . . . heavy spokeless wheels, eyes sunk in fat, bestialism, double chins, illiterate emperors, fish fed on the flesh of learned slaves. Beastliness convoluted in a triple knot like guts. There were more people in the world than there have ever been since, all crammed into the passages of the Coliseum and all wretched.

And then into this tasteless heap of gold and marble, He came, light-footed and clothed in light, with his marked humanity, his deliberate Galilean provincialism, and from that moment there were neither gods nor peoples, there was only man—man the carpenter, man the ploughman, man the shepherd with his flock of sheep at sunset whose name does not sound in the least proud (This a reference to Gorky's famous saying, 'Man whose name has so proud a sound.') but who is sung in lullabies and portrayed in picture galleries the world over.'

It is marvellous stuff, but is it true? No doubt you *can* interpret the message of the Gospels, as Pasternak does here, simply as humanism: as a sort of extreme, mystical, anarchic individualism, which is intolerant of all social groups: of nation, of class, of anything outside the supreme individual. (Pasternak makes it clear in other passages that this is indeed his meaning.) But the Gospels have not always been so interpreted, to put it mildly. Again, can this extreme contrast between the Christian and pre-Christian world really be sustained? Could not some of Uncle Kolya's denunciations of the Roman Imperial court apply just as well to the courts of, say, the Renaissance Popes? It may be replied that after Christ there was always an ideal to be betrayed, while before him there was 'no suspicion' that there was anything wrong with beastliness. But that ignores the existence of all the great pre-Christian and non-Christian moralists, prophets, philosophers, teachers, and artists. Pasternak's strictures on the courts of the Roman emperors do not apply very well to the great centuries of Athens, to say the least of it! Socrates and Sophocles, Pythagoras and Pheidias, Pericles and Thucydides and, in Asia, Confucius and Buddha, Lao Tze and Asoka, have all clean disappeared from his history of humanity! This is surely downright naïve. Even if we can agree that there has been an advance in ethical standards over the last two millennia, it must surely be attributed not only to Christianity, but to each of the higher religions, and for that matter to all the major philosophers, teachers, and exemplars of mankind. And when we have admitted that, have we not come pretty near saying that there has been, over the millennia, an all-round process of development, of which the creation of higher ethical standards is a part and an expression? Can it be denied, for instance, that the abolition of, say,

chattel slavery, accompanying and made possible by the rise in
productive technique, has been a part of that development?
And when we have said that, are we not back quite close to that
view of universal history which Pasternak so dislikes?

Pasternak's religion must be judged, of course, not by this or
that example, but from the book as a whole, since the book is in
one way an enormous parable. It may be too soon to attempt
that. But I have the impression that in spite of all his peculiarities
and historical naïveties, we have here a religious statement much
richer than other such contemporary attempts. It is a statement
full of all the Byzantine mysticism of the Greek Church, yet it
appears to be in essence simply a particular view of universal
history: a view independent of supernaturalism or of authoritarian
revelation. It is therefore in no ultimate conflict with inductive
reason. Pasternak is simply putting up a great warning sign
to contemporary reason that there are still whole vast areas of
human life—the essential areas at that—which cannot be fruit-
fully approached by any rationalism which is not much more
humble and cautious, and so, much more truly scientific, than
heretofore. But Pasternak does not specifically assert that these
areas of consciousness can *never* be approached empirically and
rationally. And unless and until a writer does that he has not
joined the retreat from reason.

What does all this come to politically?

The priority of the love of human beings for each other, of
aesthetic creation, and of religious meditation are each asserted, as
Wilson says, with immense power. In a sense this triple assertion
is Pasternak's political programme. For good or ill, however (but
no doubt inevitably), he has by no means left it at that. The book
has a whole specifically political, or, if you will, anti-political
aspect, and it is this aspect about which there has been all the
trouble. What the Soviet authorities could not stand, I suspect,
was that Pasternak's attitude to them (although not to the
revolution) is simply contemptuous. Is this contempt justified?

For the revolution itself, even in its second Communist aspect,
Pasternak has comprehension, although not acceptance. He
makes Pasha—Lara's husband—at the very climax of the book,
when Pasha comes in flight to the beleaguered house, a few hours

after Yury and Lara have been parted, and a few hours before Pasha shoots himself to evade his Chekist pursuers—he makes Pasha attack Yury for his reactionary attitudes. He explains how Lara, who in youth had been seduced by a rich lawyer, was for him the symbol of everything that was being outraged, trampled upon, degraded by capitalism—'you could indict the century in her name, out of her mouth. It was no trifling matter, you must agree.' Yury replies: 'How well you speak of her. I too saw her in those days, just as you have described her . . . I still remember her. . . .'

Pasha: 'You saw and you remembered? And what did you do about it?' It is the fierce Communist accusation against the monumental complacency of the world: against the feebleness, as it seems to them, of all the Yurys who deplore and do nothing.

At the time Yury merely answers: 'That's another story altogether.'

But Pasternak's answer in the book as a whole is, I suppose, Simone Weil's answer to the same question: 'It is better to fail than to succeed in doing harm.' Pasha and the Bolsheviks were splendidly virile, effective, robust, compared to the rest of us. But 'life is not as simple as to cross a field'. (A Russian proverb quoted by Pasternak in one of his poems.) A little less vigour, and a little more insight might have got them further in the end; on the whole they have probably done a little worse, even, than our apparently so ineffective and muddled democracies.

But Pasha rushes on to give a magnificent speech on what the revolution has meant to him:

'Yes. Well. So you see, the whole of this nineteenth century— its revolutions in Paris, its generations of Russian emigrants starting with Herzen, its assassinations of Tsars, some only plotted, others carried out, the whole of the workers' movements of the world, the whole of Marxism in the parliaments and universities of Europe, the whole of this new system of ideas with its novelty, the swiftness of its conclusions, its irony, and its pitiless remedies invented in the name of pity—all of this was absorbed into Lenin, to be expressed and personified by him and to fall upon the old world as retribution for its deeds.

'And side by side with him there arose before the eyes of the world the immeasurably vast figure of Russia, bursting into flames like a light of redemption for all the sorrow and misfortunes of mankind. But why do I tell you all this? To you it must be so much empty noise. . . .'

(Incidentally the last sentence hits off perfectly the Communist's maddening assumption that no one but he has the faintest clue to what everything is about. Yury-Pasternak, who has thought about all this, up, down, and sideways, a thousand times, is told that it must be so much empty noise to him.) Nevertheless the passage as a whole shows a commanding realisation of the grandeur of the Russian event. After this, and after several other important passages in the book (for instance, Yury's thrilled reaction to the first Bolshevik proclamations on the seizure of power: '. . . what splendid surgery! You take a knife and you cut out all the old stinking sores. . . .') it is merely silly to say that Pasternak never understood the revolution. The whole gravity of his offence to his government is that he understood it and has rejected it.

That rejection is, however, in many respects a measured one. It seems to have been widely overlooked that Lara is made on balance to accept the revolution, while Yury on balance rejects it. Lara says that she accepts the revolution because she saw much more poverty in her youth than he did:

'I mustn't let myself be influenced by your way of looking at things. You and I don't really think alike. There is something intangible, marginal, we both understand and feel in the same way. But on the wide issues, in our philosophy of life, it's better for us to stay on different sides.'

There is subtlety in this recognition that what matters between two people politically is usually not *which side* they come down on, which with intelligent people must be a question of balance, of 'on the whole'. What really matters is *the way* in which they champion this or that political cause, attitude, or party. Any politically experienced person knows that he will know people with whom he has much in common on the other side, and people with whom he has not much in common on his own side. But that does not mean that he will not work wholeheartedly with *all* the people on his own side or that he will not work wholeheartedly against *all* the people on the other side. For this is the way in which politics must be conducted, the only way in which, out of their dialectic, a workable system of governing a country can emerge.

Perhaps it was not only the fact that Yury-Pasternak comes down against the revolution which proved so galling to the Soviet authorities when they received the manuscript of *Zhivago*. It may have been even more *the way* in which the rejection was put. In the course of the above conversation between Yury and Lara, which takes place when they first meet again in Siberia after several years of separation, Lara notices his changing attitude. He replies that, yes, he has changed: in all this time something definite should have been achieved. 'Why haven't the Communists done better? It's because they haven't any real capacities, they are ungifted.' Probably they minded that comment a good deal more than if they had been vulgarly and foolishly denounced as robbers and murderers. After all, in war, revolution and civil war, we are all robbers and murderers; such terms lose their meaning. But it is depressing to be shown to be ungifted robbers and murderers. For then it is all for nothing.

The Communists, of course, have a comprehensive answer to all this. For them Pasternak's, or anyone else's, 'rejection of the revolution', when it is not simply a disguised way of fighting for the counter-revolution—that they understand—is simply irrelevant and ridiculous. They see the revolution as an absolute historical necessity. The sufferings it inflicted on the Russian people, the damage it did to Russian civilisation, are simply the price that had to be paid for survival into a new epoch of human development. In so far as there is any point in blaming anyone for performing their inevitable historical role in such events, the entire blame for all the suffering and social damage lies on those who resisted the revolution or failed wholeheartedly to support it. Pasternak, in their scheme of things, is just a sentimentalist, whining about the necessities of the historical epoch into which he was born.

History, however, has shown that this is an insufficient answer.

A revolution was no doubt indispensable in Russia. But the full Communist theory of class-war-to-a-finish, as the sole reality of social life, has proved to have been a monomania. Pasternak is doing an immense service to the Russians of the mid-twentieth century by reasserting the truth, that men and women are not *only* workers, peasants, intellectuals, capitalists, or aristocrats, but also men and women. Is not this becoming 'the truth'—becoming, that is to say, the relevant, needed, appropriate approach—for Russia also—with every year that passes? While any claim that Russia is, on balance, more classless than the West can hardly be sustained, yet what can be said of Russia is that there, as in the West, the general merging and melting of classes is taking place. Therefore the Communist theory of total class conflict will become less and less relevant. The Russians will inevitably wake up to find that what matters to them are, precisely, Pasternak's 'values': that their happiness or misery is being determined by their personal relations, their aesthetic powers, and their religious capacity, rather than by their class relations.

There is something else in the book to which the Soviet authorities were bound to object intensely. And that is, not its anti-Communism, but the contempt for politics of any kind which Pasternak sometimes, though not always, expresses. It is true that in some passages there is a recognition of the practical achievements of the revolution: but even in them there is a total dismissal of the philosophy on which it is founded. For example, Sima, a religious friend of Lara's, is made to say:

'In everything to do with the care of the workers, the protection of the mother, the struggle against the power of money, our revolutionary era is a wonderful era of new, lasting, permanent achievements. But as to its interpretation of life and the philosophy of happiness which it preaches—it's simply impossible to believe that it is meant to be taken seriously, it's such a comical remnant of the past.'

Moreover, more often than not even this tribute to the practical aims and achievements of the revolution is left out. Yury attacks

Marxism to an endlessly kind and good Communist, who goes to infinite trouble to help him:

'Marxism a science? Well, it's taking a risk to say the least, to argue about that with a man one hardly knows, but all the same Marxism is not sufficiently master of itself to be a science. Science is more balanced. You talk about Marxism and objectivity. I don't know of any teaching more self-centred and further from the facts than Marxism. Ordinarily, people are anxious to test their theories in practice, to learn from experience, but those who wield power are so anxious to establish the myth of their own infallibility that they turn their back on truth as squarely as they can. Politics mean nothing to me. I don't like people who are indifferent to the truth.'

There are two objections to this. First, although the criticism of the rigidity of the Communists is fully justified, yet it is a *non sequitur* to say that this proves that Marxism is not a science. You might as well say that Einstein's demonstrations that physical theory up till then had been false, in the sense that it did not cover all the facts, proved that physics was not science. Marxism is an *attempt* at a social science. It is a very early attempt, and in the hundred years which it has now existed it has already been shown that it cannot cover some very important social facts. But the trouble is that no one has come along and given us a comprehensive hypothesis which *can* cover all the social facts, and until someone has done that we had better be very careful about calling Marxism unscientific. So it may be, but it is not nearly so unscientific as an incoherent jumble of social prejudices without any guiding hypothesis of any kind; and *that* is only too often the only possession of the critics of Marxism.

Second, if politics really mean nothing to Yury-Pasternak, then it is a pity that he writes about them at all! And this is an issue which Pasternak never faces. He never faces the fact that 'anti-politicism' is simply the politics of social despair. Again and again he writes as if decent, sensitive, cultivated men and women should have nothing to do with this dirty business. With respect, this is a vulgar attitude. We are familiar with it all over the world.

It is as if the crew of a ship in a storm suddenly remarked that navigation and seamanship generally were a very boring, wet, cold, and disagreeable business, which should be given up immediately. Ships, however, do not sail themselves, and the sole effect of the crew going on strike is to hand her over to the first gang of toughs who come along. They will sail her all right: but they will sail her entirely in their own interests. The crew will soon be working again, but not for themselves.

Even the well-known speech of Yury on 'the re-shaping of life' seems to me open to this criticism:

'When I hear people speak of re-shaping life it makes me lose my self-control and I fall into despair.

Re-shaping life! People who can say that have never understood a thing about life—they have never felt its breath, its heart—however much they have seen or done. They look on it as a lump of raw material which needs to be processed by them, to be ennobled by their touch. But life is never a material, a substance to be moulded. If you want to know, life is the principle of self-renewal, it is constantly renewing and re-making and changing and transfiguring itself, it is infinitely beyond your or my theories about it.'

Well, admittedly the Communist attempt at the re-shaping of life has proved extremely crude. But life—social life—does not just go on automatically 'renewing and re-making and changing and transfiguring itself'. Someone or other, representing some social, economic, or political interest, is constantly re-shaping it whether we like it or not. If we do not attempt to do the job consciously then it will be done unconsciously, and totally without regard for us. It is the glory, as well as the guilt, of the Communists that they attempted to re-shape social life consciously. They did it so badly that the results have been worse instead of better, on the whole, than the results of our Western semi-conscious, piecemeal, empirical efforts. But that does not alter the fact that the supreme challenge to the human race today is precisely to achieve a far higher degree of consciousness in the inevitable process of the continual re-shaping of social life.

At the very end of the book Lara is made to say the same thing, in the midst of her exquisite lament over Yury's bier:

'The riddle of life, the riddle of death, the beauty of genius, the beauty of loving—that, yes, that we understood. As for such petty trifles as re-shaping the world—these things, no thank you, they are not for us.'

This is exceedingly arrogant! To achieve a tolerable social system which will allow geniuses such as 'Yury-Pasternak-Lara' to live, love, and create is not a petty trifle. The work may be too rough for them, but they really need not scoff at the honest journeymen who attempt it.

It will be seen that on this issue of 'anti-politicism' which I understood was, unofficially at least, the Soviet authorities' greatest objection to the book, my opinion is that those authorities were right and Pasternak wrong. Moreover, the concern of the Russian authorities on this issue is understandable. 'Anti-politicism' is an old Russian disease, to which the intelligentsia have always been prone. Dostoevsky is its other spokesman of genius. It is the strangled cry of the Russian people, when their government seems to them too hopelessly evil to have anything to do with. It is the inevitable result of the lack, alike under the Tsars and the Communists, of institutions by means of which the people, or even the politically conscious section of the people, can influence their government. It is the result of the gulf which has always stretched in Russia between the Government and the governed. It is understandable that the Soviet authorities should have been dismayed when the first spontaneous, enormously powerful, work which came to them after the relaxation of the censorship turned out to be supercharged with this tendency.

It should be needless to say that this is no justification for the Soviet authorities' suppression of the book. On the contrary, it is pitiable that this vast, apparently omnipotent government, monopolising the means of expression, has cowered back in terror before one man with a pen. Of course they ought to have published *Zhivago* and then stood up for themselves against it like men. For against what they perhaps most fear in it, namely Pasternak's 'anti-politicism', they have a convincing answer. Moreover, it is an answer which would allow them to by-pass all Pasternak's other accusations. Even if they were driven to admit them all, they would still be a thousand times right to contend that, however bad they were and are, the more, not the less urgent it is that the Russian people should participate in political life. It was Lenin himself who said that the object of the revolution was to enable every cook to take part in the government of Russia. Why on earth haven't the Soviet authorities the guts to publish *Zhivago* and to answer it with arguments from their own classics, instead of making the pitiful pretence that the book would 'interest no one in Russia'? No doubt the true reason for the members of the Russian literary establishment behaving like poltroons before the phenomenon of *Zhivago*, is that to Pasternak's other accusations they have no reply. Or rather they have a reply, and one which has much practical force; but it has implications so humiliating to themselves as to be unusable. In the face of the book's description of the dreadful consequences for, above all, the ordinary Russian people, of fighting out the class war to a finish, they can say nothing—except that all that is over and done with now. It is not an elevated plea, but it is a familiar one:

'Thou hast committed...'
'Fornication? But that was in another country:
And besides, the wench is dead.'

It was not in another country, but it was a good many years ago now. Some of it was forty years, some of it twenty years, ago. Did it kill 'the wench'? If by the wench we understand the Russian people, then of course it did not kill them. This massive and marvellous race survived, and will survive, as one of the very great peoples of the earth. But if we mean by 'the wench' the poetry and genius—the Yury-Lara element—in the Russian people, then we must answer that we do not yet know whether that has been killed or no. For a time it seemed that it had been. And if now, and as by a miracle, the moral and aesthetic genius of Russia seems to have been resurrected, that is partly because of the heroic survival of Boris Pasternak until he had written his book.

V. Quarrelling with History

There they are, the colossi, the giant powers. They seem almost omnipotent and yet, because they suppose themselves to be antithetical, they are almost powerless, stalemated in a balance of mutual terror.

There is something moving about these two huge communities, each so unfitted to rule the world, which yet each feel that they must. How will it end? It might end any day, of course, in a full-scale thermo-nuclear exchange—1,500 missiles in the megaton range each way, and that would be that. But on the whole, 'the nuclear ending' seems decreasingly probable. At any rate it is necessary to assume that it is improbable, or all speculation—and everything else for that matter—becomes futile.

There is something extraordinary about the contemporary British relationship to America and to Russia respectively. On the level of daily life we know America a thousand times the better. Without barrier of language, with a hundred interlacing ties between our economies; with large-scale, long-continued migration from Britain to America; with frequent and free intermarriage; with political systems which are different enough to be mutually interesting, but which, when compared to a party dictatorship, are fundamentally similar, we are not quite foreign countries to each other. True, our very nearness produces intense friction: the degree of mutual irritation frequently rises to remarkable heights. British jealousy, American *hubris*, the memory of past wars, a thousand things, makes this a relationship as restless as it is close.

But close the relationship is, whether we like it or not. You may measure its closeness by a simple contemporary test. No one in Britain, not even the most anti-American Britons—especially them, for otherwise they would not care to indulge their feelings so freely—is frightened of America. And that is a remarkable thing. For after all, the American Strategic Air Force could render the British Isles totally unhabitable any afternoon, with only a chance of relatively minor retaliation on the United States; and it is a new thing for the British to live completely within the

E

power of a foreign government. But the fact is that none of us gives the matter a thought! We quite simply know that the Americans will not do it. They are not quite a foreign government to us, at least in this crucial respect. There is no way of proving that we are right. But the mere fact that we really are not frightened of them probably means that we *are* right. For if you are genuinely unfrightened of someone, you can usually get along with them in one way or another.

Compared to all this, Russia is for us still in many ways a *terra incognita*. Her language is too difficult, her national traditions too strange, the intercourse between us too slight, her political system and her conduct too alarming for, one would have thought, there to be any comparison in the intimacy of our relationship. And yet there is one factor to be put upon the other side. Many people may say that it is too slender even to mention in the same breath with the solid ties which unite us with America; but this may be a hasty judgment. This counterbalancing factor is simply the works of the great Russian novelists. Every educated Briton has read Tolstoy, Dostoevsky, Turgenev, Chekhov, and now Pasternak. By means of the genius of these 'master story-tellers, master moralists' (Edmund Wilson) we know what the Russians are like; we actually know them better in many respects than we know even our personal friends in America. The Russians have found interpreters more eloquent than any the world has known. Thus there is a respect in which we in Britain are undeniably closer to the Russians than to the Americans, for we see in the classic Russian literary tradition a flowering of the culture of all Europe.

It may be objected that this tradition no longer corresponds to any living reality in present-day Russia. Was not Pasternak, in particular, writing of an extinct race, battered to death by the terrible forty years since the revolution? Pasternak's own view on this desperate question appears to be undecided. On the one hand, he ends his novel with the agonising fable of Yury's and Lara's abandoned child, Tanya. He declares, both through this fable, and in so many words, that everything has been coarsened and debased.

After Yury and Lara have been parted, Lara bears a child to

him while she is wandering with her protector and ex-seducer in the Far Eastern emigration. During these wanderings, the child, Tanya, gets abandoned and is brought up by some Siberian peasants. After a ghastly episode of robbery and murder, she has to fly from the house and become one of the child vagrants who roamed Russia in those years. However she is from time to time put into 'homes', given a little elementary education and, during the Second World War, turns up as a regimental laundress. Here two of Yury's old friends, and his mysterious half-brother, Yevgraf, now a Soviet general, both hear her story and recognise who she is. She is a nice, tough, simple sort of girl: she has become the sort of girl she has had to become to survive such a childhood. After hearing her story, one of Yury's surviving friends comments:

'This has happened several times in the course of history. A thing which has been conceived in a lofty, ideal manner becomes coarse and material. Thus Rome came out of Greece and the Russian Revolution came out of the Russian enlightenment. Take that line of Blok's, '*We, the children of Russia's terrible years*': you can see the difference of period at once. In his time, when he said it, he meant it figuratively, metaphorically. The children were not children, but the sons, the heirs of the intelligentsia, and the terrors were not terrible, but apocalyptic; that's quite different. Now the figurative has become literal, children are children and the terrors are terrible. There you have the difference.'

This is Pasternak at his most remorselessly realistic. If you break society to pieces, so that, in particular, half the next generation are dragged up without homes or parents, the price is an immense debasement. The child of the marvellous Yury and Lara is merely poor Tanya. But this is not Pasternak's last word. 'Five or ten years later,' the surviving friends are reading one of Yury's books:

'Although the enlightenment and liberation which had been expected to come after the war had not come with victory, a presage of freedom was in the air throughout these post-war years, and it was their only historical meaning.

'To the two aging friends sitting by the window it seemed that this freedom of the spirit was there, that on that evening the future had become almost tangible in the streets below, and that they had themselves entered the future and would, from now on, be part of it.'

Pasternak is no doubt identifying himself particularly closely with Yury in these passages. He is really writing about his own survival and the survival of his book. He is thinking about the possibility of it reaching the Russian people. He wonders, no doubt, whether it will be suppressed by the government, but more anxiously still he wonders whether the forty terrible years may have rendered the Russians unable to hear such a message as his. But he was hopeful, I think, on both counts.

Nor does it seem that his hopes need be unjustified. On the first and simpler issue of whether the Russian Government will in fact be able to keep *Zhivago* from the Russian people, the evidence seems encouraging. Informed observers who have recently been in Russia report that in the circles of the now rapidly growing educated classes in Russia, 'everyone' is talking of the book. Moreover, 'everyone' is claiming to have read it, or parts of it. For it is in clandestine circulation, in whole or in part, by means of an ingenious method which it is more discreet to refrain from mentioning. It is 'the done thing' to have read, or at least to claim to have read it, and that is surely extremely significant.

Nor do the risks and penalties seem to be particularly grave. Khrushchev's Russia is evidently a genuinely different place from Stalin's. No doubt Stalin's degree of totalitarianism could have effectively suppressed the book and would probably have physically destroyed Pasternak for writing it and for publishing it abroad. There is no denying the terrible efficacy of suppression and persecution pushed through to their logical conclusion. But once, for any reason, suppression and persecution are modified and moderated: once a limit is set to them, they become ineffective. Then they may actually become self-defeating by awaking an irresistible appetite for the forbidden fruit.

But is there still in existence a Russian public which can understand and appreciate *Zhivago*? The evidence of an intense interest in a forbidden book is in itself inconclusive. It may be argued that if the Russian Government had had the nerve to publish a legal edition of *Zhivago*, the book would have proved to be too far from anything which the present generation of Russians had ever heard of to make any impact. A generation of 'Tanyas' could not be expected to make much of Yury and Lara, even if they were their own mothers and fathers. And indeed so well-informed a Soviet-ologist as Mr Wolfgang Leonard, himself a graduate of the Lenin School, takes the view that *Zhivago* is too far from anything which the young Communist students in the advanced party academics have ever heard of for them to be able to make head or tail of it. Again Mr Isaac Deutscher has called Pasternak 'a voice from the dead'. For the more highly-conditioned members of the present Russian generation this may be so, but will it prove so for either the earlier or the coming generation? A voice from the dead may speak with tongues to the new-born. *Rex quondam, Rex futurus*. Moreover the opinions of such highly-trained ex-Communists as Mr Leonard and Mr Deutscher do not prove that there is not deep appreciation of *Zhivago* even amongst the present generation of Russians. After all the graduates of the party schools are a very small proportion of the educated classes in present-day Russia. The rest of these classes have no doubt been fairly severely conditioned: but not to the same extent. It seems possible to believe that Edmund Wilson was right when he ended his review of *Zhivago* with these words:

As for his (Pasternak's) enemies in his fatherland I predict that the children, over their vodka and tea, will be talking about the relations between Larissa Fyodorovich (Lara) and Pasha and Yury Andreyevich, as their parents, as I don't doubt they themselves, have talked about Tatiana and Lensky and Eugene Onegin, and Natasha and Prince Andre and Pierre.'

If Wilson is wrong, and there no longer exists in Russia a genera-tion capable of hearing Pasternak's voice, then the prognosis for their society, and so for the world, must be grave. Not all their physics, their 'years of economic triumph', their military might, their rising standard of life, will, unfortunately, avail them in the end. They may annex the barren moon and probe the galaxies for all I know: they may produce 'fantastic' weapons and terrorise the world: they may 'overtake and surpass' America in production, so that Ivan has ten times as many television sets and motor cars and refrigerators as he can use, while Sam has only twice as many. It will not be enough. But if Wilson is right, it will mean that one man, possessed of a courage and pertinacity of the rarest kind, has preserved across the forty years those things which give meaning to life.

It would be wrong indeed to suggest that it is particularly in Russia that Pasternak should be heeded. In many respects his old-fashioned warning that neglect of the unseen things leads only to dust and disaster, is more needed for us in the West than for Russia. A materialism, more crass than Russia's, because un-illuminated by Communism's messianic faith, menaces above all the more successful Western societies, such as America and Britain. It would be ignorant and arrogant in the extreme to suggest that Britain, in particular, was exempt from this menace. In some ways she is especially vulnerable to it. Nevertheless there is one respect in which we British may perhaps presume to preach: and that is to preach against the unification of preaching. It is perhaps a fair claim that we in Britain value especially highly the spontaneous individual dissenting opinion: that we value it even when it seems to be manifestly mistaken: that we value spontaneity for its own sake and even when it leads to opinions which seem to have little relation to reality.

For Britain is the traditional land of dissent: of dissent not only in its original religious connotation but of dissent itself: of—if you will—dissent for dissent's sake. In this respect there seems a persisting difference between the mental climates of Britain on the one hand, and Russia and America on the other. It has been well said that both Russia and America are 'unanimous countries'. The concensus of opinion at any one time is so strong in each of them that it is difficult indeed for an individual to swim against it. For Russia this is well shown by the letter sent by the editors of *Novy Mir*, a 'highbrow' literary magazine, to Pasternak rejecting the manuscript of *Zhivago**. It is quite an able, careful, and well-

* The full text is printed in Mr Edward Crankshaw's *Khrushchev's Russia* (Penguin, 1959).

reasoned letter, but its essential sense could have been expressed in two of its sentences. The first is: 'The spirit of your novel is that of non-acceptance of the socialist revolution.' There follow several thousand words establishing this proposition, which, for that matter, a backward child of ten could find out for himself by glancing through the book. And then comes the conclusion:

'As people whose standpoint is diametrically opposite to yours, we, naturally, believe that the publication of your novel in the columns of this magazine *Novy Mir* is out of the question.'

It is as simple as that. The idea that it might be useful, forty years after, to hear a dissenting voice does not so much as enter their heads! There is something both barbarous and panicky about the persistence of such attitudes. When will the Russian authorities get the self-assurance to be civilised?

There is some force in the accusation that the relative mildness of the enforcement of the American consensus is merely a reflection of its overwhelming power, so that there is no need of relatively clumsy compulsions. But what, it may be objected, is wrong with such an, in a sense, voluntary consensus? If a consensus is self-enforced by a vociferous, but yet genuinely spontaneous, unanimity of opinion what need is there to leave room for dissent? What is wrong with a genuinely voluntary unanimity? There is only one thing wrong with it, and that is that it will be sure to be wrong. All experience shows that any such universally held, unchallenged, social dogma will almost certainly be erroneous, in the sense that it will fail to correspond with objective reality. Even if it does not so fail to begin with, it will do so sooner rather than later, for objective social reality will be changing all the time, while the social dogma will remain frozen.

It is for this reason that social dissent, especially, has a value of its own and for itself: that it has a value even when the dissenting opinion appears to almost all of us to be manifestly foolish. The first half of our century has taught us—if it has taught us anything —that we are simply not competent to tell with any high degree of certainty which social opinions are valid and which are not. Therefore a heavy responsibility lies upon anyone who attempts, whether by physical persecution, or by the subtler, but in some respects more deadly, method of monopolising the means of expression, to stamp out a dissenting opinion no matter how apparently foolish. For the foolish opinion has the daunting habit of reappearing, in the next phase of social development, as a precious clue to social reality. If we suppress it we may well commit the suicidal sin of what Pasternak calls 'quarrelling with history'.

When Lara is telling Yury how much she loves her husband Pasha and why, in spite of that love, their marriage has been a failure, she says of him: 'He sulked at the course of events. He quarrelled with history.' How many others, as well as poor Pasha, have in our day 'quarrelled with history'? Whole nations, whole classes, to say nothing of political parties, groups, sects, and individual thinkers have each and all quarrelled with history. They have all adopted ideas, systems, ideologies, social standpoints which, in the event, have proved to be disastrously out of touch with the real course of development.

First, the old governing classes of Europe quarrelled with history when they blocked social reform before the First World War. And then, between the wars, the governing classes failed everywhere to see that they must, as a minimum, prevent mass unemployment, slump, and economic chaos. Next, in the thirties, the Fascists and their allies were far more horribly wrong still. The Fascists grasped, it is true, that 'the contradictions of capitalism' were fairly readily solvable by means of central control and planning without social ownership. That was so; but in their case this piece of economic, or social, insight merely gave them the power necessary for an attempt to conquer the world by playing upon the most primitive, odious, and degraded aspects of human nature. They never dreamt that by such outrages they would rouse an almost universal resistance, which duly crushed them.

Or again, the British Conservatives in the nineteen-thirties supposed that they had only to sit tight in total selfishness in order to survive; and thereby took their country to within an ace of destruction. And then after the second war we socialists, in Britain and elsewhere, supposed that we had only to enunciate the not very profound platitudes of our creed to inherit the government of our countries. It was not so. And now we may confidently predict that the American conservatives, who suppose that the tawdry, trivial, ideal of personal self-enrichment will suffice for a great people, will sooner or later be similarly disillusioned.

Finally, the Communists who are sure that they have put history into their pockets, have again and again quarrelled with the course of events. Marxism attempts to use the historical experience of the race as 'a guide to action'. That is its glory. Unfortunately that has not prevented its uncritical disciples from getting the whole phasing and timing of the process disastrously wrong. They were wrong, for example, in thinking that capitalism was producing the ever-increasing misery of the masses; in thinking that the break-up of world imperialism must cripple the major capitalisms; and, gravest of all, they were wrong in their appreciation of Fascism. They disastrously underrated Fascism, in one respect, and equally disastrously overrated it in another. For while Fascism by no means turned out to be, as the Communists confidently predicted, an immediately self-contradictory aberration which would be impotent to resolve the economic crisis, yet, on the other hand the Communists grossly overrated the *generality* of Fascism. They taught that Fascism was not an Italian or German phenomenon. They taught that Fascism was the inevitable political form which every decaying capitalism must adopt if it were not overthrown in good time: that Fascism *was* the politics of last-stage capitalism. Seeing capitalism as a more or less unified world system, the Communists thought, and think, of the guilt of Fascism as resting not upon the German or Italian capitalists alone but upon all capitalist societies everywhere. Regarding the distinction between the different nations as of secondary importance, they see capitalist development culminating inevitably in Fascism, and contrast it with development in the socialist world culminating, as they fervently believe, in Communism.

History, however, has taken another and more devious course. It did not turn out to be true that every capitalist society, when apparently trapped by the 'closing in from all sides' (to recall Chambers' phrase) of economic crisis would turn to the Fascist 'way out'. The great slump drove Germany into Fascism, but it drove America into the New Deal and it drove Britain towards social democracy. Fascism turned out to be merely *one* of the 'ways out' towards which a capitalism might turn when struck by crisis: there was also a liberal and a social democratic 'way out'. And each 'way out' was practicable.

Who, then, has not 'quarrelled with history'? Everyone has been proved wrong, or is in the process of being proved wrong. No one has got hold of more than a bit of the truth. The best that anyone has been able to do is to contribute something necessary and useful. But no sooner have they done so than it has become apparent that their creed was one-sided and had to be superseded to make room for other, and equally one-sided, ideas. After such an experience, how *can* anyone imagine that they know it all and have the right to suppress, by either the hard or the soft method, a contrary opinion? How *can* anyone any longer doubt the immense value of, precisely, dissent? For any real, genuine, spontaneously held personal opinion *may*, for all we know, contain the grain of truth without which we are all doomed.

In Lara's speech which has just been quoted, there occurs Pasternak's well-known protest against all mechanical unanimity:

'The great misfortune, the root of all the evil to come, was the loss of faith in the value of personal opinions. People imagined that it was out of date to follow their own moral sense, that they must all sing the same tune in chorus, and live by other people's notions, the notions which were being crammed down everybody's throat. And there arose the power of the glittering phrase, first Tsarist, then revolutionary.'

It is perhaps in respect of the valuation of scepticism, empiricism, and so of personal dissent, at their true worth that the British tradition (with all its marked inferiority in some respects: its flatness, its mediocrity, its lack of inspiration) may be worthy of attention.

VI. The End of the Reaction

Zhivago completes, and at the same time transcends, the reaction against mechanical, or 'mechanistic', materialism. Pasternak

triumphantly demonstrates that analogies, conscious or unconscious, between the working of a machine and the springs of
action of a human being are hopelessly misleading. The complexities are of a different order. And, since we have still no
means of direct description, let alone of measurement, of these
complexities, the crucial aspects of human life remain mysterious
to us. They can be approached by the older, much less direct,
methods of aesthetic, ethical, and religious experience alone.

As a matter of fact there is a large element in all this that *should*
be acceptable to minds educated in the Marxist tradition. Marx
and Engels were continually inveighing against what they called
'mechanistic' materialism. They repeatedly criticised what they
considered to be the narrow, oversimplified materialism of the
eighteenth- and nineteenth-century enlightenment. They were
pioneers in emphasising that life was an incomparably more
complex phenomenon than was allowed for in either the French
rationalist or, still more, the English utilitarian traditions which
flourished around them. It is strange and sad that the mighty
social system which has now been set up in their names should in
practice, and whatever its verbal protestations to the contrary,
have become more mechanistic—more intolerantly contemptuous
that is to say, of everything which is not susceptible to exact
measurement—than any Western society has ever been.

Presumably the explanation is that although Western rationalism was in itself crudely mechanistic, it was always balanced and
offset by the older, humanistic, aesthetic, and religious traditions,
which lived on vigorously by its side. Communist rationalism,
on the other hand, though in origin much less mechanistic,
because based on relatively subtle dialectical distinctions between
'the laws' supposedly governing inorganic, organic, and social life
respectively, has been offset by no surviving pre-scientific
traditions. In the event Communist rationalism has run amuck
and continually tends to turn into its opposite of a 'faith', as
arbitrary, authoritarian, and rigid as any the world has ever
suffered.

Against the awful sterility of this new dogma, the strangled cry
of the writers of the literature of reaction has been raised. These
writers have convinced us that our attempts to rationalise the

social fields have so far been crude and presumptuous. Unless we give far greater weight to the subjective side of man, unless we recognise the power of Pasternak's *troika* of values, we shall achieve only disasters. The creativeness of personal relations, of aesthetics, or of religious experience, is what matters today, wherever at any rate the economic problem is on the way to solution. And that will prove equally true whether we are trying to make Communism or merely to make money.

Nevertheless the literature of reaction has now done its work. It is now time to turn our faces in the other direction. The catastrophe of Communist rationalism must not make us despair of reason: reason must for ever strive to encompass all that the old rationalism ignores. We cannot achieve such encompassing reason yet; we do not know how to bring those things which Pasternak celebrates within our universe of rational discourse. It can be argued that we never shall, but I do not know why we should suppose that. Is it not possible dimly to conceive of a science which re-embraced, as did the science of the ancient world, at its own level of complexity, everything that we today think of as 'not-science'? If so it would, no doubt, become our aesthetic, our ethic, and our religion. That may be centuries or millennia away; in the meanwhile scepticism of the social conclusions of reason is our most rational attitude. To doubt, to suspend judgment where the evidence is still inadequate, is one of the highest applications of the reasoning faculty. It is the opposite of unreasonable to recognise the existence of mystery. We can hardly begin to explain the things which, when once we have our daily bread, make life worth living. But that is merely a reason for caution and empiricism when we are forced to take our social decisions.

In so far as the literature of reaction has been a protest, however frenzied, against a reckless failure to take all that into account, it has been justified. If both in intention and in effect it had stopped there, there would be little in it to criticise. But inevitably it has not stopped there; it has sometimes crossed, intentionally or unintentionally, a critical line. On one side of that line are those who point to the unsolved mysteries of social life in order the better to approach their comprehension. On the other side are those who point to the mysteries in order to dissuade us from even attempting to apply reason to society. That is the test. Those who pass this line have deserted, whether they know it or intend it, and whether their inner motive be weariness, class-prejudice, or simply despair, to the enemies of civilised life. Who can deny that at its worst and most extreme, some of this literature has thus deserted? that some of its authors have sometimes gloried in our ignorance, exalted our folly, sought to forbid the extension of the frontiers of the known and declared with unmistakable satisfaction that all the most important things in life can never be understood? The effect of this part of the literature has been to promote that 'loss of nerve', as Koestler calls it in his most recent work, which has often before in the history of civilisation set a limit to scientific inquiry.

We must not blame these authors for the consequences of their words: they had to utter their cry of protest against the trap into which a mechanistic rationalism had led the world. But though we must not blame them, we must protect ourselves from them. The nightmare of the imposition of mechanism is passing. Now is the time to take up once more the unending task of reason.

The mysteries are seen to be far deeper than we dreamed; reason must become by that much the finer to comprehend them.

(1960)

Part II

War

Digging for Mrs Miller

THE little Marlow Square incident began a period of considerable strain. No further bombs came down in their sector, but each night there were heavy raids, in which many bombs fell within the borough.

At two o'clock one morning the telephone bell rang. Ford had just come down from the landing, and was about to wake Levy. He answered the telephone and heard Mrs Raymond's correctly official voice.

'Post D speaking. Control has informed us that an exceptionally large number of incidents are reported as taking place in Slaney. All Chelsea wardens are instructed to be in readiness to report there for duty.'

Ford went upstairs and duly informed Miss Sterling and Miss Dalrymple, who were on watch, of this message. There did not seem much to do or say about it. So he went to bed and to sleep. He woke to find Miss Sterling shining a torch on him. She said: 'Post D has rung through to say that you are to go to Slaney F at 8 a.m. They have more incidents than they can cope with.'

He disentangled his slept-in clothes from the blankets and mattress on the basement floor of the sub-post. He swilled water over his face, finding it cold out of the hot tap. Apparently the gas had gone again in the night. He took a bus down the Queen's Road to the next ARP district, Slaney. When he got to the Slaney F Post the Senior Warden was out; fetched, he hesitated between various tasks. Then Rumbold, another Post D warden, came. Finally they were both told to go down to Beaton Street.

A bomb, or bombs, had hit the last five houses in Beaton Street, where it joins the river, and a small tenement that forms the last block of the embankment. (Ford supposed that these were some of the incidents which Post D had reported during the night. Curiously enough no one at 46 had heard the detonations.) These

F

buildings had been destroyed. Where they had stood there was a crater, with two mounds of debris on each side of it, one some twenty-five feet, and the other some fifteen feet, high. The debris of the five houses and the tenement was completely mixed in the mounds; there was no trace of separate structures.

Ford and Rumbold found rescue squads working on each mound. After wandering about a little they found the warden in charge. He seemed unable to think of anything he wanted done. 'Just keep them from coming down the streets,' he said. He evidently felt vaguely that it must be right to stop people doing something. But nobody was coming down the streets. Between ten and twenty oldish men and women, and one or two untidy girls were standing about in the doors and on the area steps of the more or less shattered, but still standing, houses round the incident.

Ford and Rumbold saw no one to stop doing anything; so they just waited about. It was a squally October morning. As usual on the embankment, you suddenly became conscious of the weather, almost as if you had been in the country. The tide was low: gulls stood on the mud-flats. The wind flickered the surface of the channel. A biggish collier, looking inappropriate so far up the river, was moored fifty yards farther on beside the power station. The power station's chimneys stood over them. People glanced at them, and then at the mounds.

Ford began watching what the rescue squad on the nearest mound was doing. They had evidently been at work for some hours already. They had fixed a plank walk up the side of the mound, and a knot of them was concentrated near the top, apparently moving the debris about with their hands, and putting bits of it into wicker baskets. When the baskets were filled they took them to other parts of the mound and emptied them. It looked aimless. Ford climbed on to the debris to try to see what they were at. As soon as he got on to the mound he found that it was made up of an extraordinary texture of brick and plaster rubble, more or less shattered lengths of floor joists and beams, pieces of broken furniture, rugs, carpets, linoleum, curtains, pieces of crockery, often unbroken, all made into a homogeneous, tight-pressed pudding. It was rather difficult to climb on to.

When he got to the top he was gradually able to make out what the rescue squad was doing. They were sinking a small shaft vertically downwards through the mound from its top. They worked much in the same way as archaeologists open up the debris of millennia; but this was the debris of seconds. The rescue men had blue overalls, instead of the brown overalls of the Chelsea wardens, such as Ford was wearing. The rescue men took no notice of him. They had only sunk their shaft about five feet down into the mound. They seemed to him to be working in an incredibly primitive and inefficient way—with their bare hands, and without any tools even, let alone any mechanical appliances.

One of them began to let himself down into the shaft, which was encumbered by ragged ends of floor joists and beams. He got to the bottom and then wormed his body round till he was lying in a knot with his head down by a crack, where some tattered rubble was held up an inch or so by a joist end. Ford moved to the edge of the shaft to see. The rescue men stood still, and one of them called down to the people by the mound to be quiet. Ford heard the river waves lap the mud. The rescue man down the shaft put his mouth to the crack and said: 'Are you there, chum?' Everybody kept really still. But they heard nothing. The man down the shaft put his ear to the crack. The rescue man at the top, who had called to the people to be quiet, said: 'Can't you hear him any more, Smith?' Smith said, 'Yes, but he's getting very faint.' Then he began to get out of the shaft. It was 9.30 a.m. Ford had not realised before that there were people alive under them in the mound.

The rescue squad went on digging, no faster but steadily, filling wicker baskets with rubble, passing them from hand to hand to the edge of the mound and emptying them.

The one who had called down to the people to be quiet said, 'Cut away some of that stuff'—pointing to one edge of the shaft— 'the weight'll be coming down on Smith otherwise.' A couple of rescue men took up shovels and began trying to use them on that edge of the mound, pushing rubble down into the central crater. Ford felt restless. He saw a pick lying about, so he took off his coat, put down his gas mask and torch, and began to loosen the rubble so that the men with shovels could really get at it. The rescue men neither warned him off—as he feared they might—nor welcomed him. Rumbold came and worked with another shovel.

For about a foot down his pick made good progress; it was easy to loosen the broken brickwork, plaster, and the rest of the indescribable mixture of which the mound was made. Then his pick stuck in something tough and sticky. Using all his strength, he got it out. At the next stroke it stuck again. He got it out. Forewarned, he made smaller strokes, only attempting to loose tiny bits of the new material. He wondered what it was. He picked a bit up in his hands, and recognised it as the clay which is the universal sub-soil of London. If you dig down, say, ten feet almost anywhere in London this is what you come to. But he was working more than ten feet above street level. The bomb had picked up layers of the sub-soil and somehow spread them above the layers of obliterated houses.

After some little time the rescue man who had put them on (he was evidently called Frank) said, 'That's enough.' Ford was glad. His arms ached. But he didn't fancy standing about. So he got a place taking the filled baskets as the men in the shaft passed them out to be emptied. The rescue men still neither welcomed nor repulsed him. He could now see that their apparently primitive method of work with their hands was in fact the only possible way of dealing with the material of which the mound was made. It would have been quite impossible to swing a pick or shovel in the shaft, partly because it was too narrow. But even if they had dug it wider, as soon as you had got a few feet down a network of half-shattered woodwork would have prevented the use of any tool which Ford could think of. As it was, they were continually having to stop to saw through a wedged joist or beam. They used absurdly small, flimsy saws—they looked as if they had been bought at toy shops, and perhaps they had—in order to be able to get them into the corners of the shaft.

They began to smell gas—not poison gas, but ordinary domestic gas. As the shaft progressively opened up the mound, the shattered pipes of the houses permeated it with gas. 'Nobody must strike a match,' said Frank. But the rescue men went on smoking just the same.

Every now and then a rescue man would call out 'Warden', and Ford or Rumbold would go over and take charge of some bit of personal property that had been unearthed. Ford got several pots and pans, a china dish, unchipped even, two ration books in

the names of Andrews and Miller, and a lady's handbag, undamaged and full of its owner's make-up equipment. When he
had collected a small heap of these he took them over to a partly
ruined, but still standing, house on the other side of the street.
Here a dump of miscellaneous and trivial possessions had been
established. A man, a boy in his teens, and a girl who was crying a
little, stood in the doorway of this house. Ford was surprised to see
them, because the police had twice moved away onlookers from
under this house, owing to the evident danger of more of it falling
down. As Ford put down his handful of dust-encrusted possessions, the man said: 'Don't matter about those. What I want you
to get out is my boy.' Ford didn't say anything. 'Is there any
hope—for him?' said the man, jerking his head towards the
mound, and speaking more gently. 'I don't know,' Ford said,
shaking his head. He went back to the mound. 'Is it a boy under
there?' he said to one of the rescue men. 'Lad of about fifteen,
we're told. Some say there's two, some says there's three of them,'
he replied.

Smith wormed his way down again to the bottom of the shaft,
which was now several feet deeper. He put his mouth to another
and larger crack, and said rather softly, 'You there, chum?'
Again they were silent, while Smith put his ear to the crack,
screwing up his face at the stench of the gas. After a little he began
to worm up again. 'Can't hear nothing now,' he said.

They went on filling the wicker baskets. The morning wore on.
Once a doctor came. Work on the shaft was stopped and Frank
and Smith, who were in it, came out. But the doctor couldn't see
what was below the bottom of the shaft any better than they could.
He stood quite still, peering down it—a big, very well turned out
man, with a spotless mackintosh and black soft hat, and a rather
arrogant face. There was a point in the doctor's *tenue* amidst the
encrusted grime of the rest of them, Ford noticed. It actually did
give confidence. However, the doctor said nothing and went away.

Frank said, 'Warden, telephone for a mobile canteen.' Rumbold
went to the nearest telephone box and got through to the Town
Hall. About half an hour later a canteen, drawn by a private car,
arrived. After that the rescue men, and everybody else, went to
it for a cup of tea at intervals.

The next arrival was a smallish, quick-moving man who said,

'Where's my rabbits?' He received no answer. 'Four I 'ad,' he said, 'kept 'em in the Anderson, and this morning I saw two of 'em up the top of Beaton Street.' Ford wondered if his warden's training should have included elementary rabbit catching. But one of the rescue men said unexpectedly that he had seen a rabbit on the embankment. 'There,' said the small man, 'how they do stray!'

But he didn't demand that the wardens should institute a hunt. He wanted to talk. 'It's my belief,' he said, 'that this 'ere was done by one of them 'igh-explosive bombs.' Frank said, his face not moving a muscle, 'You may be right at that, chum.' But irony was lost on the rabbit keeper. He nodded his head. ' 'igh explosive,' he said. 'I was up the other end of the street with my lad Bert, and Bert had just said "Good night" to this poor lad here underneath, when it comes down. Bert was blown through the door of No. 12 and I were blown through No. 11. "Come on, Bert," I says, and we went down to the shelter to find the Missus and my little boy Sam, what I couldn't send away on account of his 'ealth. When we got there the Anderson wasn't to be seen under earth and bricks. But we soon found it, and tapped on the steel. As soon as they 'eard us, my little boy Sam, what we 'ad to keep 'ere on account of his 'ealth, calls out, "Come on, Dad, be quick and take this earth off." So Bert and I digs 'em out, and not a penny the worse they were.' Ford said nothing. The rabbit keeper went off.

The morning wore on. The 'All Clear' went. The shaft was imperceptibly deepened. The gas stank. An ambulance drove up. The driver came up and asked Ford where she was to park it. Ford said, 'I'm afraid you won't be wanted.' The driver said, 'Oh,' but she backed the ambulance up to the mound.

Ford spent some time taking an old lady, who was pretty badly shocked, to the post. The old lady was shaking all over and kept repeating, 'Find me somewhere to go before tonight: before tonight: before tonight.' Ford put the First Aid people on to her; they were glad to have something to do, and finally took the old lady off to hospital.

Ford went back to the mound and emptied more baskets. Smith and Frank could now both work at the bottom. It was now twelve noon. Frank said to Smith, 'You're finished. Go up and have a cup of tea at the mobile.' Smith came up, all in. Ford talked to him while he stood on the mound. 'Do you think they can still be alive?' he asked. 'No,' said Smith. Then Smith said to Ford and Rumbold, 'I wish other bloody civilians helped like you.' Ford was shocked to hear wardens called civilians by a rescue man. But he appreciated a compliment from Smith.

The other rescue men went on filling baskets. The shaft got lower. It was about ten feet deep now. The atmosphere of the group working round it began to change. Everyone began peering at the bottom of the shaft. But there was still only the rubble, the bits and bats of broken furniture, the joists and beams, the twisted gas and water pipes, to see. Then Frank and the rescue man who had taken Smith's place straightened up, stopped filling, and looked round. Ford peered at the bottom of the shaft. There seemed to be nothing new there except one more greyish-yellow joist, which ended in a curiously grooved knob. After looking at it for some time Ford saw that it was a rubble-coated fist and an arm, bare to the elbow. It seemed far too big a hand for a boy of fifteen. The rescue men filled a few more baskets with rubble from the very bottom of the shaft and sawed through several more joist ends. They uncovered a large, untorn and apparently new, though intensely grimy, blanket. Ford noticed that it had a narrow light blue stripe in it at the ends, exactly like the one on his own camp bed at the post. So that's what it would have looked like if 'he' had let go his stick ten seconds earlier, flying east to west, or ten seconds later, flying west to east, he thought.

A smallish man in brown plus-fours, with no uniform, nor badge, nor armlet of any description, appeared. Frank and the other rescue men called him 'Sir'.

'How are they lying?' he said.

'Directly at the bottom here, sir,' said Frank.

'Well, get them out then; what are you waiting for?' said the man in plus-fours, sharply. But the rescue men did not want to pull off the blanket at once. They moved about, collected their saws, took off their gloves, wiped their faces. Smith came back from the canteen. He looked down the shaft. 'Which way are they lying, Frank?' he said. 'Head here, legs there, body bent round here,' said Frank. 'Very awkward,' said Smith. Then he got down

the shaft again and pulled off the blanket. Ford could not instantly see anything underneath it except a good deal of white and
red, and a good deal of white and blue, striped material. Then
he realised that these were the pyjamas of two bodies, lying face
down, on top of each other, or, rather, with their arms and legs
intermingled both with each other, and with the network of
boards, joists, bits of bedsteads, and the omnipresent rubble,
which made up the bottom of the shaft. There was no blood or
gross mutilation. But the bodies had become part of the debris;
they had become one constituent of the many constituents of the
mound. They had been crushed and pressed into the decom-
posed raw material of the five houses. Like the clay of the London
sub-soil, their clay had lost its individual existence and become
indissolubly a part of its environment.

'Well, get them out; come on!' said the man in plus-fours
again. But again the rescue men paused. Then Frank took hold
of the edge of the white and red material and pulled an arm up
from under the two bodies. He began putting this arm down
beside the white and red material, straightening it. He had to
use a good deal of force. 'None too soon,' said Smith, noticing
this. His meaning was that they would never have got the bodies
out of the narrow shaft if they had had time to stiffen thoroughly.
Gradually the contours of human forms began to take shape as
Frank folded arms and legs down beside the main mass of white
and red, and white and blue, pyjamas.

'Now lift, get on with it,' said the man in plus-fours. Frank and
Smith got their arms under the main white and red mass and
lifted. Immediately the two bodies became distinguishable from
each other by their outlines instead of merely by the colour of
their pyjamas. Ford saw that they were those of a woman, in the
white and red, and a man in the white and blue, pyjamas. The
bodies had been driven, whether by the blast itself or by the
falling debris, not only into the material of the houses, but also
into each other. They were locked in a reluctant intercourse.
Frank and Smith got the woman's body a couple of feet up. But
they could not move it any farther; so they put it down again.
Frank took up one wrist, round which was an identity disc.
'Mrs Miller,' he read off. Mrs Miller had been a very big, strong,
and vigorous woman.

'Get a rope,' said the man in plus-fours. When the rope came Frank took it. 'Pass it under the buttocks,' said the man in plus-fours. With some difficulty they did. 'Now pass the blanket under her,' he ordered. Ford noticed that he seemed to know his business. 'Now raise her.' Frank and Smith got their arms under her again and pushed upwards. Mrs Miller's body seemed to loll for a moment on the blanket. Her black hair was mingled and matted with the brick rubble. Her face was covered thick with it, like an actress in her dressing-room, taking her make-up off with cleansing cream. She bled a little at the mouth, as her head sagged.

'Cover her up,' said the man in plus-fours. They got the blanket wrapped over her as well as under her. 'Heave on the rope and pull the corners of the blanket.' Ford got on to a ledge halfway down the shaft and took the weight of one corner of the blanket. Two men pulled on the rope. Gradually Mrs Miller's heavy body came up. They had a light metal stretcher ready at the top of the mound and put her down on to it.

The sirens went. They straightened themselves and looked up, before tackling the man's body. Before the sirens stopped they heard 'planes. A gun or two wuffed. One cracked nearer. Between two clouds they saw the raiding squadron pass, high, aloof, preoccupied, flying fast across the river to the south. The stretcher party began to carry the body down from the mound. There was a heavy thump as a big bomb fell somewhere south of the river. The mound shuddered. So they took Mrs Miller away, and the sounds of the new raid were her only requiem.

Ford stayed to help get the man's body out of the shaft. When they had done so Smith said to him, 'It's a funny thing, but you hardly ever find what you're looking for at this game. I expect that lad who was talking is in another part of the mound alto-gether. Dead, of course, by now. Shouldn't wonder if they all died of the gas in the end. Hope so. It's quietest that way.' It was one o'clock and another warden came down from the post to relieve Ford. So he went home to wash. He found two people whom he had asked to lunch just going away, after waiting for him for half an hour. He washed, got out of his uniform, and they all went out to lunch at a restaurant in Soho. Ford thought that this was the first peculiar thing that had happened that morning.

(1940)

The Big Bomb

AT five minutes to seven on a Friday evening Ford was getting into his overalls when the Blitz began, noisily. He put on his tin hat and went to the door to have a look out, wondering if he ought to go along to the post without eating his dinner, which was ready.

As he put his head out, a man said, 'Warden,' out of the dark. 'Warden,' went on the voice irritably. 'Come and see these dreadful lights. Don't you think you ought to put them out at once?' Ford went down the street a few yards and found a man in a trilby hat pointing towards the trees in Bedford Court. There were the lights all right, two of them behind the trees and, as they watched, three more came slowly drifting and dropping through the higher sky, red, white, and orange. 'I'm afraid I can't put *those* lights out,' Ford said. 'You see, those are flares dropped from German aeroplanes.'—'Oh, are they?' said the man; his voice was still censorious. The plane droned lower and lower. The guns thumped, spat and crashed. 'Don't you think it rather unwise to stand about without a tin hat just . . .' Ford said. But he failed to complete his sentence. A swish had begun. He dropped like a stone full length into the gutter.

The man in the trilby hat took no notice whatever, either of the swish or of the disappearance of his interlocutor. He began explaining how he had always said that the 'best way to deal with them 'Uns . . .' Ford, however, listening, his ear very much to the ground, heard the swish end in a thud without a bang. He thought, 'DA and near.' So the war plans of the man in the trilby hat passed, literally, over his head. Ford picked himself up; another swish began. Something in its note seemed to him menacing. He flung open the area gate and had crashed down the steps by the time this swish ended, with what then seemed to be a loud bang (although a little later he was to think of it as having been an almost incredibly small bang). Emerging from the area—he hoped with dignity—he found the man in the trilby hat still explaining his own method of bombing Berlin. He had apparently again not noticed that he had been speaking to the black-out alone. Ford heard, not very loud, but unmistakably, the tinkle of falling glass and the cracking of broken masonry. The man, it may be at length disgusted at this warden's inattention, remarked, 'Well, I must be going on now,' and passed into the night.

Ford began to run. He ran in what he thought was the direction of the noises, along Marlow Square, past the sub-post, deciding (probably wrongly) not to go in and report first, but to go straight for the incident. It did not cross his mind that there would be any difficulty in finding it. Nor did there seem to be. He ran into Gage Street, crossed Royal Walk and the top of James Street, which he glanced down. It touched his consciousness that the outline of its houses—a quarter seen in the blackness—looked unfamiliar. But he thought nothing of that. Now he saw a masked torch, switched on at the far end of Gage Street. In a moment he found Ivy Rawlings standing over a very small crater, just where the street joined the pavement. They used their torches and saw that a couple of cellars were broken in, but the houses seemed undamaged.

'It was quite a small one, then,' Ford said.

A white hat came up—Mr Strong on his bicycle. 'Come with me to Royal Walk.'

'Is there another incident there?' Ford asked as they walked.

Strong said, 'Considerable damage reported in Royal Walk, but no crater found yet.'

Just then a car came up. Strong said, 'Stay and stop the traffic.' They were just back at the top of James Street. Ford stood about for a bit.

There was no traffic. He began to sense that they were on the fringe of something. He looked down James Street. He could see nothing at all. Surely even tonight one should be able to see the outline of the rows of houses? The darkness down James Street was, he now realised, something yet again. Thick, like rough woollen curtains. You looked into, or on to, total blankness. He felt that something simply wasn't there. (Nor was it.)

He began to walk down James Street. Immediately he was in another world. People were moving about and coming up. He saw that the houses opposite him were very considerably shattered. He looked farther down the street and saw that there were no houses. He became conscious of the smell. The unmistakable, indescribable, incident smell flooded into his nostrils. It is more than a smell really; it is an acute irritation of the nasal passages from the powdered rubble of dissolved houses; it is a raw, brutal smell. He realised that the particular darkness which hung over James Street was due, not to the moonless night, but to the fact that the whole of this area was still covered by an unsettled dust cloud. Here's the incident all right, he thought.

Before he had got opposite to the part of James Street that did not appear to be there, he met Miss Sterling. She pointed at the shattered-looking but still standing houses and said, 'There's a good many people in there.' Mrs Morley came up, smooth and undisturbed. She said, 'The mobile unit' (a sort of medical advance guard consisting of doctor, nurse, and stretcher-bearers) 'has just gone in there,' pointing to No. 50.

Ford went into this house. The ground- and first-floor rooms were more or less all right—nothing more than blown out window frames and shattered plaster. But up from the first floor the stairs were ankle deep in rubble. He went up, passing the second-floor rooms. The two top-floor rooms and the top landing were deeply encumbered with debris, rubble, slates and roof timbers. He looked up; there was no roof overhead. There were dark clouds, picked out with momentary sparkles of shell bursts, reflected gun flashes and an uneasy searchlight waving its futility.

In the first room two men of a stretcher party, a nurse and another man were bending over a figure lying on a heap of the plaster rubble. Ford saw that it was an injured man. His breathing was violent and laboured. They seemed to be trying to get something down his throat through some sort of tube. One of the stretcher-bearers saw Ford. Pointing to the back room he said, 'There are two more in there.' Ford looked in, cautiously using his torch, supplementing its metal hood with his hand. This room was wrecked. One side of it was heaped halfway up to the ceiling with debris. Several roof timbers lay across it. Ford began to

clamber his way into it. He saw something dark lying at his feet.
He put the beam of his torch on it and saw that it was a girl. She
lay partly in, partly out of, the heaped-up debris of plaster and
brick, her body perhaps a third buried, like a high bas-relief. She
lay in a pleasant attitude, one hand curved behind her head, her
legs a little pulled up, to form, with her body, a gentle S shape.
He had seen that attitude once before, in the little Museum of
Prehistory in the Dordogne; a skeleton of a prehistoric girl of the
Mousterian Age, from one of the abri (they had their abri too).
Celia had said, 'I never knew that a skeleton could be attractive
and elegant; that one's bones may be chic after twenty thousand
years.' Here in the top floor back of James Street was the same
charming position.

Ford hadn't much doubt that she was dead. She looked so
small for one thing; and there was a severe head wound. But he
wondered what could have caused fatal injuries. The roof timbers
were fairly light and had had only a few feet to fall. With a feeling
of intimacy, he took up her unresisting hand and felt for a pulse.
To his surprise he felt, or thought he felt, a very feeble beat.
He went back to the front room and said, 'Is there a doctor here?'
One of the stretcher party said, 'He's a doctor, but he's busy.'
He pointed at an oldish man bending over the other casualty.
Ford said, 'I think the girl in here is alive. Will you come and
see?' The doctor gave no sign of having heard. But after a time he
came. He ran a hypodermic into the grey, debris-encrusted flesh
of her arm—'just in case,' he said. He felt for the pulse, but said,
'Very improbable.'—'Where's the injury?' Ford said, 'Her head,
I think.'—'The *head*?' said the doctor, as if astonished. Then he
ran his fingers over her skull, under her blood and rubble matted
hair. But he said nothing. Ford said, 'Shall I take her downstairs?'
The doctor said, 'No.' So they left her, lying easily on the debris,
looking through the roof at the sky.

II

When Ford got back to the street he found that Strong had
taken over as 'incident officer', and got the two masked, light-
blue lamps burning to mark his position. This is an excellent

arrangement by which a light-blue flag is hung out by day and light-blue lamps are lighted at night, to mark the spot where stands the incident officer. The incident officer is responsible for co-ordinating the work of the wardens, the rescue squads, the stretcher parties, the ambulances, and the AFS units (if there is fire). No one who has not experienced a major incident, can well conceive of how necessary is this arrangement. This is especially true when, as in this case, an incident occurs with eleven hours of darkness, during the whole of which it may be risky even to use a torch, lying ahead. The endless confusion caused by the simple fact that it is usually impossible to recognise anyone without stopping them and asking them who they are; the fact that, as in this case, the geography of one or more streets may have been appreciably changed by the destruction; that the mounds of debris are decidedly hard to climb over, and sometimes almost impossible to carry casualties over; that continuing gunfire and, still more, the swishes and detonations of even quite distant bombs may be having an effect on the nerves of those inhabitants of the bombed area, who, although they have not suffered physical injuries, will be more or less severely shocked; that several distinct organisations, each with its own responsible officers, will be at work—these and other similar factors fully justified, Ford had concluded, the rather rigid and at first sight red-tapey form of organisation which had been set up.

He found Tyne, radiating competence and confidence, with Strong. Someone came up with a written message (all messages, and this also has proved a correct arrangement, are sent in writing even over a distance of a few hundred yards whenever possible). Strong said, 'More wardens are wanted at Lothian Cottages. Will you both go there, please?' They went round by Gage Street, passing what Ford and Ivy had mistaken for the incident, out of their own sector, into Leavon Street. You got to Lothian Cottages through a narrow entry. A group of wardens, stretcher-bearers, nurses or other Civil Defence personnel were standing about at the mouth of the entry. Tyne said, 'Do you want any more wardens?' 'No,' said a woman's voice. 'Where is the incident officer?' said Tyne. 'Up there,' said the woman's voice, adding, 'He's busy, you can't go up.' After a bit they went up the opening. At the end of it they came to a completely devastated area, on which a rescue squad was already working. A white hat (Tapplin's antagonist from Slaney) stood on the first mound of debris. They went up to him and reported. He began cursing them for not coming before. 'Why the hell haven't you people from Lees taken over your own filthy incident before this?' he said. Tyne said, 'Is it in our district?' 'Of course it is, you bloody fool,' said the white hat. (As a matter of fact, the district boundary ran down Leavon Street, so that, although nearly all the damage was within their sector (which was the most westerly sector of the Lees district), this part of it could only be approached from Leavon Street, one side of which was within Slaney.

Ford began to be able to see that here, too, a number of houses had been demolished; and a good many of those still standing were well shattered. He supposed vaguely that this was the result of another bomb, falling close to the one which had evidently come down in James Street. He began climbing across the debris-covered area. He went about twenty yards, not without difficulty. The darkness seemed even thicker here; no doubt there was more unsettled dust. He found half a dozen or so rescue men digging hard at a mound. Fairly strong cries and groans were coming from this mound. He took off his coat and gas mask (keeping his torch hung on its strap round his neck) and put them over the shattered door jamb of the nearest house that was standing. This necessitated a tiresome twenty-yard scramble over the debris. But he felt the necessity to put the things on some definite landmark, if he was ever to find them again. He noticed for the first time that it was now raining steadily. He joined a couple of rescue men who were digging at one particular corner of the mound. They were not troubling to fill the wicker baskets, but were simply throwing the stuff back with their hands. Ford did likewise. The debris here was mostly composed of whole, or at worst half, bricks. So they made rapid progress, throwing the bricks back through their own legs. He thought that they must have looked like a line of gigantic and insane rabbits, furiously digging their burrows into the mound. He noticed that in even ten minutes they had made an appreciable impression.

The cries and groans went on unnervingly from underneath. Ford began to distinguish one woman's voice saying, 'Oh, my God, we're done for—I know we are—I know we are—Why don't you come?' Then he noticed a figure which seemed to be neither a rescue man nor a warden, nor a stretcher-bearer. This figure was moving about uneasily in order to avoid the stream of flying bricks that they were throwing backwards through their legs. The figure began to talk to whoever was in the mound. It said, 'That's quite all right, Mrs Wells. Now *don't* become frightened. We're getting to you *very* rapidly. There is *no* cause for alarm. All will be well.' Ford felt certain it must be the Vicar; it was. He saw the dog-collar glint in the light of a torch. Ford thought, 'Well, he's a bit in the way, but not much; and it's right and proper he should come out.' Mrs Wells did not seem to hear the Vicar. At any rate, she took no notice of these well-meant consolations from an outside world of which she could, no doubt, see nothing. Both her cries and groans and the Vicar's assurances that she had nothing to worry about went on monotonously. After half an hour or so of this the rescue man working next to Ford suddenly shouted into the mound, 'Shut up—shut up!' The rescue man was neither brutal nor callous. He was sweating his guts out to dig down to her. But her groaning and calling had got on his nerves. Mrs Wells did shut up, and so did the Vicar.

They were making the beginning of a shaft through their end of the mound, and other rescue men to the left of them were sinking another.

Every now and then the gunfire would get heavier, and they would hear an enemy plane, apparently directly overhead. Then the rescue men would all shout 'Lights—put that light out', and insist on every torch, even the most carefully masked, being put out, so that they had to work on in total blackness. The rescue men were extremely fussy and particular about this. An hour of labour, scrabbling in the gritty rubble and brickwork, now turning slimy in the rain, went by. About every ten minutes the rescue men would shout for silence. Everyone would stop dead. The rescue men who had burrowed deepest would ask for the buried people to give their position. Ford found these silences eerie.

At first there seemed to be two other voices as well as Mrs Wells'. But the last time there was only one other voice. Gradually the outlines of an unshattered floor, the boards still holding to the joists, began to be revealed in the mound. They all guessed at

once that this floor must be held up, if only a foot or so, by something. Only this could account for the fact that there were people
alive underneath. For there were many tons of debris on top.
Human beings could only have survived if at least one end of this
floor was being held up off them, so that a sort of tiny lean-to
had been formed. They dug on, trying to reveal the general
contours of whatever trace of structure must be there. Before
they had succeeded, Ford and the two rescue men working next
to him abruptly uncovered a man's leg. It stuck out of the debris
from the knee down. This leg gave one convulsive kick or twitch
and then hung still. It would have been quite useless to attempt to
pull on it, since the body to which it was attached was deeply
buried. So all they could do was to go on digging, in general round
the leg, but more with reference to the still audible voice than to it.

Gradually the chance-built construction which had kept the
buried voices alive became evident. They had unearthed the edge
of the unbroken floor along ten feet or so of its length. And, sure
enough, a very low cave—not more than six to nine inches high,
could be detected under about half its length. A rescue man who
appeared to be leading this squad called out 'Jacks'. A couple of
men began clambering back over the debris and after a bit came
back with two short, strong jacks and some wooden blocks. For
some time it was impossible to get a jack, even when fully closed,
under the uncovered floor joists. But by means of scrabbling
debris from under it this was finally done. Then the jack was
cranked open. One corner of the floor shifted a few inches upwards. They got blocks under it and, with some trouble, shifted
the jack along. They began to raise the floor a little farther. But
now the base of the jack itself kept slipping and giving in the
shifting debris. The floor rose an inch or so, only to fall back on
to the blocks. The rescue men began to feel baffled. The soaking
rain was turning the rubble into a disgusting gritty paste which
covered them from head to foot. The droning overhead never
ceased. One of the rescue men said, 'Can't do nothing here—let's
go.' Another said, 'Shut up, you bloody bastard, they'll hear you.'

Apparently the suggestion of giving up had not been serious,
because no one took any further notice of it. They all began
digging with their hands again, hoping to find a new point of
attack from which the floor could be raised. Mrs Wells began

G

groaning and crying out again. At any rate it showed them where she was.

Unexpectedly a new voice began complaining, with plaintive precision. 'Where—are—my—spectacles?' it said. 'Oh—who—has—got—my—spectacles?' For some time no one paid any attention. Gradually Ford became aware that an elderly hospital Sister was floundering, like an outraged goose, about the edge of the debris. Eventually a rescue man said that 'he had just put 'er glasses down for a minute'. It was only too apparent that, if he had, the spectacles had long ago been ground to powder under-foot. But why the old thing had ever taken them off, or why, having taken them off, had given them to somebody else to hold, Ford never knew. The Sister wandered irrelevantly away into the darkness, repeating, 'My spectacles, my spectacles.'

The rescue men at the far end seemed to be making progress. They had got the jack into action again and raised the floor several inches. They had succeeded in getting several new blocks into place. The rescue man next to Ford said, 'We could get a prop under here.' Ford went off to look for a stout bit of debris. He found it almost immediately and came back with it. 'Not wanted,' he was told. 'They're out.' Ford saw with amazement that in the, say, 150 seconds he had been away the whole scene had been transformed. The floor had evidently been raised just sufficiently to take all pressure off the buried persons. Two women had either crawled or been pulled out, and there they were on the two stretchers that had been lying waiting for them. The stretcher-bearers were giving them cups of tea out of a thermos. Both women seemed quite all right, and were talking excitedly. The stretcher-bearers picked them up, carried them laboriously over the debris, and out through the entrance into Leavon Street.

III

Ford went to fetch his coat and equipment. He found them soaking wet and disgusting to handle because of the now sticky grit with which everything was covered. Anyhow, he was soaked, so he put them on. He now began to wonder just where he was. He knew that if he went through the entrance into Leavon Street he could walk back the way he had come to the main incident in James Street. But he was curious to know what relationship, if any, this apparently subsidiary area of devastation bore to the other. He imagined that he was now somewhere at the back of James Street. So presumably if he went on across this piece of devastation he might be able to get back through the gaps that had evidently been blown in the row of James Street houses on this side.

He set off, clambering over the debris. Within fifteen yards he came on another squad of rescue men, whom, such was the darkness, he had not realised were there. These men were doing something with the wreckage of an Anderson. The tough, corrugated steel sheets had been split open and the shelter itself lifted out of the ground on to its end. The ragged ends of the steel seemed in the uneven, moving light of the torches, to wave in the air. It looked like a huge sardine tin which had been opened with a road-drill. The rescue men were trying to push back the jagged pieces of steel in order to get at whatever was inside. 'Give us a hand, mate,' said one of them. Ford clambered nearer and began getting a foothold in the debris in order to push with his shoulder under a piece of steel which had to be bent back. He felt something different under his right foot: a supple thing which gave a little and yet was much more solid and substantial than most of the debris. He knew instantly that it was a body and jumped off as if his foot had been stung. For the first time in the evening he felt horror. (Or did he? Was it mainly, at any rate, that he thought he ought to feel horror? Afterwards he was by no means sure.)

The nearest rescue man, seeing him jump, said, rather un-necessarily, 'Hi there, you're on one.' Ford found another foot-hold and they began pushing back the stiff, heavy steel. When they had got three of the separated strips back it was possible to get out the bodies of a man and a woman whom they found inside. These bodies were very dead. The process took some time, and the debris seemed to get more and more nightmarish to deal with. They were all beginning to tire somewhat. It was surprising how long it took to perform the simple operation of getting these two bodies, and the one which Ford had trodden on, on to some stretchers that the rescue men had to hand. But at last it was done.

Ford saw that they had disentangled the bodies of two men and a woman from the chaos into which they had been blasted. They lay in a little row. They seemed to await some adequate tribunal, before which they could lay the consequences of dropping a bomb upon a London street. But there was no tribunal: there was only the rescue men and Ford, who had done nothing for them, who could do nothing for them, who had nothing to say, who, at that moment, at any rate, had no judgment, no protest even, to make. Ford wondered if, far from having wronged the body with his blundering boot, he should not have trodden it still deeper into the debris, rather than drag it out, as now he had, to stare and be stared at in this hideous world.

The rescue men took up the stretchers and began to carry their load towards where Lothian Cottages had stood. They moved through the entrance into Leavon Street, which had become the gateway to one end of this devastated region.

Ford moved on heavily in the opposite direction. In a dozen more yards, which took a minute or so to traverse, he came round the corner of the row of tall, shattered houses on his right (on the window jamb of one of which he had hung his coat). He saw, off to his right, more lights moving and heard men calling. He began to realise that he was getting back to James Street and to understand that these were not two devastated areas, but one large area, stretching from the middle of James Street up and back through Lothian Cottages to Leavon Street.

Suddenly conscious of acute fatigue in his knees and ankles, he determined to make for the blue lights of the incident officer, which he now dimly distinguished. He turned half right. But he had not gone five more yards when a void faced him. He flashed his torch and found himself standing on the extreme lip of a crater. It seemed to be about thirty feet deep. Its sides seemed vertical. It was much the largest bomb crater that he had ever seen. It was not possible to climb down and up its sides in the darkness. He turned left along its rim, intending to get back into James Street a little lower down.

After about twenty yards of heavy going he realised that he was climbing steadily upwards. The black bulk of a house appeared before him; he found himself looking in through the

shattered window openings of the first floor. He couldn't make
out what street this house, or remains of a house, stood in, or had
stood in. With difficulty he climbed on and found himself descending to the level of the crater's rim again. But another upward slope began. He found that this time he was in fact climbing
up a house. This house had indeed lost all structure. No trace
remained of separate rooms, staircase, roof or anything of that
sort. But yet it was not level to the ground in the same sense as were
Lothian Cottages, for instance.

A good many bricks were still upon each other, and whole
floors were sticking together, propped up at varying angles like
crazy lean-tos, against still standing bits of wall. He found next
morning that this construction of destruction, this deposit of the
blast, was itself supported by the house one beyond it from the
area of the crater. This second house, or about fifty per cent of it,
definitely stood, although there was no part of it which was not
shattered. It stood in the sense that it was possible to recognise
clearly its main features, such as the staircase, various floors, and
even some individual rooms. Taken together these two still,
in a sense, standing houses made in the darkness a quite formidable obstacle. They had, however, to be traversed in order to
get back to James Street, since their disorder extended to the
edge of the crater. (Next morning Ford found that he could perfectly well have made his way past their backs. But at the time
he did not realise this.) His feet began to take him upwards
again. It was soon too steep for walking. He began to clamber,
the debris shifting in the dark underneath him. His legs stopped
moving. He did not feel exhausted from the waist up. But his legs
kept still. So he sat down on the debris and waited. In a few minutes his legs became mobile again. He climbed to the top of
the heap, and from there got down again quite easily into
James Street. He found that the street was blocked between
himself and the blue lamps of the incident officer. However,
he had no trouble in making his way across the block, and
reported.

Strong was still incident officer. Miss Sterling, Mrs Morley,
King and Miss Petty, and several other wardens were there.
Mrs Strong arrived with a jug of tea. Ford got a cup of it. He sat
down and drank the hot, sticky, sickly stew. It tasted disgusting,

but was restorative. It was just after half-past eleven, or, as they technically said at the post, '23.33 hours'.

Tyne loomed up. Strong told him and Ford that they were off now. They were to come on again at '04.00 hours' next morning. They walked up James Street towards Gage Street. Ford asked Tyne what he thought about the hole in Gage Street: what had made it? If it wasn't a DA (delayed-action bomb), what was it? Tyne said, 'Let's have a look.' So, instead of turning left into Marlow Square, they turned right down Gage Street to what Ivy and Ford had thought, as it now seemed childishly, was the incident.

There was nothing overhead at the moment, so they used their torches. Ford saw again that two or three cellars had been bashed in. But there was not a single window-pane broken. They concluded that the hole could have been made by nothing but an unexploded bomb, or, just conceivably, a huge lump of masonry flung clear over the row of houses on the other side of Gage Street from the James Street crater. Tyne said that the borough authorities had been sent for to determine whether or not the suspicion of a DA was sufficient to necessitate the evacuation of the street. This idea reminded Ford of the ambulance drivers—three girls who lived at No. 10. He told Tyne he thought he would go and see if they were all right. So they rang at No. 10. Julia Thynne, a girl whom Ford had known for the past fifteen years, came to the door. Tyne refused to go in; he went off to lie down till four o'clock. Ford went up to the girls' flat.

IV

The ambulance drivers had had their windows broken—or rather, they had had the felt blown out which had replaced their windows when the Marlow Square bomb had broken them.

They had all happened to be off duty that night. They had been round to their ambulance station as soon as the James Street bomb had gone off, but found that no one beyond the normal staff on duty was wanted. So they came back. They gave Ford some bottled beer. His throat was parched by the rubble-dust. He drank three glasses quickly, and felt better, although in the

act of feeling better he realised that he was very tired, indes-
cribably filthy, and soaking wet. The ambulance drivers were
each of them six feet tall, good, large women. It was very nice to
see them.

They seemed to have felt a need to emphasise their aliveness,
for each of them had put on bright, sharply coloured clothes and
had done their faces carefully and emphatically. Julia began
doing her face again while Ford was there. 'Good God,' said one
of the others, 'that's the third time she's done her face since the
incident began.' But Ford thought she was right.

They talked about the incident. The drivers had had a longer
experience of bodies than Ford. Indeed, these were only the
second lot he had had to deal with. They all agreed that corpses
were quite all right so long as one had an official relationship
with them. It would have been intolerable to see so many of them
unless there had been definite things which had to be done about
them, such as digging them out, covering them with blankets,
putting them on to stretchers, taking them away. But so long as
one had something to do it was all right.

The worst part of a bombing, they all agreed, was the smell:
the harsh, rank, raw smell. They tried to analyse it. Its basis
certainly came from the torn, wounded, dismembered houses;
from the gritty dust of dissolved brickwork, masonry, and
joinery. But there was more to it than that. For several hours
there was an acrid overtone from the high explosive which the
bomb itself had contained; a fiery constituent of the smell.
Almost invariably, too, there was the mean little stink of domestic
gas, seeping up from broken pipes and leads. But the whole of the
smell was greater than the sum of its parts. It was the smell of
violent death itself. It was as if death was a toad that had
come and squatted down at the bottom of the bomb craters of
London.

Ford told them about the possibility of the DA in their street.
They complained at the idea of being evacuated. He drank some
more beer, felt better still, if wet, and thought he really must go
home and change. There was a ring at the door. Julia said, 'My
God, is that the DA?' She went down. In a minute she came up
and said, 'It is. We've got to be out of here in three minutes.'
Ford said, 'Nonsense! Take as long as you like to pack. They

always try to scare one over DAs. But why don't you come and sleep at my place?'

They said they would. So he went on to get them some beds made up, and to change. They duly came along and he disposed of them on his bed and two mattresses on the floor in his room. They made a little over six yards of ambulance driver in all. Then he went back to the sub-post. Mrs Morley was there on the telephone. It was pleasant to exchange a few words with her un-ruffled, immaculate personality. He noticed that, although she and King had actually been the first on the spot at James Street, such a thing as a big bomb had entirely failed to put a spot of grit on to her uniform. He lay down on one of the camp beds.

But either he was too tired to sleep, or he was tired in the wrong way. The sights and sounds of the night passed through his head in procession. He saw again the dead girl and the smashed young man upstairs at No. 50; heard Mrs Wells cry out for release; saw the twitching leg; felt the hidden body give from his boot; upheld the sagging weight of the man and woman who had been in the Anderson.

At 3.30 a.m. Miss Sterling called him with a cup of tea. She had one herself. They talked while they drank and Ford, reluct-antly, put on the soaked and filthy overalls of his uniform again, and pulled at his heavy rubber boots. Miss Sterling told him that Aarons was to come on to the incident with him. Ford said, 'Tell him to go straight to the incident officer if I've gone on.'

Miss Sterling said, 'Oakadidoke,' and then added, 'Or, as I should say, "Onkadidonk".'

Ford began laughing.

'What are you laughing at?' she said.

'At the precision of your slang, Miss Sterling.'

She said, 'Mr Strong, who also weighs his words, tells me that "Oakadidoke" is *so* old-fashioned.'

Ford said, 'I'm afraid I still say O.K., or, at best, Oke.'

'Oh!' said Miss Sterling.

Ford said, 'These forms would both be marked "Obs." in the dictionary?'

'Or "arch.",' she replied. As they were overtired they laughed at each other immoderately.

Aarons came on duty as they went back to James Street and

reported to Quin, who had taken over from Strong, as incident officer. Quin told them to keep in contact with the rescue men. They found a squad at work on the house, the remains of which Ford had climbed over. Some men from the Gas Light and Coke Company were wandering about disconsolately. They said they had been sent for to deal with an escape and that now nobody seemed to want them. So he went to find the leader of the squad.

He found him, or rather found his legs sticking out of a sort of crevasse which opened where two houses had, as it were, flowed into each other in their incomplete collapse. When the squad leader emerged he knew exactly what he wanted the Gas men to do. 'You come down here,' he said, leading the way into the basement of the house, half of which was still standing. Ford went down, and found that, although it was about half full of rubble and the ceiling was very dicky, this basement could quite easily be got into. Four or five rescue men were at work here. The stink of gas was bad, and the Gas men were put on to deal with it. They were set on to it as you would set hounds on to a fresh scent. They went smelling round, trying to find the source of the escape.

The squad leader explained to Ford what he was doing. A young man in ARP overalls had come down two hours before to report that he had lived in the almost demolished house over which Ford had climbed (No. 30). His mother slept in the basement and was almost certainly there. Would they dig for her?

It seemed a particularly difficult task to try and get at this basement by sinking the usual shaft vertically down. So the squad leader had decided to get into the basement of the still partially standing house, No. 31, and then attempt to tunnel through the base of the party wall into the basement of No. 30. This he had now succeeded in doing in two places. He was evidently proud of the job and asked Ford to come through the tunnel and have a look. Aarons said he would be available outside in the street to deal with anything else. So Ford went down.

He found that he could just squeeze, on hands and knees, through the nearer of the two holes that they had knocked in the party wall. He found himself in what must have been the front basement of No. 30. A large part of the house, and much of its furniture, had collapsed inwards on itself and shot into the basement. The room's space was now wedged tight into a kind of moraine of house and furniture—like the after-effect of a glacier or avalanche. Into this solid, rigid, yet heterogeneous mass the rescue men had tunnelled about three yards. Altogether it was one of the prettiest bits of work Ford had seen. The squad leader had every right to be proud of it.

They had come to a more or less intact settee. 'We think she's under that,' the squad leader said. Ford concluded that there was no real hope of her being alive.

He wormed his way out of the tunnel again. Aarons was all right in the street, so he stayed in the basement of No. 31, and helped push back the debris which was being got out of the two tunnels. The man whose mother it was came back. He had a look at the situation, and said that he knew there was no hope she was alive. He said, 'I drive one of the Council's mortuary vans, so if you get her out let them know at the Town Hall and they'll send me down.' He went off.

One of the rescue men said, 'Didn't oughter send him on a job like this.' Just then the squad leader came out of the tunnel. 'We've found her, or at least as much as we're likely to find till all this is shifted. The back of that settee is soaked in blood. I shall take the men out of the tunnels. I can't let them run risks for corpses.'

The rescue men came out. The man who had thought that the son ought not to be sent for said, 'A corse I could 'ave told 'em she was dead before ever they started digging.'

Ford said, 'There wasn't much hope, but I don't see how you could tell.'

'Yes, I could,' said the rescue man. 'I can sniff 'em. Always know when they're just corpses.'

'Oh, I say,' Ford said, 'but bodies don't begin to smell for several days.'

The rescue man said, 'It ain't that. I just know when those that are underneath are alive and when they're dead. I can sniff 'em.'

Ford noticed that the rescue men, like most people—sailors, for instance—who work at a certain hazard, and in the presence of death, were building up a body of superstition and traditional lore. For example, their extreme aversion to even the most carefully masked torches, if any raider could be heard anywhere near, was probably only partly rational. For they were quite willing to take what might well have been considered greater risks from, for instance, falling debris, by working in the complete dark, rather than use any light.

Ford went back into James Street and rejoined Aarons. It was now six o'clock and the darkness began to give a little. In a quarter of an hour more there was appreciable light. The 'All Clear' went. The various squads of rescue men worked on steadily; but no more people, either dead or alive, were found.

By seven o'clock it was light. Ford climbed up to the rim of the crater again. It was not till then that he got a clear grasp of what had really happened. Now he saw that all the damage had been done by one very large bomb which had landed perhaps twenty feet from the back of the houses on this side of James Street. (The official report stated that it was almost certainly of the largest size being dropped by the Germans on London at that time.) It had fallen directly upon several Anderson shelters which had been built in their backyards. The crater itself was a surprising distance across and was much deeper than any which he had previously seen. Round its rim the earth was piled up in an extremely regular, circular mound. For some distance from the rim of the crater everything had been levelled to the ground. Beyond that the houses, although shattered, still stood. Many of them, as Ford had found on his night clamber across the devastated area, had debris piled against them, up to the level of their first-floor windows. It looked as if they had been washed by some night tide, bearing on it the remains of distorted ships, rocks and sea growths.

The official summary of damage in the sector subsequently showed that, in all, nine houses had been totally demolished and eighteen more so badly damaged that they would have to be pulled down. During the next few days they discovered that a good many more houses in the sector were habitable in the basements alone.

Ford came back to the street. Nothing more happened except that from time to time the rescue men would retrieve some clothing, blankets, a shoe, some papers. Ford and Aarons took them and put them on a bedraggled heap, in one of the abandoned houses.

At eight o'clock Mrs Morley and King came out and relieved Aarons and Ford. They were told that they were off till two o'clock that afternoon. They went back to the post, and this time Ford slept like a log.

V

When Ford got back to the incident at two in the afternoon he noticed that the rescue men seemed moody. They were picking about on the top of the mounds of debris without much apparent purpose. It was raining. One of them came over and sheltered beside Ford in a doorway. He complained that the borough did not provide them with adequate mackintoshes nor with a change of overalls.

'No good catching your death for a lot of stiffs,' he said, excusing himself for having knocked off.

Just then Ford noticed a change in the atmosphere of the incident. The nearest squad of rescue men had become alert again. Quin, who was again incident officer, came over and told him that they thought that they had heard tapping. Ford asked Quin's permission to join the squad working on the mound formed by the segment of the arc of the crater which impinged on James Street. Quin gave it, kindly taking over Ford's job of receiving salvaged property himself. The two houses which had taken the full force of the blast had stood here. Three or four men had dug out a small cave, almost at the top of the mound. One crawled inside; he called for silence, and again there was a stillness while they listened for the sound of life. The rescue man in the cave began shouting down, 'All right; stick it. We're coming.' Evidently he heard something.

The whole squad began working strongly and fast. One or two men would from time to time get excited and begin to grab at the debris, flinging it aside. But that didn't pay in this case, for it was evident that tons of stuff would have to be moved before they had hope of coming on anyone. Ford took off his equipment and began the usual filling of baskets, and the passing of them back, along a chain of hands to be emptied. Every fifteen minutes or so one or other of the rescue men would ask for stillness, would listen for

the tapping and would call down. After two or three times some
of the rescue men began saying, 'Cut it out. Get on with it.
You're holding up the work. We haven't much time.'

Ford guessed that the rescue men were thinking not only of
getting to the buried person, or persons, as quickly as possible,
but also of getting the job done before the dark and the raiders
came back again. But he couldn't conceive that there would be any
difficulty about that. The idea of another night and another raid
beginning was a remote and repulsive hypothesis—the last night
and the last raid seemed only just over. In any case, it was a
difficult matter to decide how often it was justifiable to hold up the
work in order to get a signal from below. It was necessary to do
so from time to time, because by means of such signals alone
could they hope to locate the buried persons. And unless he, she,
or they could be located, with gradually increasing exactitude,
hours might be wasted in sinking shafts and tunnelling in the
wrong places.

The rescue men were attacking this very large, irregularly
shaped mound of debris from three different positions. After a bit
one of the parties working some way away from the cave from
which the tapping had first been heard, insisted on silence. He
claimed that he could hear a voice as well as tapping. After two or
three more bouts of digging this rescue man definitely got into
touch with the buried person. A voice responded several times,
and they all got a much better idea of where to dig. It became
apparent that the original cave, which had been deepened into
the beginning of a shaft, was much too high up the mound. With
reluctance the rescue men who had been working up there were
induced to come down and join those who were cutting into the
side of the mound. It was now half-past three. The rescue man
who was deepest into the tunnel, near the bottom of the mound,
began to shout.

'Who are you?' he called. He listened. 'What name?' he
repeated. He listened. ' "Bee", did you say—"Bee"?'—'It's
a woman,' he said, turning his face upwards. 'Bee, or Lee, or Tee,
or some such name.' Quin consulted his records of who should
have been sleeping in the house. (Each sector kept a record of the
occupants of each house, for occasions such as this, with, if
possible, an up-to-date note of where every person in the sector

slept—whether in a public shelter, an Anderson, their own base-ment, or wherever.) But this record was of far less use than usual on this occasion, as the bomb had come down at seven o'clock in the evening, before most people had gone to bed. (Ford later discovered, for instance, that the girl who had been killed up-stairs in the house which he had first visited had been a casual visitor.)

'There should have been a Miss Lee,' Quin said.

'That's right,' said the rescue man. 'That's what she's trying to say.'

They worked on, obviously encouraged by knowing now that it was a definite person, whose name they knew, that they were trying to reach.

It was now half-past four. The light was perceptibly weaker. Ford realised that, far from there being plenty of time, it was going to be a race to get her out before the darkness and the fireworks began all over again. After filling and passing down an infinity of baskets, they found that they were uncovering a more or less intact area of flooring. It looked as if the same story as in the case of the Wells' house at Lothian Cottages was to be repeated. If Miss Lee was alive, it must surely be because something had held up this flooring and made a tiny lean-to for her. The men working at the bottom of the mound were driving their tunnel well in, and getting under this area of flooring.

It was now five, and the wet, clammy dusk was rapidly gaining on the daylight. The rescue men said nothing, but they began to get a little short and abrupt with each other, working against time. There was more in it, Ford felt, than the rational fear of working in the difficulties of the darkness and a new raid. There had been reawakened in them all an older fear, of the beasts, the spirits, and the dark.

They dug. At six-twenty the sirens went. 'He's back,' said the man working next to Ford. The guns began. At first they heard the thud of distant batteries, south of the river; then the sharp note of their familiar local guns, and then the rising and falling drone of the bombers' desynchronised engines. The rescue men took no notice. It was still possible to work fairly effectively with-out the use of torches. Then they heard a wailing from the mound. It was Miss Lee. She too, imprisoned, had heard the new raid begin. Her shattered nerves gave way. An incoherent, terrified sound, occasionally crystallising itself into words, came from her. Ford heard, 'It's there again. They'll get us all; they'll get me.' The rescue men began to shout back to her, 'No, they won't; you're all right; stick it now.' But the wailing shouts went on. 'Can't you save me? Don't be so slow. Why don't you come?'

'Shan't be ten minutes now,' answered the rescue men.

They dug. The light failed. The fact had to be faced that it would be necessary to work on during another night; and, not for ten minutes, but for several hours, as far as could be judged. Miss Lee kept up an intermittent, usually inarticulate, wail, like an animal.

At half-past six the leader of the squad told the two men working on what was now the face of a two or three yards long tunnel to knock off. They refused. Ford had noticed that rescue men were almost always angry at the idea of being relieved when they thought that they were getting near some buried person. And naturally. Every such attempted rescue involves a scheme or plan, based upon a guess of the buried person's position, the lie of the debris, what is holding it up, and many other factors. It is intolerable to leave before you come to the solution of the riddle.

The squad leader saw that he would have to work on to the end with these same men. He sent for a big tarpaulin from the rescue lorry. This he had stretched, like a sort of rough tent, over the mouth of the tunnel so that torches could be used. The two rescue men and two stretcher-bearers, who, as they neared Miss Lee, had begun to take an increasing part in the work, got in and around the mouth of the tunnel. Ford also got under the tarpaulin at the back of this group. The tarpaulin was held down at the top by piles of bricks on its corners, but the bottom ends were left loose. They kept it up by letting it rest on their heads as they sat or squatted under it, their steel helmets taking its weight fairly comfortably. The two men at the end of the tunnel, which was now steadily cutting inwards and downwards, filled baskets, and the rest of them passed them back. Ford swung them out from under the edge of the tarpaulin into unseen hands. These hands grasped them, took them off, and gave him back empties. Before long George, the rescue man who had forced his way farthest in, called back, 'I can touch her hand now.'—'All right,' said one of the stretcher-bearers (he was a corporal, and in charge of the party), 'the doctor says she can have this morphia tablet.' They passed down the tiny tablet. 'Can you take this in your hand, Miss?' George said. Ford could not hear the answer. But George said, 'She's got it.'

The tarpaulin made a little, private torch-lit world of their own, cut off from the rain-soaked, gun-thudding, bomber-droning world outside. They felt safer. Unfortunately it did not seem to help Miss Lee. For her terror of the guns (they heard no bombs, fortunately) seemed to increase. Her wailing became worse. The stretcher-party corporal whispered, 'The morphia always makes 'em worse to start with.'

They worked on. It was seven o'clock. Miss Lee had been buried just twenty-four hours. 'I can see her head now,' George said. Then, after a bit, the other rescue man said, 'That ain't her head—that's her arse. She's lying this way.'

'No, she isn't—She's in an S curve, this way. Aren't you, Miss?' said George, appealing to the patient to settle this argument as to her anatomy. Ford couldn't hear the reply. But it was clear that as the rescue men got nearer and nearer, so that she could hear them properly and even probably see them by now, she was getting calmer. She had stopped wailing, and was quiet except for an occasional sob.

There was a shout from the outside of 'Warden.' Ford put his head out of the tarpaulin. 'Party here wants to see Miss Lee,' said a rescue man.

Ford came out to find a tall, elderly, rather infirm-looking man in a black coat and white wing collar—a confidential clerk or shopkeeper.

'I am Henry Edward Lee, Miss Lee's father,' he said. 'Is there any hope that my daughter is alive?'

'But yes,' Ford said. 'Certainly she's alive. We shall have her out very shortly now. Don't be alarmed. I think I can arrange for you to speak to her now if you like.' Henry Lee seemed to be overcome, but he bowed his head as if he wished to speak to her.

Ford went back under the tarpaulin and said, 'Miss Lee's father is here. Can we let him come down to speak to her?'

The rescue men said, 'Stand back for Miss Lee's father.' Ford fetched the old gentleman and they half-pushed him into the mouth of the tunnel and about halfway down it. The rescue man at the end said, 'Here's your father come to speak to you, Miss—' 'Speak to 'er, Dad.'

Henry Lee said, "Is that you, Amy?' but in such a tiny voice that she could not possibly have heard him. 'Speak *up*,' said the rescue men in chorus. 'Speak up, Dad, do. She can't 'ear you.' This time he did speak a bit louder, but his voice broke. Ford could just hear Miss Lee from below saying, 'Is that you, Dad?'

Then they handed the old boy out again. Ford thought that he had probably made a mistake in ever having him in. But, anyhow, it had only held the work up for a couple of minutes.

They dug. Ford began to hear Miss Lee's voice much more clearly. She was saying something about a dog. 'Right across my knees,' she said. They had evidently got much closer to her now. After a bit Ford bent forward, craning over the back of the stretcher-bearer corporal in front of him to have a look down the length of the tunnel. To his astonishment he found that George and his mate had now cut their way right through to her. For there she was.

Miss Lee sat facing him, in a tiny torch-lit cave, clear of the debris from her waist up. But her legs and the lower part of her body were still deeply covered by something. She looked to be a slight woman in her early forties, her face and hair covered with the greyish debris. She was perfectly calm now, comforted by the actual presence of her rescuers. She sat there contentedly and innocently, like a dishevelled child sitting up in bed in its night nursery. George, by lying full length, could get at the debris on her right side; he was slowly filling a basket with it. She went on talking about this dog. 'Scratched for me, he did,' she said. 'As soon as the first lot came down on me, I heard him scratching for me and barking. And then the second lot came down, much more heavy, and killed him, right across my legs.'

Ford began to realise that she was explaining that the body of this dog was across her legs now: that its body was part of what was holding her legs down. 'Saved your legs, lying soft on 'em like that,' George said to her.

'Now let's see if we can shift him.' Ford couldn't see what George was doing. But he heard him grunt as he tried to move something heavy. Then Miss Lee cried out, 'Oh, my legs!'—

H

'All right, Sister, all right. Bound to hurt a bit as we shift him off.' But evidently they couldn't get at the dog's body. For in a minute they called for a rope. One was fetched by the unseen hands from outside and passed to Ford under the end of the tarpaulin. They gave it to George. He took some time passing it under the dog's body, as Miss Lee cried out whenever the weight on her legs was shifted.

But she was perfectly calm and rational now. She went on talking to them as they worked. 'I know I'll never have the use of my legs again,' she said, her voice pleading for reassurance. 'Oh yes, you will, Sister,' George told her. 'In ten minutes' (it was always ten minutes) 'when we gets you out, you'll find the use of them legs coming back to you prompt. That poor beast's body has saved them legs of yours.'

Miss Lee said, 'I'm a seamstress. Work for Halliday and Knight. Don't use power machines in our shop. All treadle machines. Wouldn't think a big firm like them would have treadle machines, would you? Old-fashioned.'

'You'll be all right,' said George. He had got the rope fixed under the dog. 'Now, Miss, we're going to lift this dog off of your legs. May hurt a bit as the blood comes back into 'em.' He turned to the rest of them—'Now heave.' They all pulled on the rope and Ford felt it slowly coming. Gradually a darkness was pulled back through the tunnel; it was deposited on to Ford's knees, as the last man in the line. It was the heavy, soft, black body of a very large Labrador retriever. Ford had considerable difficulty in lifting it and passing it out from under the tarpaulin. But in the end the hands from outside got hold of it, and the body was taken away.

There was now enough space in the actual cave in which Miss Lee sat for George to get down into it beside her. He and she sat there quite peacefully together; she, reassured and happy now that she was in actual physical contact with another human being; he carefully digging round her legs so as to free them. The conversation went on, Miss Lee talking gently about her life and her job; wondering if she'd be long away from work, and would someone at the hospital tell the firm what had happened? George managed to make a good deal of progress towards freeing her right leg, which was nearest to him, though not without causing her sudden sharp pains at intervals. 'That's good, Miss, that is,' he kept saying, 'shows you've got the feeling down your leg.'

But he had great difficulty in getting at the debris over her left leg, since to do so he had to reach right over her body. After several not very successful attempts, he said to her, 'Could you shift any of it yourself, Miss?' Miss Lee began picking quite strongly with her right hand (her left was slightly injured) at the debris over this leg. Ford remembered what intolerable stuff it was to handle with one's bare hands. He took off his right glove and said, 'Here's a glove for her; pass it down.' They took it, saying, 'Glove coming down,' and Miss Lee put it on her right hand.

By this time George had got her right leg free and was able to lean over more easily and help her with the left leg. After about another fifteen minutes' work he announced that this leg, too, was coming free. The corporal of stretcher-bearers called out to his men outside the tarpaulin, 'Ready for the doctor.'—'Doctor coming down,' they answered, and almost at once the end of the tarpaulin was lifted and the trim, mackintoshed figure of the doctor appeared. 'Doctor coming down; all out for the doctor,' ordered the corporal. The doctor made his way down, guided by the hands of the men, and, not without difficulty, reached Miss Lee, taking the place George had left. He began speaking gently and firmly to her. She was scared as he began to examine her legs. 'They're broken, Doctor, I know they're broken,' she said. 'No, no, I don't think they are at all. Let's just see, let's just see.' After carefully feeling each leg, he asked for a splint and two triangular bandages. These were passed down to him, and he bandaged her right leg to the splint. 'That's all we need do here, Miss Lee,' he said. 'Now you're coming out,' and he wormed his way back down the tunnel.

Ford did not quite see how she was to be got out, though. It was clearly impossible to get a stretcher down that narrow, irregular length of tunnel, still less into the cave. But the corporal called to his men—'Fetch the Neal Robertson.' In a little while two stretcher-bearers appeared with a curious-looking white object. They put it down near the entrance to the tunnel. The tarpaulin was now rolled back, and they worked for a time with unscreened torches. Fortunately it didn't sound as if there were any German planes particularly near overhead. The white object

was unwrapped; it was like an enormous pair of stays, only
this stretched the full length of the body. It was made of white,
tough canvas, reinforced with struts which were made either of a
light metal or some pliant wood such as ash. The whole thing
bent and rolled up into almost any shape. This ingenious device
was passed down the sloping tunnel. George was at his old place
beside Miss Lee in the cave. Gently and expertly they slid the
Neal Robertson stretcher under her—she was able to help quite
considerably herself, by rolling on to it. Once on, they carried
straps, with which the sides of the stretcher were fitted, across her
body, and strapped her firmly on. Then they began the still by no
means easy process of working the laden stretcher back through
the tunnel. Miss Lee must have been quite a light woman, but it
is amazingly difficult to get enough purchase to lift any inert
body when one is working in a confined space. However, little by
little, and without, as far as they could judge, hurting her, they got
the stretcher backed out of the tunnel. Once it was clear they lifted
it and Miss Lee together on to an ordinary stretcher. Meanwhile
the waiting ambulance was backed close up to the mound. It was
just nine o'clock. Miss Lee had been buried twenty-six hours.

While they were doing this Ford came close to the stretcher, and
looked down at Miss Lee. She was lying there very still, but seemed
calm and unshocked. He saw that his glove was still on her right
hand. He bent down and slipped it off. She took no notice. It was
really a perfectly sensible thing to do; the glove could not
possibly have been of any further use to her. And yet afterwards
Ford couldn't help feeling that he had been mean in taking it
back. It was rather too careful a thing to do, in the circumstances. But Ford had always particularly hated losing one glove
of a pair, as he not infrequently did. So that even after twenty-
six hours of the James Street incident the impulse to prevent
that happening was still strong in him. Of all the things that
happened in the course of this long incident this lending and
recovery of his glove stuck most obstinately in his mind.

The stretcher party picked Miss Lee up, put her in the ambulance and drove off with her. Ford went up to the doctor and
asked him whether she had been badly injured. 'Not at all, not at
all,' he said. 'So far as I could ascertain—from the very superficial examination that was all that was possible down there—

there is no grave physical injury. No limb is broken and there appears to be nothing else serious the matter with her.' Ford and the other wardens present—Miss Sterling, Mrs Morley, King —felt elation. There was triumph in the wresting of Miss Lee, without serious injury, and after twenty-six hours' work, from the chaos of the big bomb. There was triumph in the stubborn digging of the rescue squads, in the use of such a well designed device as the Neal Robertson stretcher by the stretcher-bearers, and, for that matter, in their own efforts. Ford went off duty and slept.

VI

Next morning Ford was on the incident from eight o'clock (when the rescue squads began work) to ten-thirty. There was first of all a lot of fussing with the police about the DA in Gage Street. As usual, people were now beginning to doubt whether it really was a DA at all, to wander about nearer and nearer to it, and finally to trickle back towards their houses. There was an argument about where the police should post constables, and where the ropes, carrying 'unexploded bomb' notices, should be hung. While this was going on a brisk little man drove up to the barrier in a tradesman's van labelled, 'Ironmongery, Wireless, Electrical Goods'. Ford stopped him. He touched his hat and said, 'I've called for the stiffs, sir.'

This, Ford realised, was one of the vans hired by the borough for use when their own mortuary van (driven by the man who had lost his mother) was busy elsewhere.

Ford said, 'They're in that shop there.' The man drove off and was loaded up by the rescue squads.

Julia Thynne came down the street; she wanted to get something out of her flat. He persuaded the constable to let her past by pointing out that she was a Civil Defence worker and should be allowed to go to places at her own risk. He went up to the flat with her and saw the beer glasses and bottles on the table, as they had left them. Julia said, 'Let's go and talk to the Bomb Disposal Squad and see if there is any chance of us getting back.' So they went down to the DA crater. They found four men of the Bomb

Disposal Squad working there under a lance-corporal. Or, rather, they were not working; the men were sitting about at the bottom of the small crater. The crater consisted in the two broken-open cellars under the pavement, now a good deal enlarged by the squad's digging. The men's faces wore disgusted and resentful expressions, their tin hats pushed far on to the backs of their heads. The lance-corporal came out of the crater. Julia asked him when she would be able to go back to her flat. He said, 'Now, as far as I'm concerned. Don't believe there's aught here.' He began questioning them as to whether they had heard one or two bombs come down. They were able to reassure him that there had been two quite separate swishes, separated from each other by something like thirty seconds. The lance-corporal was not much reassured.

'It's like this,' he said to Julia, 'We don't mind digging for a *real* bomb. But we hate digging for nothing; moving all this stuff; it's not worth it.'

They felt by no means so distressed as he at the idea that his labours might prove fruitless.

Ford went back to the site of Lothian Cottages, where thirty-six hours ago Mrs Wells and her daughter had been dug out. He found an unshaven, rough-looking man poking about in the debris, and from time to time loading salvaged goods, such as bedding and pots and pans, on to a hand barrow.

'I'm afraid the borough will be on to you if you do that,' said Ford. There was a strict and perhaps necessary regulation that all salvaged objects without exception must be taken to the Salvage Department at the Town Hall, there to be sorted, and only claimed by their rightful owners when they had established their identity. No one was allowed to go to the site of his own house to pick up even his most personal possessions.

'Aye, them,' said the man. 'I've been seein' them from the borough. I told them it was me sister, Mrs Wells, who lived here. I know the house fine.'

'But didn't they stop you?' said Ford.

The man said, 'Stop me, stop me! And who could be stopping me? I'm a free citizen, aren't I?'

Ford thought that apparently he was. It was evident that the theory of natural rights, however discredited in the schools, was alive in the mind of Mrs Wells' brother. Moreover, it seemed that some such theory of the existence of certain inalienable rights, appertaining to the citizen as such, rights which when they conflicted with official rules and regulations, overrode them, must have been present also in the mind of the borough official who had had to confront Mrs Wells' brother on the site of her house. At any rate, the official had left him in possession.

'Can you tell me how Mrs Wells and her daughter are doing?' Ford asked.

'Very weell, very weell indeed,' said the man, amiable at once. 'I'm Mr Ross, her brother, and I saw them last night in hospital. Lily has not the use of her legs yet, but they say there's no serious harm done to them. And Mrs Wells had no more than severe contusions, they say.'

'What hospital are they in?' Ford asked.

'St Andrew's Hospital, over in Stane Street,' said Mr Ross.

Ford went back to James Street. A couple of rescue squads were still working there. But it was doubtful if there were any more recoverable bodies. The wardens' lists showed that there was one woman still unaccounted for. If this woman was reckoned as dead, the total casualty list was thirteen dead and six injured. Once again such a total was most unexpectedly small, considering the extent and area of the devastation. On the other hand, the proportion of double the number of dead to injured was an extremely high one. The rescue squad would be probably working for another couple of days trying to find the missing body, and pushing down any particularly precarious walls. After that the site would be left alone until such a time as the Pioneer Corps came along.

Ford was as usual on night duty at the sub-post; so as soon as the special pressure was over he was not asked to do any more day periods on the incident.

On the following day he was free to go and see Mrs Wells and Miss Wells at St Andrew's. He found it a nice little hospital, run by the LCC with less red tape and prison-intimidation about it than he had experienced whenever he had been to one of the big 'Voluntary' hospitals. They let him go into the women's air-raid casualty ward, although it wasn't visiting time, without any fuss.

There were ten or a dozen women in bed in a row. Ford had to ask for Mrs and Miss Wells, for he had scarcely seen their faces amidst the darkness and the debris. He brought them some fruit. Mrs Wells seemed to want to talk about the incident.

'We didn't hear a thing, did we, dear?' she said to her daughter. 'We were all three just sitting round the fire when the house began to fall in. Then it went black and we didn't know nothing till we woke up under the debris. I could hear Lily here calling, and Father too. But we couldn't say much because whenever we opened our mouths we choked with the dust. It was the dust more than the weight that killed Father.'

Mrs Wells' eyes filled with tears. 'Of course we could feel that terrible weight on our legs, couldn't we, Lily? But it was the dust that was choking us. The worst was that Father couldn't have gone directly when the house fell. He kept saying to me, "I'm going now." He knew they wouldn't reach him in time.'

Ford remembered the twitching leg; he said, 'Did you hear the rescue men working?'

'Of course we did! Weren't they splendid?' she said.

'Did you know they were using their jacks to lift the floor off you? Before they got the jacks they were pretty well stumped, you know.' Ford wondered if they had heard what the fed-up rescue man had said. 'Did you hear that chap say they might as well go home?' he asked. Mrs Wells said, 'Certainly we did. But, of course, we knew he didn't mean it. Baffled he was: baffled like.' She turned sharply to Ford. 'Were you there?'

'Yes,' he said. 'I was there.'

'Lily,' Mrs Wells said, 'do you hear that? He was there digging for us.'

Ford asked them if the borough had arranged any place for them to go when they came out. Mrs Wells said, 'Oh, we've had more than a dozen offers from friends to take us in. Don't you worry about that.'

Ford said, 'I want to find a Miss Lee, who was also dug up. Is she in this hospital?'

Mrs Wells' face changed. She said, 'Ah, Miss Lee—she died yesterday.'

This news affected Ford extremely. He had an intense impulse flatly to deny it. He turned instinctively to the other women in the ward. They nodded their heads.

'She was along in the end bed there. Went yesterday,' they said.

'But why?' he almost shouted. 'Why did she die? She seemed all right. Surely she can't have died?'

The ward sister came up. Ford said to her, 'Why did Miss Lee die? We dug her up after twenty-six hours. She was perfectly all right. She talked to us just as I'm talking to you. Now you say she's died.'

The Sister said, 'Shock partly, also multiple internal haemorrhage.'

Mrs Wells nodded. 'It's my belief it was mostly shock. She seemed all right when she first came in. Talked to us all. But at night the guns began again. Turned her fair frantic. She was all right in the daytime. But she couldn't stand the guns and the nights. Kept calling out and calling out, she did. And last night she went.'

Ford said 'Good-bye' to Mrs Wells and to Lily. He was too depressed by Miss Lee's death to feel much pleasure even in their preservation, recovery and staunchness. He went home and told the post. They were all equally depressed.

The incident had now become a business of endless clearings up and sortings out. The job of the wardens was largely to help people to use the well organised, but complex, services made available to them by the borough, such as having their furniture moved out of shattered houses and stored, free of charge, by the Salvage Department, getting alternative accommodation, reclaiming salved possessions, and the like.

Three days later Miss Sterling told Ford that Mrs Wells had come out of the hospital. She had taken her to the Town Hall to register the death of her husband. Mrs Wells had said to the Registrar, 'We're all right; we'll come out on top.'

The Registrar, evidently a mild man, had said. 'I hope so.'

To which Mrs Wells had replied, 'Have some guts, man.'

Ford thought about these words of Mrs Wells'. Many people would, no doubt, consider them very old-fashioned, not to say jingoistic. They sounded so 'British', in the most conventional sense of that term. But Ford could not say that he found them in bad taste. They would, no doubt, have been in bad taste if they had been said, even in the slightest degree, for effect; but they had not been. Again Berlin would undoubtedly have regarded it as far more appropriate on the part of Mrs Wells if she had been too cowed to speak. Moscow, on the other hand, would have considered it incomparably more correct—more contemporary—if she had denounced 'both camps of Imperialist brigands'.

Be all that as it may, the fact must be recorded that what she said was, 'Have some guts, man.'

Mrs Wells was an obstinate woman. You may drop big bombs on her; you may kill her dearly loved husband before her eyes; you may bury herself and her daughter under her home; but you do not alter her.

Miss Sterling said, 'Mr Wells' and Miss Lee's funeral will be the day after tomorrow at eleven o'clock. I think the wardens should be represented. Will you come?'

Two days later they went, in uniform, to the Parish Church, just out of the sector to the south. It had had some incendiaries on it, and the roof had been burnt out. The only usable part was the vestry, so the service was held there. Miss Sterling was a little late because the sirens went just as they were setting out and she had to get another warden to man the sub-post. When they got there the Vicar had already started the service. He was reading a passage from the Book of Common Prayer. He did not read it very well, but he read it.

'Man that is born of a woman hath but a short time to live and is full of misery. He cometh up and is cut down, like a flower: he fleeth as it were a shadow, and never continueth in one stay. . . . Forasmuch as it hath pleased Almighty God of his great mercy to take unto him the souls of our dear brother and sister here departed, we therefore commend their bodies to the ground; earth to earth, ashes to ashes, dust to dust.'

(1940)

Troopship

SAILING on a troopship was a good deal more like ordinary travelling than Ford had supposed. There was the same problem of how much luggage to take; the same question of which suitcase to label 'not wanted on voyage' and which to have in the cabin, and what to pack in each. The chief difference was that everything was better and more systematically arranged. It all took longer, but, on the other hand, there was no rush or bother whatever.

The first impression of the ship, too, was exceedingly normal. In the first place she was the old *Illyria*. Ford had travelled on her in peace-time. He had come back from New York in her eleven years ago. The officers' quarters were not very different from a particularly crowded ship in peace-time. Moreover, they were all positively shaken by the goodness of the food. It was the old, solid, sound company's food, served in the first-class dining-saloon by the same old stewards. There were even the same little white printed menu cards. The company evidently didn't let a little thing like a world war change its ways.

It was not until the first evening that Ford got any impression of strangeness. Then he had occasion to go to the orderly-room, which was aft, about ten o'clock. The way led along what had been the main promenade decks, now converted into combined mess decks and dormitories for the troops. He made his way down one of the largest of them. It was dark, and the lines of hammocks, slung from the ceiling and weighted with sleeping men, receded into the distance. Ford tried to slip along silently between the rows. Every ten yards or so he had to bend double to get under the bodies, where the rows were too close to pass between. He began to realise that a loaded troopship in war-time is not, after all, very like a liner in peace-time. The breathing of all the sleeping men who were aboard her made an undulating, persistent sound, like a light sea upon shingle. The effect was murmuring and plaintive as if, in sleep alone each man could express his underlying sorrow at the necessity which had brought him there.

Ford had been on his way to the orderly-room to get permission to send a letter off to the shore. The ship was still lying in the river and Harry Cole had got hold of an evening paper which someone from the shore must have brought on board. Ford had looked at the paper over his shoulder and had seen that Hitler had invaded unoccupied France. For some reason the news made him think of the last time he had been in this ship. In 1929 he had been a different man in a different world. He certainly did not mourn his own youth—he had hardly been a person at all in those days. Nor, when he thought it over carefully, could he regret the purposeless, meaningless world of the nineteen-twenties either. Those were the years in which it would have been so wholly possible to prevent what had happened now. And no one had lifted a finger. The sole thing that could be said for his own youth was that he had never for a moment ceased to revolt against that world and everything it had stood for. True, his revolt had been almost as misdirected as the thing revolted against had been odious. But still, to have revolted was something. Now men had to be packed into the troopships, the troop-trains, the lorries, the tanks, and the aircraft, fundamentally because nobody had thought of anything else to do with them. For those who held the keys of the kingdom had refused to let them work when the world was at peace.

Next morning Captain Lee, the leader of the corresponding American unit to their own, came to their cabin to discuss joint plans. He was a substantial, youngish man. He brought two neat, quiet American boys with him, naval petty officers, who operated his ciné cameras. They discussed service propaganda methods being all in that line of business. The Americans had the most beautiful personal equipment, such as their fur-trimmed leather jackets, their Colt side-arms, their belts and straps, but above all their steel helmets. The linings of them were detachable and became sun helmets. The steel outer skin was perfectly finished, very light, yet elaborately shaped—more like, though not identical with, the German than the round British helmet. Their own British equipment was very good and sound—just as serviceable as the Americans', perhaps. But this was something yet again. It was a new sort of military *chic* with nothing to do with tailoring—it was 'battle-dress *d'élégance*'. They were a little put out by it.

Ford felt the interlacing of the moral and material factors in war; it was all, he couldn't help reflecting, highly dialectical. Napoleon had rather boringly asserted that in war the importance of moral factors was as one to three compared to material factors. But Napoleon had failed to point out that morale itself largely depended on whether men had confidence—or, still better, pride —in their weapons and equipment. It depended on simple and highly material factors such as these at least as much as on grand and ideal factors such as a good cause to fight for. But, on the other hand, it might be true that only those states in which the social divisions are not too acute, and which represent, in general, progressive causes, will in the long run provide their troops with first-rate weapons and equipment. In a word, the moral and material factors go on interlacing and reciprocating endlessly. *Vive le Dialectic!*

They had their first 'Action Stations'. Life on a troopship in convoy largely consists, they found, in rehearsing for a play which may or may not be performed. The rehearsals began with four blasts on some sort of internal ship's siren. This was the 'Action Stations' signal. At that every man on board had to go to his cabin or mess deck and put on his equipment. This consisted of a haversack, containing emergency rations for forty-eight hours, a full water-bottle, a great-coat, and, for officers, a loaded revolver. In addition they had to put the life-jackets, which they had to carry with them everywhere, night and day, over their heads. Thus encumbered, like overloaded Christmas-trees, they had to try to lie down on their bunks or hammocks. A few minutes later the siren gave a very long single blast. This was the 'Emergency Stations' signal. At that they had to jump up and parade on an appointed spot on the deck. From this spot they would, if necessary, abandon the ship. They went through this performance twice a day to begin with. Gradually all the men began to know their way about the ship. The time which elapsed from the sounding of the 'Emergency Stations' signal to the last man being reported on parade at his station was carefully taken.

When the time became satisfactorily short they were made to rehearse only once a day.

Ford's unit, which consisted of Public Relations Officers, ciné-photographers, and the like, took a poor view of being held downstairs on their bunks during Action Stations. For this would be the time when any attack on the convoy would be taking place. So they made representations through their CO and the 'OC Troops' to the Captain of the ship himself that immediately on Action Stations being sounded they should be allowed to equip themselves and then to go to two points on deck, one aft, one forward, which they had chosen. Rather to Ford's surprise, permission was given at once. So on all future Action Stations Ford went to his position, which was aft, immediately above the anti-submarine gun in the stern and immediately below one of the AA guns. If an actual attack ever did occur, the place, Ford thought, might be noisy.

Just after noon that day they began to move down the river, other liners and some freighters in company. They passed naval craft, destroyers, corvettes, and then an aircraft carrier.

The liners steamed gravely on into the winter sunset. They looked bulky and galleon-like; top heavy, yet at the same time deep laden. What targets! Ford couldn't help thinking. A couple of surfaced submarines moved briskly past them. One flew the White Ensign and the other the Dutch horizontally striped tri-colour. But they were a reminder of what the sea contained.

Ford stood watching with an American Brigadier from Michigan until last light. Next morning the convoy had closed in and was formed into several shorter lines. A Sunderland circled them monotonously. Ford turned his glasses on to the destroyers and corvettes of the escort, then back on to the solid masses of the transports. It was all very different from, and far more interesting than, the lonely voyages of peace-time. A score or so of ships, in close company, so that the half-dozen nearest are only three or four hundred yards from each other, must impress the onlooker with a sense of weight and purpose. The heavy ships bear onwards through the resisting sea. It was visibly an expedition. Or rather, Ford noted, in this case it was one small part of an expedition— of an expedition for which convoy after convoy such as this had sailed, and would sail.

Thus far it has been possible to produce these major collective efforts for the purpose of war alone. What could not be done if an expedition of this scope could be fitted out, not in order, as was this one, to decide who should have the right to develop Africa, but in order actually to develop Africa! Ford felt, however, that, not so much this reflection in particular, as reflection in general, was out of place on the convoy. So he noted a passage which he found in Diderot's *Neveu de Rameau*, a book which he was a trifle self-consciously reading, partly in order to try to salvage something from the wreckage of his French. He translated the dialogue.

'MYSELF: That is enough of your reflections. Go on with your story.

'HIM: That is not possible. There are days on which I have to reflect. It's a disease which must be left to run its course. Where was I?'

Each day Ford spent a long time on deck gazing at the convoy. They were now in the open Atlantic and the liners looked like large, solemn sea-creatures, pushing their noses into the swell, rhythmically lifting and sinking their broad, buttocky sterns. The weather was surprisingly good for a winter Atlantic. Ford was grateful, for he knew from experience that he would have been sick if they had hit a storm in the first two days. Now that he had had time to accustom himself he felt that he would survive. He thought again of all the men on the packed mess decks below. What would happen if they were all sick? Already even a very moderate degree of motion had caused some trouble. But so far the thing was within bounds. He flinched at the thought of what must happen when a troopship, as crowded as this, hits heavy weather on the first day of its voyage.

That morning they reached their Emergency Stations in six minutes from the sounding of the siren. It wasn't good enough, said the OC Troops, through the ship's broadcasting system. He threatened them with having to go back to doing it twice a day for the rest of the voyage if they didn't improve. He also scolded them for leaving orange-peel about the decks. This must cease immediately, he said.

At the next practice their time for Emergency Stations was a minute better. This was reasonably satisfactory, said the OC

Troops' voice. But the orange-peel was as bad as ever. The issue of oranges would be stopped for twenty-four hours: 'Dismiss your parades.'

From the day on which he joined the RAF Ford had found the atmosphere of armed forces very different from what is commonly supposed. What seemed mainly to characterise the military life was a certain dry primness. He wondered, rather sadly, if the famous armed forces of history had been like this; if the orders of the day of the Grande Armée had been concerned, nine days out of ten, with instilling the smaller, neater virtues—with tidiness, punctuality, and accuracy. He wondered if Pizarro had expressed his 'serious concern' at the stretching of his men's webbing equipment, 'due to the practice of carrying gold nuggets in belts, which practice is to cease with effect 10/7/33'; if Hannibal had qualified his congratulations on Cannae with a stiff paragraph on the unsatisfactory grooming of the elephants of his armoured division; if the Golden Horde, on parade, had had to listen to Genghis Khan's threat to discontinue looting for forty-eight hours unless all decapitated bodies were removed from the camp before twenty-two hundred hours? He expected it had been pretty much like that. Alexander must have nagged, must have had a fad for this; Marlborough a whim for that; the great captains must all have appeared to their men for the most part in the role of scolding nursery governesses. Probably there was no other way in which great masses of men, living together in the insane proximity of armies, could be kept even tolerably efficient. Still, the OC Troops of the *Illyria* had an aggravating voice.

The voyage went on. In their cabin they kept up a light barrage of *unterseeboten* jokes. They had been ordered to sleep in their clothes, but they did not. Ford felt a little guilty about this, especially one night when he went up on deck just before going to bed. It was a beautiful, mild, clear night. A half-moon shone through broken clouds on to the water. It was remarkably light. Ford could see the silhouette of each of the fat transports, picked out precisely against the horizon. And so, presumably, could an eye at a periscope. He got into bed in his trousers, but they tickled and he took them off. Nothing happened.

The next afternoon at a quarter to three Ford went to the

lavatory. In a minute or so he heard the siren for Action Stations.
There was a notice up to say that they would never sound it without notice for practice purposes. Ford 'adjusted his dress on
leaving' at record speed. By the time he got back to the cabin he
found his five colleagues throwing on their coats, equipment, and
life-jackets. The siren went on blaring. They felt both exhilarated
and scared, and at the same time sceptical (they were newspaper
men). Ford knew exactly where his equipment was and had it on
as quick as the rest of them, so that they all went out to their
Action Stations in a bunch. When they got there they found that
the crews were ripping the covers off the guns. But there was
nothing to be seen on the sea or in the sky. Nor had any of the
escort left their stations. After some minutes the gun crews got
the word that it was an unidentified aircraft, now recognised as
friendly. So they went in again.

Later that evening their CO was informed by an Intelligence
Officer, who was doing watches on the ship, that the Action
Stations had not been caused by an aircraft but by two subs,
which had been spotted on the tail of the convoy. They had
submerged, he said, and contact with them had been lost. As this
was given them by their CO as more or less official 'gen' (in-
formation), they all believed it. It made them think a bit, because,
although these subs had no doubt been shaken off all right, it
meant that the enemy now knew the position of the convoy and
would be signalling to every sub in the ocean. It made them feel
that their daily rehearsal might be for a play which would be
performed after all.

Ford lay on his bunk. He tried to envisage the three-dimensional
theatre of war through which the convoys were sailing. The top
layer consisted of aircraft droning on and on till they found their
opportunity to swoop on a surfaced U-boat. On the middle layer
the convoys thrust forward heavily and powerfully, veiled by their
escort screens of destroyers and corvettes. Below, on the third
level, were the U-boats shadowing them, waiting their chance to
close for a shot. It was curious to envisage those highly specialised,
efficient, disciplined German sailors sitting there behind and a
little below them in their weird boxes of tricks, at that moment
patiently waiting for the opportunity to send a torpedo into them.
He wondered about those Nazis. No doubt the ones off duty

I

were lying about on their bunks, sleepily talking or reading, just as he was doing. Were they very much the same sort of men as the Englishmen (four ex-newspapermen and a young doctor) in the cabin with him? Ford was of the generation of the aftermath of the First World War—formed by the internationalist, left-wing, anti-war ideology of that time. He had been taught, and had taught, that 'the men on both sides of the trenches' were fundamentally the same, with the same sufferings, the same needs, the same confusions, the same exploitations, the same desires, the same good intentions. What had to be done, the doctrine had implied, was to get together against those who had sent them out to kill each other. But was that any longer true, at any rate at the immediate, and perhaps most immediately important, level? Was it true that these young Nazis, cased in the stressed pressure-hulls of their *unterseeboten*, were the same sort of people as the tens of thousands of Englishmen and Americans on the convoy? Undeniably it was no longer certainly true.

Undeniably the young Nazis had been very highly conditioned. Their responses to stimuli were visibly different from other people's. But to what extent, how irrevocably, and in what numbers, had the Germans been turned into Nazis? Had the fellows out there in the pressure-hulls been fundamentally and irredeemably de-humanised? If so, it was by how much the greatest and by how much the worst event in history. Or were those submarine crews still made up of ordinary, some decent, some not so decent, average humanity merely suffering temporarily from the obscene Nazi mind-controls? Would they, if they got the chance that night, fire their torpedoes *as Nazis* or simply as no doubt pretty tough, but basically run-of-the-mill North European sailors, rather reluctantly earning their 'danger money' by taking on this shaky U-boat job? Ford hoped very hard that they were the latter. It would be far less alarming to him, for one thing, to be torpedoed in the ordinary way of business by young Hamburg or Flensburg sailors, out to earn some extra marks, than by highly conditioned Nazi fanatics. The specifically nightmarish—Brave New Worldish—element of the Nazi decade had arisen from the undeniable ability of the Propaganda Ministerium to produce synthetically the attributes of fanaticism and, indeed, heroism. Ford hoped very hard that what those

U-boat sailors were really concerned with was their danger money. But he wasn't at all sure. That was the worst of it. Ford didn't know; and he very much doubted if anyone else did either.

Yet this question of the extent to which the German people had been de-natured, as it were, by ten years of Nazi control was all-important. What ought to be done with them, when we had the power to do it, entirely depended on what they were really like. And nobody knew.

Ford was interested to note that being called to Action Stations at the reported presence of the U-boats set going a conversation about survival after death that evening in the cabin. It started naturally and was quite unforced, but it started. Two of the four officers believed in survival, two of them didn't. The arguments used were not original, to say the least of it. Ford found himself stating an exceedingly undergraduate version of the materialist position. He was a little shocked to find that neither those who believed nor those who did not appeared ever to have given the matter a moment's attention before in their lives. They seemed to find each argument, however crude, quite unanswerable until they heard the opposite; then that seemed equally convincing too. Yet they were shrewd and capable men. Was there ever a generation so naked of any kind of rooted world-outlook, good or bad, as the generation of Britons at present under thirty years old? Ford reflected that it made it all the more remarkable that his juniors had proved so stubbornly willing to fight. For it seemed that they were all fighting for something which they had either forgotten or had not yet heard of.

Both his speculations as to the Nazis astern of them in their pressure-hulls and as to this conversation about immortality gave Ford a touch of a sensation, said to be experienced by every generation if it lives on into a new period with new values and assumptions. Ford was reminded, rather comically, of the position of the eighteenth-century rationalists who lived on into the evangelism of the early Victorian world. Already, in early middle life, he seemed to have lived on from a period of rational scepticism into a period of blank inattention—which might so easily change at any moment into its opposite of some unquestioning faith.

That night there was some chat in the cabin about the order to sleep in their clothes. Ford kept on his socks, partly because his feet tended to stick out of the end of the bunk and get cold, and partly as a sort of acknowledgement of the supposed presence of the U-boats astern.

Next day they gave out a book of 'gen' addressed to all officers of the First Army (apparently the RAF officers counted, for this purpose, as attached). 'Dwight D. Eisenhower, Lieutenant-General,' commanding the whole theatre of war, contributed a Foreword. 'For the first time in history Great Britain and the United States have jointly prepared a military expedition and dispatched it overseas, under a single Commander, to attack a common enemy,' he began. The C-in-C evidently thought that he was presiding over an historical occasion of great significance; and so he might be—at that.

'Kenneth Anderson, Lieutenant-General,' commanding the First Army, had written his own Foreword too. What was more, he had put his own private war aims into it. He wrote that we British could suffer and sacrifice just as bravely 'as do the peoples of Russia or Greece or Norway' if we really believed in our cause. Then he went on to ask, 'What is that cause?' That sentence brought the text to the bottom of the page. Ford was all impatience to find out what the Lieutenant-General considered our cause to be. On the top of the next page he read:

'In essence, it is to give each individual and nation security and a fair chance in life. We must eradicate the desire of individuals, classes, and nations to better themselves and live softly at the expense of others, and replace it by desire and action to help others.'

Ford, to his surprise, found that he agreed.

By the next day they had reached southern waters. The wind carried a sense of easy excitement. Ford spent the day on a sort of platform above the bridge, to which the Public Relations Officers had managed to get access. Every hour or so a rainstorm swept up to the convoy over the now dead-calm sea. First the escort screen would be shrouded by it. Then a rainbow put one foot on a destroyer and the other on a corvette. A circling Catalina flew low over the water to avoid the cloud. Then the liners, on their never-ending zigzag, reached the fringe of the rain. Line by line they went into it. The warm, un-serious, splashy rain of the South came down on them, wetting them, but only in fun. In ten minutes the storm had passed and they were sailing through the bright, mild sunshine again.

Towards midday Ford noticed that a part of the escort screen ahead had begun to converge on a central destroyer which was winking its Aldis signalling lamp. It looked exactly as if the escort were putting their heads together about something which they couldn't quite make out. And apparently that was just what it was. The destroyer farthest to port began to turn on her heel. She had run a few hundred yards back past the convoy when up went a high white fountain sixty yards or so from her stern. They could hardly hear the explosion of the depth-charge, but the white water seemed to hang in the air. Ford watched it through his glasses as it slowly subsided. The destroyer went quietly on and dropped nothing more. 'She must have had a tickle, but not much,' said a naval officer. After a bit the destroyer turned through 180 degrees and slipped back to her place. The confabulation of corvettes and destroyers ahead began to loosen out. The incident was, it seemed, closed.

That evening they sailed past Gibraltar. It was after dark, but the moon was full; they could see the dark outlines of the Spanish mountains. It was the first sight of Spain which Ford had had since he had been in Barcelona and Madrid during the other war. Then they saw the photo-familiar outline of the rock.

'An impertinent piece of Imperial architecture,' Ford said to the young doctor who shared their cabin.

'Line!' said the doctor.

Then they went over to the other side and saw Ceuta all lighted up. It was the first lighted town they had seen for three years. They could hardly believe that it was really quite all right for those people to show *all* those lights, without *any* attempt to screen them at all.

They steamed due east up the Mediterranean, through warm, rather cloudy days and clear nights of bright moonlight. The convoy and her now larger escort made a lovely sight, in an easy, slightly picture-postcardish way. Your first sight of it was breathtaking, but you did not really want to look at it for long. The seascape, as always, lacked the humanity of landscape.

Ford studied the small advertisements on the back page of a copy of the *New Statesman and Nation* which he had brought with him. He read with relish the columns of announcements of the political meetings, lectures, picture exhibitions, film shows, plays, ballets, rallies, entertainments, which were being held that week in London. Ford found that, far from regarding such activities as futile, or inappropriate for a time of war, his reaction was to feel a deep satisfaction at being reminded that they were all going briskly on. It added to his conviction that the elaborate expedition in which he was taking a tiny part, and consequently the war effort as a whole, did, as a matter of fact, happen to be as important as they were supposed to be. For one of our war aims might be defined as being to ensure that this kind of thing should go on. Ford had had twenty years of participation, in both Britain and America, in 'progressive activities', and he knew to the full the odour of futility which sometimes arose from them. But now he saw that it was precisely the right to experiment— which meant being futile ninety-nine times out of a hundred, and so really getting somewhere on the hundredth experiment— which he for one was out to defend. His eye travelled on to the *New Statesman*'s equivalent to an agony column. He read about a—

'Capable, intelligent, young grass widow with young baby, wld. hsekp. professional's flat or sm. hse.; West End, Bloomsbury, Hampstead pref. Salary a secondary consid. prov. sole charge of congenial, prog. home.'

Then there were 'prog' (progressive) schools, 'prog' restaurants, 'prog' country hotels, 'prog' youth clubs, 'prog' secretaries seeking 'prog' positions. The page laid out before him the whole slightly absurd, characteristically English 'prog' world. Well, Ford was a 'prog' himself. 'And with all our maddening faults we progs,' Ford thought, 'can claim to have come a good deal better out of the last three years that some other groups I *could* name. *Vive les progs!*'

Action Stations sounded again. This time Ford was not otherwise engaged, but Cole (one of the other members of their cabin)

had just got into a lovely hot salt bath. He came out swearing and
dripping, struggling to pull on his shirt over his sticky skin.
When they got on deck they found that the sun was in the act of
setting dead astern. This was the time for a low-level attack by
torpedo aircraft out of the sun. Soon they saw what appeared to
be the cause of the trouble: an aircraft which they couldn't
identify was flying high and distant to port. It flew away east,
towards enemy territory. 'A recco (reconnaissance) job,' said the
experts wisely. One of the destroyers ahead turned right round and
steamed straight through the convoy, fast. She passed within
fifty yards of them, looking good. Then she began patiently to
weave from side to side, covering every inch of water behind the
convoy. The sun's disc began to be bisected by the horizon. The
moment his upper rim was gone, they became conscious of the
moon, and within ten minutes it was a moonlight night. The
authorities evidently thought that there was still enough light for
an attack to develop, because they kept them at their stations for
a long time. But again nothing happened.

When they got up the next morning they found that they
were in sight of their destination. In half an hour they began to
turn in towards the harbour.

They steamed on only a little farther and then stopped. When
you sailed in convoy, coming into harbour was not, it transpired,
something you could do just any time you arrived. As in so many
other spheres of war-time life, there was a queue to be waited in.
The *Illyria* lay all that day anchored in the bay; and it became
known that she and the rest of the convoy would be there for at
least that night also, before there would be a place for them
alongside.

A twin-engined aircraft flew over them, pretty high. Ford
couldn't identify, but two young pilots standing next to him said
decisively, 'One of ours. A Mosquito; didn't know we had them
out here.' As they spoke AA fire from the port opened up on her.
Ford was always pleased when the experts failed to identify. As
it turned out, however, he should have felt less pleased this time.
The enemy aircraft flew away without dropping anything. 'A
recco,' said the experts. They were right there.

The torpedo hit the *Illyria* well forward. A liner is a remarkably large object. Somewhat grim scenes may be taking place in one part of her, while another part is, for the time being at least, only mildly affected. For instance, as the Public Relations Officers' cabin was amidships, they didn't feel any overwhelming shock from the explosion. Still, they all knew that something very serious had hit the ship. 'She's had it,' Cole said. They lurched to their feet. The ship didn't heel over much—she would go far farther over in a heavy sea. But the blow was giving a deep impression of injury.

The Emergency Stations signal went before the ship had steadied. The siren had a scream in it. Ford crammed the rest of a hard-boiled egg which he was eating into his mouth; they struggled into their equipment and moved quickly and heavily off towards their Emergency Stations.

When he got on deck again Ford was startled by the brightness of the moon. He noticed that they were well ahead of the crowd. So he ran over to the port side where she had been hit. There wasn't much to see, only a few dark things in the water, but there was that acrid smell of explosive. He hurried on to their station. As the troops began to assemble, he looked down the long rail of the ship. He could not help noticing that she was beginning to settle by the head. Until now he had not known that he was scared. But now he found himself arguing hotly against the fairly slight, yet definite evidence of his senses. 'That rail isn't pointing downwards,' he heard his mind saying. 'It is,' said his eyes. But their evidence was overruled. 'For,' said his mind, 'if it were pointing downwards it might mean that the ship was sinking—and I shouldn't like that.'

'Objection sustained,' said some arbiter. And his senses could go and put their head in a bucket, with all their evidence.

The deck began to fill with men. In three minutes every inch of it was packed with the serried ranks of the troops. Ford was very glad they had got up from the cabin ahead of the crowd. He wouldn't have enjoyed the feeling of being trapped behind those thousands of men. The troops were coming up beautifully calmly, however. Ford felt gratitude to them for their solid, steady habit.

As a matter of fact the PROs ought none of them to have been down in the cabin at all. Ford oughtn't to have been eating the egg and they ought to have had all their equipment on. For Action Stations had sounded some hours before, when the second attack had begun, and had never been dismissed. But the truth was that, after being scared during the beginning of the attack, the PROs had begun to get tired and bored. The two attacks had lasted almost all night and nothing much had been happening for a long time. The PROs had all been at their various Action Stations on deck all the time. Round 4.30 in the morning it had become cold. There had not been even distant gunfire for some time. One by one it had occurred to them that the attack must have petered out; that even if another enemy aircraft did come up there would only be the same barrage to watch—and, though it was spectacular, they had been watching that all night; that it would be nice to go and sit down, to compare notes with the other chaps, to have something to eat, etc., etc., etc. So four of them found themselves back in the cabin. They began to loosen, then to slip off, their heavy equipment. They knew that if anything happened they could still reach their Emergency Stations as soon as the rest of the troops, whose Action Stations were all below, in any case. And, in the event, so they did. Nor did they miss much, for this last attack on the *Illyria* seems to have been almost exactly like the previous two or three which they had seen (except that this one ended in the torpedo).

The torpedo attacks had only begun towards the end of the night. The earlier raiders had been bombing. In fact, the performance had begun while they had been in the middle of their dinner the evening before. While the Action-Stations siren was still going, the ship shook and seemed to jump forward. But somehow they guessed that she hadn't been hit. They heard a burst of gunfire above them, but by the time the PROs had got to their stations it had died down.

Ford found the gun crews aft rather shaken. A bomb, they told him, had burst on the water about twenty yards off the stern and they had got a lot of blast. While they were telling him about it, they heard the next e/a (enemy aircraft) coming in. Ford had always found that the noise of air-raids on land was greatly exaggerated. But this was rather a different matter. The orchestra

of the barrage was led by the *Delia*. She was what is called 'an
anti-aircraft vessel'—in effect a floating battery of AA guns. She
was lying a few hundred yards to port. A moment after they heard
the e/a coming, *Delia* appeared to burst into flames along her
whole length. For a moment Ford thought she had been hit. But
then he saw that it was simply the effect of her opening up with
her whole armament. Above this preliminary din Ford heard the
e/a diving towards them. Then all the convoy except the *Illyria*,
which was the outside ship to starboard, opened up. Each ship
mounted a remarkable assortment of weapons.

The most spectacular, perhaps, were the various types of small
automatic cannon. It was they which fired the streams of red
tracer with which the air was now filling. They 'hose-piped' a
little, swinging their barrels gently through a short arc. The
tracer flashed out of the guns almost too fast to see. But as it
mounted the sky the impression of speed was lost and the little
red balls seemed to hang almost lazily before they went out. The
swing of the gun muzzles distributed the half-spent tracer shells,
at the end of their flight, in sweeping arcs and semicircles.
Suddenly Ford's ears were startled by a far sharper sound. It was
the *Illyria*'s own automatic cannon coming into action. He turned
to watch them. They were firing almost directly into the moon.
The tracer flashing out of their muzzles looked like exquisitely
thin red rapiers jabbing at the sky.

Ford had only a few moments in which to consider this
spectacle, however. The barrage was now complete. Every piece
in the orchestra was playing. It was the first time that Ford had
known war to live up to its reputation for noise. He was scared
by the existing din rather than by the apprehension of any
bombs to come. He huddled himself closer under the cover
provided by the towerlike turret on which the upper AA gun
was mounted. The noise was really painful. The guns went on
firing with a sort of sustained madness. He had time to think of
one of the very first realistic descriptions of fighting, which,
as it happened, he had been reading that afternoon. For he had
passed on in his French lesson to *Le Chartreuse de Parme*. The
day before yesterday he had read how Fabrice had reacted to the
noise of Waterloo. 'At that moment the barrage became so heavy
that Fabrice could not answer him. It must be avowed that our

hero was not at all heroic at that moment. All the same, fear came
to him only as a secondary effect; he was above all scandalised
by this noise which hurt his ears.' Like so much else in Stendhal's
great, if preposterous, book, it was true.

As the thought of Fabrice and his scandalised ears glided
through Ford's mind the engine note of the e/a grew louder and
louder. It began to dominate the barrage. He looked back at the
Illyria's light automatic cannon and saw the gunners leaning
back like gymnasts on the straps with which they swung their
guns till they were lying on their backs, their muzzles pointing
vertically upwards. The slender streams of tracer shot up in red
passion. Suddenly the engine noise ceased to grow; a second later
it was far less. The e/a had pulled out of his dive. He evidently
hadn't liked the top end of the barrage any better than Ford had
liked the bottom end. They heard him swing over to starboard,
the barrage, rather uncertainly, following him.

Ford saw the point of this apparently wild firing into the
blackness: it performed the indispensable function of preventing
the e/a's coming near enough to hit their targets. The barrage is a
defensive weapon, but an effective and indispensable one.

There was a pause. Ford had time to look round. It was only
now that he realised how deplorably bright the moon was. Then
he looked towards the harbour. He could not see it at all. He
realised that it was completely covered by a smoke-screen. That
was an excellent idea; but why wasn't it round *him*? He saw the
liners of the convoy riding there like so many fat ducks on a pond.
Surely something could be done to cover their nakedness. Sure
enough, destroyers began to steam out in an arc round them,
pouring out smoke. They had started on the other side of the
convoy. Ford watched their progress with eager interest. They had
still a long way to go before they could draw their nice dark
blanket round the *Illyria*, the 'outside-right' ship.

Ford looked up at the moon with increasing distaste. It was
most indecently bright. The glittering track of its rays led straight
up to the *Illyria* in a most unnecessary way. The destroyers
seemed a long time; even now while they were crossing the
Illyria's bows it would be a little while before the smoke billowed
down over her. Ford heard aircraft again. Then he saw first two,
and then three more, lights in the sky to the left of the officious

moon above the smoke-screen. They had begun dropping flares. Thank goodness these were a bit short. The tracer began going up. Here it all was again. Just as the first smelly wreaths of smoke reached him, the barrage broke out in full strength. Again its variegated flash and din outraged Ford. He crouched closer under the mounting of the aftermost gun. The sky filled with tracer shell-burst and gun-flashes.

He was looking along the length of the ship down the rows of her automatic cannon and rockets when there was a violent flash somewhere over the bows. He wondered if it could be a bomb. He found afterwards that it had been. It had been near enough for the men in the bows to be drenched by the splash. But the barrage was so loud that he didn't hear the burst at all. The e/a must have pulled out of his dive as he bombed. For the barrage swung away to starboard after the retreating sound of the engines. There was evidently more than one Jerry about, because the barrage kept going for a few minutes more. Just at the end Ford saw the splash of a stick of bombs dropped at least a mile away over the other side of the bay. Evidently the barrage was performing its essential preventative function. All in a minute the barrage died away. There was no sound of engines. This attack was over.

After a quarter of an hour or so Action Stations were dismissed and the Public Relations Officers went to bed. They got some sleep before they were wakened by the siren calling them back. They were quite expecting it, got into their gear and headed for their Action Stations on deck. They had been a good five minutes on deck before the first e/a came in to attack. From then on for several hours the attack went on. The e/a's came in singly, so far as Ford could see, one about every quarter of an hour. For the first three or four attacks exactly the same scene reproduced itself. A few seconds after the first sound of engines the whole convoy let everything go. You heard the alarming, mounting rumble of an e/a's engines as she began to dive. The barrage became vertical and frantic. The e/a pulled out and went off. Each time this now familiar sequence began, Ford felt a little pull of reluctance to face it. But his curiosity was far too strong to allow him to go below. (As a matter of fact it was really only the noise of our own barrage that had to be faced. For during this part of the attack Ford wasn't aware of a single bomb falling anywhere near them.) So he crouched and squeezed with the spare members of the gun crew under the gun's tall steel turret. It gave them quite good cover.

About the fifth or sixth attack something quite different began to develop. The attack started in the same way as the others, with a distant engine note, and a few moments later the switching on of the tracer like a red fountain. But this time the fountain was playing horizontally along the surface of the water instead of up into the air. It was a pretty variation, Ford thought; then he wondered what it meant. The engine noise grew and so did the barrage. The convoy began firing a variety of weapons along the water. It began to dawn on Ford that if the e/a were coming in at sea-level they obviously weren't bombing. They must be torpedo-carrying craft.

About this time Ford found himself standing next to a figure in khaki. He could not see anything of his face under his helmet. But Ford could imagine the face from the suburban London voice which rather surprisingly emerged from the figure. The figure said, 'A lot of destruction.'

Ford said, 'Well, so far tonight there's been nothing but noise so far as I know.'

'I was thinking of what caused it all,' said the figure. 'It's all caused by money.'

Ford was mildly interested, supposing that the speaker was exhibiting a certain political consciousness.

'Yes, but how do you mean—money?' he said.

'Why, money,' the voice said, 'the misuse of money.'

'Well, this *is* rather an expensive way of staging a fireworks display if that's what you mean,' Ford said.

'I don't mean that at all,' the voice said. 'I mean the way the nations have been misusing their money in international trade. That's what's caused the whole war.'

'How do you mean?' Ford pricked up his ears.

'Why, they've been using money as a commodity instead of using it as money. Don't you see? That's been the cause of the war.'

'Oh, I think there's a lot more to it than that, you know.'

'No, there isn't'—the voice was peevishly firm; 'the misuse of money—treating it as a commodity—that's the root of all this trouble.'

Ford felt astonishment. Monetary theory happened to be one of his principal interests in life. He held views almost exactly opposite to those which the voice seemed to be expressing. There was nothing he liked better than an argument on the theory of the uses and misuses of money by the governments of the world. He was just beginning, 'Oh, but . . .' when a wave of weariness came over him; he really *didn't* feel he could explain his views on a controlled economy and its external relations plus the changes currently taking place in the nature of money just then. He moved a step or so from under the gun mounting. Now the moon shone upon the face under the helmet. It was thin, sensitive, rather harried-looking, as Ford had supposed it would be. The man had persistence.

'It's all the way they used *money*,' he repeated.

'But, you know, you couldn't go on trading in the old way— it had broken down. The money trouble is only a symptom of a far deeper break-up—of a whole economic, social, polit . . .' Ford heard his own voice with dismay; it really *was* no time to go into all that.

The barrage began again. They were still firing low along the surface of the water. Ford noticed that he had heard no engine note this time. Perhaps the money-man's conversation had distracted him. The tracer began to swing to starboard across the *Illyria*'s bows. The ships to port had to cease fire. But one ship's guns still seemed to bear, because she went on pumping out the tracer. A quite new noise came from her. Tam, tam, tam, tam, tam, tam, with rapid, steady persistence. Ford recognised it immediately. It was her multiple pom-poms, or Chicago piano; it was exactly as heard on the sound-track of Mr Coward's film. It occurred to Ford that the ship might well be called on to pay Mr Coward a royalty for the effect. Still, reality was at least imitating art quite effectively. The barrage was more intense than ever before. Ford pushed his way farther under the tall gun-mounting. He found that by getting behind a largish sort of box he could get more cover. He felt the money-man pushing in behind him. Then, unfortunately, he wondered what was in the box. It was presumably ammunition. But he couldn't move now.

There had still been no sound of the e/a's engines. He heard a strong silky swish and woosh immediately to starboard; the sound rushed past fairly close to them, from bow to stern. A second later there was a roar of engines to stern. Ford had no doubt what it was, though he never got any confirmation. The e/a had dived past them with her engines out, and switched on a few hundred yards to stern. Now the barrage was seeing her off the premises. Ford was startled by an e/a having come by him so close, like a large silent bird. It was strange that he had not been able to see it. The moon was still bright, but there was a good deal of smoke at that particular moment. As soon as the barrage abated, Ford heard the money-man grumbling away about 'all this destruction'.

The next few attacks were very similar except that nothing seemed to come so close to the *Illyria*. Then the intervals between the arrival of each e/a got longer. The attack was dying away. Finally, nothing had happened for forty minutes or so. It was then that Ford, and, as he found, several other of the Public Relations Officers, began to feel chilly, bored, and, in Ford's case at least, hungry. They began to trickle down to the cabin. Soon they were sitting down to a pleasant discussion of the incidents of the night. Harry Cole got out the sort of picnic packet of sandwiches, etc., with which the thoughtful authorities had provided them. Harry tried a sandwich, but didn't like it. He fished in his package and produced a hard-boiled egg. He looked at it with distaste and offered it to Ford. Ford had a package of his own, but it was put away somewhere and he felt too tired to rummage for it. Harry said the idea of a hard-boiled egg at that moment made him feel sick. So Ford took it with pleasure. As he was peeling it the barrage began again. They began getting into their equipment, which they had half taken off. The shell of the egg stuck a little and it was a minute or so before Ford had it peeled. He took a bite. It tasted exceptionally good. He couldn't think why Harry hadn't wanted it. They felt—not heard—the torpedo strike the ship. As they got out of the cabin Harry said, 'You'll always have associations with hard-boiled eggs now.'

They found themselves jammed together (as they had been each day at the practices) in the solid pack of bodies which covered the deck. They stood facing the rail in the approved manner, leaving a foot-wide gangway along its length. Ford's height enabled him to see back over the heads of the ranks behind him. The men stood still and rather passive: in the moonlight they lacked detail; they became an undifferentiated mass of human forms.

Ford noticed the classicism of the scene. It was exactly as preparations for abandoning ship are always described. Nothing happened for some minutes. Ford had time to wonder what the effect would be if another e/a came in and the barrage started up again. How would the men take it; for, since they had been below, they had neither seen nor even properly heard the barrage all night. And what would be the effect of shell fragments, such as he had heard from time to time, clattering down on the decks and splashing into the water, on these thousands of men standing pressed against each other shoulder to shoulder and back to chest? Still, his main preoccupation was as to whether the ship would sink or not. Someone said, 'Well, if we take as long as this . . .' evidently supposing that the order to abandon ship would be given as soon as everybody was ready.

Ford said, 'But, good Lord, she isn't going to sink. They've only had us up here as a precaution.'

He did not know whether his words reassured anyone else, but they undoubtedly reassured himself. He stopped noticing the preparation of the boats, which was steadily going forward, and noticed that she seemed no more down by the head than before.

They waited. Then they heard the ship's always ineffective loudspeaker system beginning to function. As usual, they couldn't hear what it said. They heard a call being passed down the ship from bow to stern:

'Ship's carpenter to come to the bridge.'

Ford found this delightfully eighteenth-century. It was as if, in emergency, the fact that ships were now made of steel was disregarded and the traditional expert was summoned. There was another pause. Then another call was passed down:

'Ship's electrician to come to the bridge.'

This was more contemporary. The ship's principal consultant

physicians were being called in to report on the extent of her injuries.

Ford thought of the various things which he had not brought up from the cabin, including Bob's field-glasses and the earlier part of this narrative; it would be very irritating to lose them. He heard the sound of aircraft engines.

A moment or so later the barrage opened up again. 'Now this really may not be so jolly,' he thought. He looked at the dark human mass behind him. At the crash of the first shots they let out a little rather pleased sound. Perhaps they liked the sight of the pretty red tracer bounding up in the distance. The barrage swung nearer. It was going to be a high-level attack again this time. The engine note grew loud. The e/a seemed just about above them, to be diving. The *Delia*, the two nearest liners, and the *Illyria* opened up simultaneously. The barrage was at full blast again. The *Delia*'s armament flashed and crashed; her Chicago piano began its formidably insistent tam, tam, tam, tam, tam, tam.

The barrage was completely new to the troops and they had no head cover. Ford felt a sort of ripple go through the jammed men behind him. But that was all that happened. The ranks stood in calmness and order. It was pleasant and reassuring to feel that one's fellow-countrymen actually did behave as they are popularly supposed to do.

A ship's officer came up and shouted, 'Those who can, get under cover—the others get down.'

The men nearest any sort of head cover pressed towards it and a few got under. The circular area of men standing within sound of the officer's voice got down on to the deck, crouching or kneeling. The moonlight shone on to their helmets as they unconsciously assumed the attitude of prayer. But just what was the practical point of the order Ford could not imagine. He would have thought that, if anything, this crouching down made the men even more vulnerable to falling fragments than if they had been standing. He felt acute apprehension as to what would happen in a few moments when the iron that was being pumped up into the sky began to come down again.

As usual, after a minute or two the raider's engines receded, the barrage abated, and the attack was over. But no fragments

K

came down on them. The barrage had evidently never come exactly in their direction. It was, Ford thought, one of the biggest bits of luck which they had had that night.

When the attack was over, Ford looked along the rail to see whether the ship was any farther down by the head. This time he could honestly think that she was not. He began to feel confident that she would not sink. (In this he discovered afterwards, he was premature. For about four hours the water in No. 1 hold continued to gain and the ship remained in danger of sinking.)

Nothing happened. Ford began to hope that they had had the last attack. The moonlight grew paler. Harry Cole said, 'Look at that,' and pointed to the east. There, sure enough, was the other kind of light.

Harry Cole said to Ford, 'Aren't you pretty glad to see it?'

Ford surprised himself with the amount of meaning which he got into the simple phrase, 'You bet I am!'

After an hour or so more, Emergency Stations were dismissed. No official announcement was made about there being no more danger of the ship sinking. But the dismissal of Emergency Stations was a direct intimation that this was so. The Public Relations Officers went to their cabin.

Some airmen, with their clothes torn, soaked, and covered with horrible black stains, came up the passage and were shown into the officers' bathrooms. Ford recognised them as some of the ground crews of a light bomber squadron. He knew that they had been on the lowest mess deck forward on the starboard side. The PROs took their nail-brushes along to help them scrub the filthy black oil out of their skins. Ford got a word with one of them in the bathroom. The torpedo had hit the ship abreast of their mess deck, where they also slept. Earlier in the night, when the attack seemed to have died down, they had gone back to bed (like the Public Relations Officers). When the torpedo hit, they had been flung out of their hammocks by the explosion. The first thing that most of them had known was the bang of falling on to the deck, and then the black water rushing in. Ford had been down to those lower mess decks several times. The sight of human beings packed as unnaturally close as that had been painful at the best of times. He found it hard to imagine what it must have been like when the ninety-eight airmen who were on that deck had to make their way out with the sea flooding in on them from the broken side of the ship. But they had managed. The man whom he talked to had never had the water above his knees; but some of them had had, he said, to swim for it. In the end only two men were found to have lost their lives; three others were injured. There must have been not only great good fortune but also great steadiness down there.

Much sooner than Ford had expected—indeed, he hadn't really expected it at all—word came up that breakfast was ready. On the way down to the dining-saloon he popped out on to the deck to see if anything more was happening. As he was stepping out of the alley-way he heard a repulsively public-school voice hailing.

'*Illyria*,' it said, 'do you require any assistance?'

It was a young naval officer hailing them from the bridge of a tiny corvette which, far below, was coming alongside. He heard their own bridge answer in the heartier tones of the merchant service, 'No, thank you; everything under control.'

Fortified by this official communiqué (as it were) that all was well, he went down to breakfast. Everything in the first-class dining-saloon was aggressively normal. The stewards served the porridge, coffee (so called), bacon and eggs, rolls, butter and marmalade which the printed menu cards announced to them, with a certain emphasis. It was as though they wished to make it quite clear that the Company regarded the intrusion of a torpedo into one of their ships as something which should be treated with marked disregard. Harry Cole, who was ahead of him, was finishing his egg when the steward was bringing Ford's porridge.

'I'll have another, please,' Harry said to the steward. 'He' (pointing to Ford) 'ate mine in the night.'

'*Certainly*, sir,' said the steward, whipping his plate away. He was back at once with a second egg.

Harry said, 'Not bad service, I suppose.'

As Ford ate his breakfast he looked at the imitation Adam decorations with which the Company had always (until the last year or so) equipped their vessels. They were pleasant in their insipid, provincial good taste. The little chintz curtains hung in

seemly pairs on each side of the long row of port-holes. The cream
paint on the small fluted pilasters was new and clean. It was all
precisely as it had been in 1929 when he had last seen it. But that
was all that was the same. He wondered what he would have
said when he was breakfasting in that saloon in 1929 if he had
been told that thirteen years later he would be there again, the
Illyria would be a troopship, engaged in a critical operation of a
Second World War, and that he would have been spending the night
being torpedoed by an aircraft? As a matter of fact, he supposed
that he would have said, 'Quite likely.' For he could remember
the rather dreary attempts he had had to make, in 1929, to explain
to the Captain why Capitalism must always produce war. But
what if they had gone on to say, 'Ah, but thirteen years hence you
will be attacked by a German aircraft flying under the orders of
Putsie Hamstaengel's friend Adolf Hitler, who will be the dictator
of all Europe. The *Illyria* will be taking part in a joint Anglo-
American expedition, one of the purposes of which will be to
improve communications with Britain's and America's great
fighting ally, the Soviet Union'? As Lenin remarked, history is
always more 'cunning' than any of the prophets can suppose.

When he had finished breakfast, Ford went on deck again. He
was told they were to go into the harbour first. In fact, they were
under way. But at the moment they were backing slowly out
farther into the bay. Ford went first on to the upper bridge (above
the bridge proper whence the Captain controlled the ship).
When he got there a signaller was just flashing an Aldis-lamp
acknowledgment to the *Delia*. Then he handed his message-pad
to a ship's officer. Ford looked over his shoulder. The message
read:
      'Sorry you got it. But the Hun paid the price. He went in the
moment after he dropped his fish.' Which was nice, if true. (He
never got any further confirmation.)
      From where he was Ford could see some debris piled up on the
deck near the bows. He went down. There was a rope barrier to
keep people back, but by saying 'Public Relations Officer' very
loud to the sentry he got by. There wasn't much to see on deck—
just some splintered wood and bits of twisted iron. The damage
was all far below. Then he saw that the hatch was off the forward

hold. He went and looked down. There was the sea. It was un-
comfortable to see the rush of the waves right in the middle of the
ship. But there they were, surging and foaming, cascading off one
partly flooded deck on to the one below. Crates, sodden baggage,
cabbages, and broken woodwork were being banged about by the
water. Ford went back aft.

Some time afterwards they began to go slowly forward towards
the port. The ship's broadcasting system, for some reason suddenly fully audible, announced that they would be called to
Emergency Stations again, but purely in order to balance the ship.
It was, the announcer implied, a somewhat delicate operation to
manoeuvre the ship in in her present condition. A sudden
movement of several thousand men to one side or the other might
make 'anything happen'. So they all stood at their stations again
while the dipped bows of the *Illyria* were edged almost imperceptibly towards the entrance between the two moles. The
loudspeaker began to talk again. The announcer said:
'The master of the ship wishes to speak to you.'
A North-country voice, which they had not heard before, began
to speak.
'I wanted to thank you all for your behaviour during the night.
It is, of course, very unfortunate that we cannot bring the ship in
undamaged. But, considering that we were struck by an aerial
torpedo, we have done very well. I consider that everyone, ship's
officers and crew, and the troops and their officers, showed great
steadiness. Thank you.'
Ford appreciated this very much. He also derived great
satisfaction from hearing the Captain's official pronouncement
that they had been struck by a torpedo. He knew that they had
been; he had been fairly heavily jarred by the explosion. Still,
the event was not wholly real until he heard the Captain's words.
In the confusion of modern war, he realised, there ought always
to be an official commentator to tell, not merely those who have
not been there, but also, and above all, those who *have* been
there, what has happened. Again he thought of Fabrice in the
Chartreuse de Parme. As Fabrice lay at Amiens, it will be remembered, lodging with a family which was both 'complimentary and
avaricious', recovering from the wound which he had received

during the rout, 'he became adult, because he made so many deep reflections on all that had happened to him. He remained a child on one score alone: what he had seen, had it been a battle, and, in the second place, this battle, had it been Waterloo?'

Ford, more fortunate in this and, he hoped, in many other respects, than Fabrice, was now at least sure that it had been a torpedo.

(1942)

First Ops

As soon as the engines started, Ford felt all right. You could tell instantly—at least Ford thought he could—that they were running perfectly: a deep, even hum and a feathery, wingy beat of airscrews. These Manchesters are very big aircraft for two engines. They have incredibly long airscrews; you see them turning solemnly on either side of you, not very fast, like windmills.

The running engines were a sign that the operation had started, that the slight unpleasantness of waiting about was over. Actually, the time between briefing, three o'clock, and take-off, six-thirty, had gone quickly. But missing his tea had definitely upset Ford. There had been (you don't say so?) a muddle. Operational teas had been ordered for the crews, as usual. But whoever ordered them had forgotten that two passengers, 'Sailor' (the Naval Liaison Officer at Group) and Ford (an administration officer on special detail) were coming too. So there was none for them. And operational teas are not be despised—lovely bacon and eggs. At any time Ford would have hated to see it streaming by and none for him. But before going out on one's first operation, it seemed really hard, and a bad omen too. As if one weren't quite there already, somehow.

Then came emptying one's pockets (Sailor and he gave their identification cards, money, letters, etc., to the doctor to keep), borrowing a parachute, having a helmet fitted for intercom. ('So you can hear what we are talking about,' 'Dim' Woolley, the pilot, said.) Ford had known Dim, a pale young man with a superb moustache, for some time. He had met the navigator at briefing, had been shown the course. It was simply a long, straight line—very long, Ford thought. The other chaps in the lorry going across to the dispersed aircraft were new to him. Sergeants and flight sergeants, gunners, wireless op, second pilot, bomb-aimer.

They had all bundled into the aircraft now. She sat on the perimeter track, throbbing gently. Dim opened up each engine in turn. The heavy frame of the Manchester shook. The engines, Rolls-Royce Vultures, roared, but roared silkily, if you can imagine such a thing, and Ford's spirits continued to rise.

The crew were getting settled. The navigator spread out his chart on his table, pinned the corners down with drawing pins, set out his dividers, pencils, etc., very like a man settling down to a morning's work in a drawing office. The wireless op, beside Ford, was already absorbed in knob-turning. Ford looked back and saw a gunner climbing up into the dorsal turret, halfway down the fuselage, at the top. Ford stood up, putting his head into an astrodome of perspex. He got an excellent view behind and to both sides. In the front he saw the pilots' heads, the nose of the aircraft.

The wireless op said, 'I'll plug you in.' He took the plug at the end of the cord dangling from Ford's helmet and put it into a socket on the fuselage overhead. Immediately Ford heard someone talking. It was Dim, saying 'O.K.?' There were some murmured 'O.K.s,' a wave to the ground crew to take the blocks from the wheels, and the aircraft began to roll very slowly forward.

Ford looked out of the astrodome. The five Manchesters which were to take part in the operation from this station were each crawling towards the west end of the east-west runway. The aircraft were ponderous, clumsy, beetle-like on the ground. Now the first was headed down the runway. It began to charge. The impression of combined weight and speed grew and grew. Ford watched, with personal interest, to see if the take-off was all right. There had been a lot of chat at tea: 'Well, I'm last off, so if you're all in the hedge, I shan't go,' 'Well, Christ, have a heart. I've got Sailor to get airborne too,' and Dim saying, 'What about me? This chap weighs twice as much as Sailor, as much as another thousand-pounder.' Ford had seen that the pilots were really not in the least worried. But the aircraft *were* heavily loaded, though not with bombs. They carried mines. The operation would consist of laying these mines in certain much-frequented 'enemy waters'.

As the first Manchester passed the intersection of the runways, Ford saw the faint beginnings of divergence between the line of her movement and the plane of the runway. Then she was air-borne, and her dark bulk heaved over the boundary, with effort but with plenty to spare.

The second starter, with Sailor on board, went off while Dim was turning his plane from the track on to the runway. Then Dim's plane—P for Peter—turned to face east into wind. Dim opened up his engines. P for Peter gathered way. Ford had not a moment's anxiety; their acceleration was obviously ample to make them airborne long before the end of the runway. Already he felt the bumps ironing out as the weight eased off the wheels, and just beyond the intersection he saw the aerodrome surface falling away.

It was a messy evening, with lowish cloud. Even at three hundred feet the fields began to blur, as if seen through a dirty wind-screen. Ford didn't realise the plane had made a full circle until he heard Dim's voice saying, 'Setting course now,' and an answering 'O.K.,' which he supposed came from the navigator. He kept his head in the astrodome, reflecting that as two-thirds of the journey would be made in the dark he would have plenty of time to look about the aircraft later on.

As soon as the dirty edge of the sea was beneath them, he felt the nose rise, the motors open out. A moment later the plane was engulfed in cloud. The Manchester bumped very little inside the cloud. There was nothing to be seen, just even greyness. Five or ten minutes passed. Ford was about to sit down when a fleck of light passed overhead; then another, brighter. Ford's eyes followed it backwards, turning towards the tail. Then more light, then definitely a patch of sky. All at once they were out.

Is there anything better than breaking cloud? Every time Ford had done it he had found it one of the best things in the world. No doubt, he thought, in the future, when everyone flies and the images of flying have passed into the language, it will become one of the symbols for the reappearance of hope. One will read such things as 'After a series of unrelieved failures the young dramatist broke cloud with his sparkling comedy "Two in a Turret"' or, in a programme note, 'After this sombre passage, dominated by the brass and woodwinds, the symphony breaks cloud with the gay air of. . . .' But that, like all programme notes, would be a bore.

Ford's eyes were resting in pleasure upon the scene before him.

Above cloud it was an exquisite evening. As he looked back, due west, between the tail fins, the sky was red with the sunset, and in it there hung, delicately, a new moon. They flew evenly, a hundred feet or so above the light surface of the cloud. There was no break in it, nothing to suggest that below them there was that quite different evening—grey, brown, murky—which they had just left.

Ford stood gazing. Then he noticed that a part of the aircraft was moving. The dorsal turret, its unexpected, conical shape sticking up like a monk's hood from the fuselage, was turning slowly and solemnly, first to the right, then to the left. As it did so, the barrels of its machine guns waved up and down. The dorsal gunner had begun his unremitting watch against fighters. No doubt the rear gunner in his turret was doing the same.

A voice spoke in Ford's ear. 'Captain, this is the front gunner speaking. Can I try my guns?' Then Dim's voice: 'Yes, just a short squirt.'

Ford could see the barrels of the guns in the nose turn downward. Then he heard, faintly, the rrrrrrrr; then a voice in his ear saying 'O.K.'; then another rrrrrrrr; then another voice: 'Rear gunner speaking, O.K.' . . . 'Dorsal gunner speaking, O.K.' Ford felt safe and comfortable, protected by eight power-turreted guns. He looked ahead. The first stars were out. Night was falling in the east.

They flew on, peacefully. A precise professional voice: 'Captain, navigator speaking. Alter course to 170.' Dim's voice: 'O.K., 170.' Ford took his head out of the astrodome and sat down. Inside the bomber it was already dark. The wireless op and the navigator had switched on little, glowing desk lights, by which they worked.

'Wireless op, navigator speaking. You might give me a couple of fixes. When you have time; don't break off your watch' (i.e. listening to our home stations in case they should transmit any new orders to aircraft on operations). The wireless op's voice: 'O.K.'

The figure beside Ford began a complex bout of knob-twiddling. A few minutes later his voice repeated a group of numbers and letters. The navigator's voice: 'O.K.'

Ford moved forward a yard, kneeling on his parachute pack beside the navigator's table. The navigator was hard at work with pencils and dividers. When he noticed Ford he pointed to a spot about a third of the way down the course line. Ford nodded. Then, in his earphones, he heard the navigator's voice: 'Captain, navigator. A couple of wizard fixes from the W/Op. We're dead on course.' Dim's voice: 'Good show.'

The exertion of moving forward made Ford realise that, to his great surprise, he was sweating. Indeed, now he noticed it, he was far too hot all over. He had guessed that flying clothing would be unnecessary in these well-appointed 'heavies', but after hearing many grim stories of the suffering from the cold of the crews in earlier types—such as Hampdens—he couldn't help feeling that one should be warmly clad. So he'd kept his greatcoat on, had a couple of pullovers under it, and wore big, lined gloves. Now he looked round and noticed that neither of his neighbours had taken any of these precautions. He felt definitely overdressed for the party. But beyond taking off his gloves, he now couldn't do anything about it because of his parachute harness. And the heat was pretty stifling. He had noticed that Dim had come in his overcoat, too. Later he asked him why. 'You don't catch me walking about Oflag VII in my pants at this time of the year,' Dim had said, and then added, 'But I suppose in practice it would only mean this old coat leading a charge on the Russian front.'

In a little while Ford began to get a headache from the heat. He heard Dim's voice: 'Can't someone turn that damned heater off? I'm stifling.' There were murmurs of approval, and the wireless op leaned across Ford and pushed a knob over. It didn't seem to make much difference. Another voice said, 'Sir, could you open your side window a bit?' Dim did so, and a rush of delicious fresh air came through the bomber. But it made too much of a draught to keep open all the time. So Dim shut the window again, and at intervals someone asked to have it open for a bit. It was exactly like any set of English people trying to regulate the heating in a Continental train.

Ford stood up again. It was now fully night. The cloud floor just beneath them was a grey expanse. Above, the stars seemed extraordinarily bright. Ford found the Bear, the Pointers, and the North Star where they ought to be—to port. Orion was on the starboard quarter. He sat down again. Then he thought he would go visiting. He felt shy about switching on the little microphone which was in the oxygen mask hanging from his helmet. But he did so. He said into it, 'Captain, Ford here. Can I go and visit the rear gunners?' Dim's voice said, 'Yes, do.' Ford switched off the microphone, unplugged himself, hitched up the cord in his parachute harness, and began clambering back down the body of the bomber. He opened the armour-plated door just behind his seat and shut it again behind him. Now it was pitch-dark. He felt his way towards the tail; it certainly wasn't too hot here. Finally he saw a glimmer of light straight ahead of him. When he got to it he was rather surprised to find that it was empty space. The rear gunner was, he discovered, slowly swinging his turret from side to side. And as it swung it left an open space, through which you looked out into the night. Ford clambered back to the light and warmth of the body of the bomber.

When Ford had got back and had plugged himself in again, he noticed the wireless op's clock. They had been flying an hour and a half. They would be there in forty minutes. He sat still, watching the dark outlines of the crew in the glow of the working lights. It was a satisfying scene. A voice in his ear: 'Captain, rear gunner speaking. There's a light on our starboard quarter.'

Ford promptly put his head back into the astrodome. There it was, a moving glow, coming, he thought, from under the cloud layer, a mile or so away from them.

Dim's voice said, 'Searchlights, I should think. Navigator, is it from one of the islands?'

There was a pause, then the navigator's voice: 'Might be So-and-So'—he mentioned the name of an island—'but it's a bit too far out for that.'

Dim's voice: 'Might be from a flak ship.'

They flew on. Then another voice: 'Flak on the starboard quarter.'

Simultaneously Ford saw it. A medium-heavy barrage, looking just the same as a barrage looks from the ground, a longish—a nice longish—way off. They all looked at it for a moment. Then the navigator's voice: 'That's from So-and-So island. I know the barrage.'

The navigator had spent a lot of time in these parts. He told Ford later that this island's barrage always came up in that distinct shape. Anyhow, it was the only island that could put up so considerable a volume of fire.

They flew on. The island's display passed from the quarter to the beam and then began to be left behind. Now they saw flares both to the port and starboard. They seemed to be just the ordinary coloured flares, falling in pairs. Every Londoner had seen dozens of them last winter. What they were meant to do, and whether they came from hostile fighters or were being shot up from the coast and from flak ships, Ford didn't know. He supposed the Boche thought that they might illuminate one of our bombers above the cloud. But it seemed most unlikely that they would. Anyhow, they were all miles away.

Dim said (presumably to the front gunner and bomb-aimer), 'Let me know if you see any flak exactly ahead of us.'

A voice said, 'I will.'

They flew on. The note of the motors changed. Dim was throttling back; the nose went down a shade. Almost immediately the stars went out. The Manchester was engulfed in greyness. Ford knew that they were very close to their ETA (estimated time of arrival) and were going down through the cloud to try to check their exact position from a sight of the coast. When they had checked it they would drop their load.

Ford knew enough about flying to know that coming down through cloud was sometimes a slightly tricky proceeding. Met had said that the cloud base probably would be fifteen hundred feet out here at this time. If that was so, there would be lots to spare, of course. But Met could not always be right. And if the cloud base were only a few hundred feet—or only a few feet—up, then it wasn't so easy to stop yourself from flying into the sea if you persisted in trying to do your job by checking your position.

Ford could feel that Dim was going down in a very gentle glide. He looked out. He could just see wing tips and tail. A bomber in cloud is like a blunt fish swimming through an opaque sea. It is unseen, unseeing. Ford felt alone. He was beginning to wonder why he heard nothing on the intercom. He would have expected to hear the navigator telling them that there were so many minutes to go before their ETA.

Suddenly the greyness turned black; they had broken cloud. An instant later the engines screamed, roared. Ford felt the nose heave up. In a moment they were in cloud again. From his astrodome Ford could not see down. But he guessed that the sea had been there, and not far away.

Surely they were saying something on the intercom? He felt if his plug was in. Blast! It had slipped half out. He had missed some of the most interesting part. He shoved the plug home. Immediately, Dim's voice: 'Bomb doors open.'

The bomb-aimer's voice: 'Bomb doors open.'

Dim's voice: 'In thirty seconds release the load.' A pause. Then, from underfoot, a clonk.

Dim's voice: 'Shut the bomb doors.'

Navigator's voice: 'Set course for base.'

Dim's voice: 'We'll go up out of it. Fly at six thousand.'

Ford felt the aircraft bank gently, the nose rise and swing to starboard in a climbing turn. Almost immediately they were out of cloud again. Now he saw flak and searchlights on both sides, fairly close to starboard and a long way off to port.

Navigator's voice: 'That's So-and-So near to starboard, Such-and-Such some way off to port.'

Dim's voice: 'We can't have been far wrong then. Not bad for this filthy night. Couldn't get a proper pin point.' Pause. Dim's voice again: 'On course for base.'

Ford was surprised to think that they had made a full hundred and eighty degrees' turn. He looked up at the stars. Yes, no mistake about it; the North Star was now to starboard and Orion to port. He was pleased that he could check something for himself.

A searchlight shot up, much nearer than anything had been so far. Ford saw with sudden interest that it was to starboard of them. The blotch of light which it made on the underside of the cloud lay not very far off and definitely to starboard of a point which they would soon pass over on this course. He began to grasp the meaning of the fact that these near lights—the lights the navigator had said were from the nearby coast—were still to starboard of them after they had turned a full hundred and eighty degrees. He had just realised what this meant when he heard Dim's voice confirming him.

'Gone over the bloody coast. Turned too wide. I'll turn north a bit.'

Ford noticed how Dim waited till the blotch of light on the cloud layer had moved well down their starboard quarter, then turned the nose a few points to starboard. Then they settled back on to their homeward course. The island was still throwing up its barrage in an irritable sort of way. The navigator picked out one or two more familiar points by gun flashes or searchlights.

After a while Ford went forward and stood behind Dim and the second pilot in the nose, watching the pretty green illuminated instruments. Then Dim turned her over to the second pilot. He plugged Ford into the socket behind his chair. The first thing Ford heard was the navigator cursing the second pilot.

'Keep that air speed steady, for God's sake. You're all over the bloody sky.'

A new voice said humbly, 'Sorry.'

Dim said, evidently to Ford, 'Well, I'm afraid it's been a very boring trip for you.'

'Far from it,' said Ford. 'You don't suppose I wanted it to be exciting, do you?'

Dim laughed.

'The only irritating thing is I missed a bit of conversation just before you dropped the load. My plug had slipped half out,' Ford said. 'I heard you say "Open the bomb doors". Had you been talking just before then?'

'Yes. We'd discussed just where we'd drop the load,' Dim said. 'They've sent us out on such a filthy night we couldn't get a real pin point. That cloud was down to two hundred feet—thought we'd never come through it. My altimeter was knocking its bottom out. Did you see the sea?'

'No,' Ford said. 'You can't look down from that astrodome thing.'

'Lucky for you,' Dim said. 'It looked bloody cold and rough to me. Filthy great brown waves.'

'How near were we?' Ford asked.

'About two hundred feet.'

'That was when you stepped on the gas?'

'I certainly did.'

Ford put his head into one of the pear-shaped perspex blisters behind the pilot's seat—they allowed you to look directly downward. The cloud layer was far below them now. Once Ford saw a gap, and through it a black surface, which he took to be the sea.

The flight back went quickly and pleasantly. The very idea of anything going wrong with them had disappeared. The navigator seemed only to have just said, 'We've left the enemy coast now' when he said, 'We shall be crossing the English coast in eight minutes.'

Dim's voice: 'Now we'll see if you really know where we are.'

Navigator's voice: 'We're there, all right. You'll see.' Then, after a few minutes, 'Crossing the coast now.'

Dim took over again. Ford hoped the cloud base wasn't as low here as it had been over enemy water. It wasn't. Trailing a few grey wisps, they came into a darker, starless night, but the ground was visible, still quite a reasonable distance below them. A moment later a red beacon winked to starboard.

Dim's voice: 'What's it flashing? Can't see it for the wing.'

Pause. Then the navigator's voice: 'DL. It's Wentworth.'

Dim's voice: 'Wizard. I hand it to you, navigator.'

Wentworth was a fighter station fifteen miles east of their base. Another beacon. The navigator's voice, pardonably, dryly self-satisfied: 'Flashing QS. That is base.'

It had seemed every bit as sure and easy as coming back to a fully lighted airport in an airliner in peace-time with every navigational aid. This was super-navigation. Ford had been to enough post-flight interrogations to know that it didn't by any means always turn out as well as that. It was very strong corroborative evidence that they really had been where they thought they were when they had dropped their stuff.

In a minute or so they saw the string of lights—trivially pretty, like fairy lanterns at a fête—round the perimeter track. They swung to starboard a little.

Dim's voice: 'Hello, Jackal. Hello, Jackal (Jackal was their base's call sign that night). This is Starfish, P for Peter. Calling.

Can you hear me? Am circling aerodrome at a thousand feet. Can
I have permission to land? Over to you, over.'

Pause. Then, through the helmet, a louder crackle; then a new
voice, sounding just as if it had come from one of the crew in the
aircraft: 'Hello, P for Peter. Hello, P for Peter. This is Jackal
answering. Can you hear me? Continue circling aerodrome.
Over to you, over.'

Dim's voice: 'Message received and understood. Over.'

They ran on in their gently banking turn, the lighted perimeter
track slipping round below them. Now Ford saw the flare path,
like a neat, straight, lighted street. It didn't look a very big
objective to put twenty tons or so of bomber down on.

A voice: 'W for William, W for William, this is Jackal speaking.
Proceed to end of flare path, then turn starboard clear of runway
on to perimeter track.' Ford realised that he was hearing base
speak to another aircraft, which had already landed and was
blocking the flare path. He heard no answer from William. Then
Jackal repeated its instructions to William. Still no answer.
P for Peter flew on.

Then Dim's voice, explosive: 'W for William, get off the ruddy
flare path, can't you?' (That, Ford knew, was technically known
as 'irregular RT (radio telephony) procedure'.)

It had no effect. They flogged on.

Dim's voice: 'Hello, Jackal. Starfish, P for Peter, calling. Can I
land? Visibility poor. Over to you.'

Pause. Then: 'Hello, P for Peter, Jackal answering. Continue
circling aerodrome. Is that understood? Over to you, over.'

Dim's voice: 'Message received and understood.' Dim said,
'Blast!'

They flogged on. Ford had lost count of the circuits. But he
knew that, as a matter of fact, they hadn't been held up very
long—not nearly as long as he'd often seen aircraft made to circle
when something had gone wrong on the ground. He was just
resigning himself to anything up to an hour of this flogging round
when the voice came again: 'Hello, P for Peter, Jackal calling.
Land. Over to you, over.'

Dim's voice: 'Message received and understood. Am coming
in. Over.'

The motors were throttled back. Ford felt the aircraft losing

L

height; they were at right angles to the flare path. As usual, when he noticed how a landing was being made, he did not see how the pilot would get her round square to the flare path. But by degrees, wobbling a trifle as she lost air speed, the blunt nose came round. Now they were nearing the aerodrome boundary, they were practically straight with the runway, the ground was coming up fast. Ford felt so confident in the smoothness of Dim's night landings that he stayed standing up, with his head in the astro-dome. And sure enough, the wheels took the runway with gentle bump, bounced a few feet up, came down again with no more bump than the first time; then her twenty tons were losing momentum along the runway. A murmur of 'Nice work, sir,' 'Very nice, sir' from the crew. Ford unplugged his helmet.

They bundled out. The flight sergeant of the ground crew shone his torch on the steps. Ford heard Dim say, 'She went beautifully, simply perfect, Flight.' The truck took them back to the flights, then on to station headquarters for interrogation over a cup of tea. There they found Sailor. He had had by no means so pleasant a ride. Severe icing most of the way; then he had re-crossed the English coast miles off course and had had a long hunt for base. However, here he was, all right, sceptical as ever. They tried to convince him that it was the approaches to a German estuary, not, as he seemed to be suggesting, the Humber which they had mined. He reluctantly agreed that, maybe, this time they had. All the aircraft from this station were back; everybody felt cheerful. They drove up to the mess and this time there were bacon and eggs enough for Sailor and Ford.

Next morning Ford went into the Ops Room at Group. Sailor was there. 'Everyone got back all right last night, I suppose?' Ford said.

'No, they didn't,' Sailor said. 'Look.' He pointed to the board. There were two gaps in the list of times of return to base, one from each of the other two stations which had operated. 'Two missing,' Ford said.

Sailor nodded.

'Makes you think, doesn't it, Sailor?' Ford said, grinning, but wryly.

Sailor nodded again.

It had seemed so completely unalarming, so entirely under control. Ford was frankly shaken. 'Who were they?' he said.

'Munroe of So-and-So Squadron for one.'

Ford remembered Munroe; he had had some dealings with him the week before. He had thought him an unpleasant young man, as a matter of fact. (It is in fiction that 'only the best' are killed.) Munroe's longish, oiled red hair—it would be wet now—came into Ford's mind. 'And the other?' he asked.

'A Manchester crew.'

That meant seven of them.

'What on earth happened to them? They wouldn't have been hit by that flak, surely, or by fighters on a night like that?'

Sailor shrugged. 'Maybe they stayed too long in one place and got hit. More likely they got iced up and flew into the sea, I expect. So would you have if Dim hadn't been pretty bright, really. It takes experience to keep a loaded Manchester out of the sea when you break cloud at two hundred feet. If the pilot doesn't like the look of it, gets fussed, pushes the nose up too hard before he's opened out, you stall, and then down she goes on her tail. Maybe that's what happened. The Manchester captain wasn't terribly experienced.'

'I see,' Ford said.

So maybe he should have felt frightened in that soft greyness when he hadn't seen the sea. Actually, he had only felt frightened when they hadn't brought him his tea in the mess. One never seems to feel the right things at the right time.

The subjective reflection of reality is unreliable, uncertain. We don't understand much of what's happening to us, even when it's happening. We simply don't get it. The man in the modern world, the blind bomber in cloud, the blunt-nosed fish moving through opaque waters. None of us gets it. No one knows what it's all about.

(1941)

Part III

India

A Temple of Love

IT is one of the most ancient of Indian customs to make pil-
grimages to the 'pagodas' or temples in which the sub-continent
is rich. Breaking off a tour otherwise devoted to political and
economic interests, I recently visited the Black Pagoda of
Konarak in the State of Orissa, about halfway down the west
coast of India.

I was in the company of an eminent Harvard economist, a man
of immoderate height. As he curled and uncurled his legs in the
station wagon in which we travelled, a curious shrill squeaking
became audible. For some miles we put it down to inadequate
lubrication of the vehicle. But it gradually became clear that it was
the effect, on the contrary, of the eminent economist kicking our
supper which rested, in the form of several live chickens in a bag,
beneath his feet. The curator of the Orissa state museum who
accompanied us, seemed quite tolerant of this reminder of the
carnivorous habits of occidentals. But it did rather bring home to
us the good taste of Hindu vegetarianism.

We had prudently started at dawn, yet as the drive wore on, the
delays thickened; the bullock carts stuck across our path at the
half-dry river crossings, and the heat beat upon us. The country
began slowly to change from a rich alluvial plain to a more sandy
littoral; for we were approaching the sea. Yet on the river banks
there were patches of the piercing green of young rice.

'That is what irrigation can do,' remarked the economist. The
irrigation, we observed, was effected by means of a two-stage
process. Buckets, swung upon long bamboo poles were pulled by
teams of sun-blackened figures down to the water; a counter-
weight at the other end of the pole swung them, when released,
halfway up to the level of the bank, pouring the water into little
dug out ponds. Then another team repeated the process, swinging
the water by another hoist to the level of the bank. 'A bit "labour-

intensive" as to method, isn't it?' I remarked. 'Spoken like an economist,' said my Harvard colleague. 'But it's probably all right at this stage of development.' And indeed evidence of the first beginnings of progress from the depths of sub-subsistence, seemed to be brushing the face of Orissa. The river itself was being confined and controlled along its length by well-made dykes against the floods which only last monsoon, the Chief Minister had told us, had devastated the State. But as we approached the sea, sand and scrub—the hallmarks of dessication—began to gain upon the plain. At length we were in a level desert bounded by low dunes, beyond which we guessed at the sea. Upon this waste, amidst a clump of scrub and trees, we saw a pile of masonry, dark against the sands. It appeared to be on the same scale as a good-sized cathedral.

'It is the Black Pagoda,' said the curator.

We were stirred by the half-seen bulk of the temple, come upon in this waste-land, at the end of the road, where there was nothing else but sand, and the sound, clear now that we had stopped, of distant surf, and a salt, hot wind. We gazed uncomprehendingly at an apparently shapeless mass. It seemed to have no kind of connection with its surroundings. Here was no trace of ancient city—no mounds nor earthworks even to mark where houses, markets, fortifications must once have stood. There was only the temple, inconceivably alien to western eyes, looming gaunt and forsaken. As we got nearer, however, we began to see that the whole surface of this great mound of stone had been carved and cut. Not only was almost every part of it encrusted with designs in high relief: on every platform, niche or course of masonry there appeared to be statues, many of them free standing, of anything up to life size. What must be men, Gods and animals and, for that matter, men-Gods and animal-Gods, crowded its long and high façades. The deserted temple had still a thousand stone inhabitants.

We were upon the point of plunging into an inspection when the calm voice of the curator arrested us. 'It will be too hot for the Temple now. Let us wait for the evening. There is a rest bunga-low we can go to.' There was something startling to occidental impatience in this calm postponement of the whole purpose of the expedition. But then we looked again at the Temple; we saw that a universe of forms awaited our attention and our comprehension. The heat—that simple, omnipresent fact of India—mounted threateningly; it began to change our scale of values. Our resolution melted. The ovenblast of the air struck at our eyes as we tried to gaze upwards at that towering bulk. No doubt the curator was right. To try to see what we had come to see, there and then, without the preparation of rest, would be merely foolish. The tempo of Indian sightseeing must adjust itself, like everything else, to the stringent regulations of the sun. Wondering a little at our own docility, we turned away, were guided to the little rest bungalow, which lay unseen on the other side of the trees, and threw ourselves upon its cots.

By tea-time we were ready to go to the Temple. At first sight it is in many respects disappointing. Very ruinous, it has lost altogether its great dome-like tower, which was only once seen by an Englishman, in 1833. The remaining part may be thought of as analogous to the nave of a Christian church but a nave built separately from, though closely adjacent to, the tower.

At Konarak this remaining part stands over the waste like some dismasted ship. The temple must have been built on about the same scale as a medium-sized Gothic cathedral, with which it is contemporary. But it has none of an occidental cathedral's structural virtuosity. A great hull—in its present ruined state almost a great hulk—it can boast of no spring or tension of arch and vault and buttress. It is an almost solid mass. And yet how premature it would be to dismiss the Black Pagoda of Konarak because of its structural limitations. For what is marvellous is not the temple as a whole but the statuary which encrusts it. The Black Pagoda is one of the greatest, and one of the strangest, galleries of sculpture in the whole world.

Nevertheless, even when we transfer our gaze from the mass to the dazzling details of the temple, we may still be bewildered rather than enlightened. The profusion of carved men, women and beasts is very great. Highly stylised 'lions of strength' rest upon 'elephants of prosperity'. Snake King and Snake Queen entwine; they are elegant, slender pilasters, their human, happy faces issuing from their scaly necks. The horses of the Sun God draw his vast chariot, which is the temple itself, upon twenty stone wheels, each fifteen feet in diameter. And every inch of axle, spoke and tyre is covered with a concentration of carving in deep relief.

'A bit underpowered for their load,' said the Harvard economist, comparing the three or four foot high horses with the towering temple to which they are hitched in tandem. 'But aren't they graceful?'

And indeed, as each detail came into consciousness a sense of wonder at the perfect urbanity of every figure grew upon us. The very lack of realism in such features as the disproportion between these lovely little horses, arching their necks and dashing forward, and the towering mass in tow was a charming conceit. At another point, a great war-horse and its rider, in this case fully life size, are charging down an enemy. Elsewhere a full-scale elephant is tossing a man in its trunk. But even these scenes of war are some-how depicted with verve and brio—almost charm—rather than with ferocity or passion.

It is only too easy to get absorbed in all this world of detail; to stare, for instance, at a little frieze of dancing girls on one of the ruined subsidiary buildings—a frieze so light, so swift, so alto-gether airborne, that almost all other sculpture one has ever seen begins to seem the work of yokels. And yet all this is incidental. This is not what the temple is about. For the temple is about something: the temple has a theme. But before we consider that theme we must allow this intensely civilised spokesman-in-stone of the Hindu tradition to entertain us further. The temple would not dream of inflicting its earnestness upon us (for it is, like all major works of art, in the end earnest) until and unless we were ready to be earnest. As we approach what the curator tells us is 'the landward gate'—for this is the cathedral of a once great seaport—we see high above us a row of free standing statues, a little less than life size, of women musicians. These are 'Apsaras' the curator tells us, or fairies. But there is nothing airy-fairy about them: they are mature, comely women, the sophisticated entertainers of the court, playing the cymbals, the drum and the clarionet. (And if the third musician has, as a matter of fact, three heads it all looks so natural that neither I nor the eminent Harvard economist noticed her idiosyncrasy, so convenient for a wind instrumentalist, till our second visit to her.)

Mr John Murray, in his reliable guide-book on India, several pages of which are devoted to Konarak, certifies that all the statuary so far described is 'free from offence'. And so it is. If however we now begin to climb upon the hull of the temple, we shall encounter statues which, Mr Murray warns us, are 'licentious'. And it is true that they celebrate that aspect of life which, as the curator at this point aptly reminds us, 'is quite important really—actually a most necessary thing for the continuance of the race'.

It is when we inspect the longer façades—the nave as it were—that we encounter the main theme of the temple. That theme is love. It is a temple dedicated to the reiterated, the ecstatic, portrayal of the act of love. It is a temple dedicated to the proposition that the erotic aspect of life is as worthy of exemplification and contemplation as any other of the major aspects of human life—as worthy as the religious aspect for example with which, the temple asserts, it is inextricably connected.

Not that all the statues on the long façades, or on the seaward face, of the temple are erotic by any means. True, there are dozens of pairs of lovers displayed in the act of love. But then the sheer scale of this immense collection of sculptures must be kept continually in mind. There are many hundreds of statues, either free standing or virtually so, and many thousands of figures and designs, in varying degrees of relief. The erotic groups take their place in an immense stone panorama of human activity, in which worship, war, music, recreation, animal husbandry, are all depicted. Indeed it is possible that it is only our astonished western imagination which assigns central importance to the portrayal of the erotic theme. It may be that if we could cross-question the sculptors they would raise surprised eyebrows at the suggestion that the erotic was their predominant interest. They might maintain that, on the contrary, they merely gave it its due and natural place in the panorama of life.

It may be so (indeed almost every authority who has written on Konarak gives a different interpretation of the sculptures): but on the whole I doubt it. Judging not so much by the quantity as by the quality of the erotic groups I adhere to the suggestion that the celebration of love—the act of love—is the theme and message of the temple. For it is in the erotic groups that the plastic genius which Konarak once possessed found its highest expression.

Brevity, propriety and inability alike forbid me to describe these lovers. The major erotic pairs are virtually free standing groups of statuary about three or four feet high. They are moderately naturalistic in treatment—about to the same extent as western mediaeval work. One pair of lovers in particular must have been formed by the supreme sculptor of this great building. In this pair her face is pressed upward upon his, which bends down upon it as much in benediction as in passion. What is being done is unmistakably an act of love and not of lust. This statue, in particular, and the very best of the other erotic groups, cause one to reflect upon the remarkable capacity of great art to portray what might well have been supposed to be the unportrayable. The literalness, the repetitiveness which might be thought to inhere in the subject is exorcised by sheer aesthetic skill. However, an attempt to describe the best of the erotic statues (they are not all so successful) would fall inevitably into precisely the pitfalls which they so breathtakingly avoid—unless indeed the words were of equal merit to the stones. Moreover, with consummate aesthetic tact the creators of the temple have interspersed amongst these amorous images, meltingly carved in soft sandstone, four cool figures of the Sun God himself, cut in hard grey-green granite. He stands alone, still as they are mobile, formal, almost heraldic, free from the compulsions of the law of kind.

After some two hours of heavy scrambling over the great ledges of the temple, finding evermore, and ever more remarkable, statues and bas reliefs, some erotic and some not, we began to wilt in the still considerable heat. We had only begun the examination of this vast monument. But we could take no more. Fortunately, we had arranged to sleep at the rest bungalow and to resume our study of the temple in the morning. We straggled back to our dinner and our cots, reflecting on this new world.

How brassy, to my eye at least, are the monuments of India's conquerors when compared to these ruinous, incomparable achievements of the Hindus? No valid comparison is really possible between, for example, the Ajanta paintings, the Elephanta, the Ellora or the Konarak, sculptures, on the one hand,

and the pleasant fancy work of the Moguls on the other. The former are attempting the main function of aesthetic activity, namely the realisation, in one form or another, of the basic aspects of human life. The latter is merely intended to please the eye.

Not but that it must be readily admitted that in its own field the Taj Mahal, for example, is an immense success. Shahjehan, the seventeenth-century royal aesthete, did exactly what he meant to do when he built it. His Taj is everything that it is written up to be. It is astonishingly light and aery; it floats above its waters; it is perfectly symmetrical and unified; its marble really does gleam in the moonlight, the ideal foil for the dusky sandstone of its surrounding buildings. The Taj is all this and more. But it has one defect. It is pretty.

On the other hand it would be unfair to the Moguls to suggest that they were always pretty builders. On the contrary their work was often grand and solid. For example the deserted City of Fatehpur Sikri, or 'Town of Triumph', is often considered (by Mr Aldous Huxley for instance) to be their greatest achievement. Built of red sandstone by Akbar, the contemporary of Phillip II of Spain, of Ivan the Terrible and of Elizabeth of England, it was abandoned less than two decades after it was finished. Since then it has stood empty through the centuries, court upon court, audience chamber upon audience chamber, mosques, baths, seraglios—all the appurtenances of a Muslim Court. And empty it still stands, astounding upon the plain. There is nothing pretty about *it*. It is massive, masculine, handsome. Nevertheless, the intense interest which it excites is, to my mind, historical and Imperial rather than aesthetic. Why Akbar abandoned it, no one seems to be quite sure. Perhaps it was that his nomad Central Asian blood led him to wander back to Agra, his former capital, for no particular reason. At any rate he did so. And then his successors abandoned Agra also and moved to Delhi, much as we British did 250 years later—in order that, in each case, the ancient prophecy might be fulfilled, that he who makes Delhi his capital, loses India.

As a matter of fact the British, at Delhi, built something of a Fatehpur Sikri of their own in the shape of 'New Delhi'. New Delhi is a vast, highly planned 'administrative' City, built by the British Government in its penultimate years, near but separate from the city of Delhi itself. (It looks now rather as Washington must have looked before America had grown great enough really to warrant L'Enfant's splendid design.) New Delhi was planned and built by the two leading architects of the British Empire of that day, Sir Edwin Lutyens of the United Kingdom and Sir Herbert Baker of South Africa. And in my humble opinion a magnificent job they made of it on the whole. Like the Moguls, we also used that glorious building material, the sandstone of the North Indian plain. This lovely stone varies in colour from deep red, through every shade of brown, to fawn, to cream with veins of the darker colours running through the lighter. The huge main, Central block of buildings, comprising the President's House (built as the Viceroy's House) and the key offices of the Government of the Indian Union, designed by Lutyens, are a much finer architectural legacy than the Indians might have expected to get from a nation which, on the whole, built meanly and ill in its dependencies. In fact I am inclined to think that it is only that apparently unavoidable snobbery for the old, from which we all suffer, that prevents us comparing the New Delhi buildings quite favourably with Akbar's job at Fatehpur Sikri. For instance Lutyens' stylised elephants at New Delhi are probably as good as any of the Mogul work. The truth is that neither New Delhi nor Fatehpur Sikri are major works of art; they are both handsome and splendid public works.

Be such hazardous aesthetic judgements as they may: the British like the Moguls, each after building their Fatehpur Sikris, have strolled off into history. The Indians are left with the monuments. Not that New Delhi is today an abandoned city. On the contrary it seethes and clacks with the activity of a major bureaucracy in full spate. The eminent Harvard economist said that it reminded him of Washington at the height of the New Deal. The Indians have a use for every inch of office space which we have left them; indeed they are feverishly building more.

It might have been better if the Indians had been left to build their own capital for themselves. We British might have stayed on, till the Indians were ready to take over, in the Victorian discomfort, the still semi-commercial atmosphere, of Calcutta. It is true that in Calcutta our Governors and Governor-Generals were continually being potted at by pious Bengali nationalists;

but then they seldom hit them. Instead we set up a bogusly Viceregal establishment at New Delhi. It was aesthetically a success, politically an error: the opposite of the usual British form.

Not, of course, that staying on at Calcutta would have prevented us having had to leave India. The British guest in present-day India is continually being told, sometimes even by Indians, that we should not have 'lost India' if only we had done this or that— used more force, or less force, put more, or less, people into prison, been firmer or less firm, more active or less active, developed education more or less, etc., etc. There is not a word of truth in all this. I was a member of the Government which passed the Independence of India Act and the fact is that we left India because, in the inimitable Chinese phrase we had 'exhausted the mandate of heaven'. In other words, it was time we went, not for this or that reason, but for every reason. If there is any credit in the matter, and I think that there is, it is that, just in time, we recognised the situation for what it was.

'Mais alors, c'est tendre,' said the young Frenchman in surprise, when we showed him the supreme pair of lovers at the Temple the next morning. He and his fellow travellers had loomed up out of the dark, just as we were going to bed the night before in our rest bungalow. He fairly jumped into the circle of light round our lamp, introducing himself with that perfection of positive good manners possessed by cultivated Frenchmen alone.

'Could he possibly borrow anything in the way of bedding to doss down on the veranda, as there was no room in the bungalow?'

We were preparing to see what we could do for him when his fellow travellers appeared. At first all that was visible were some intensely bright colours, low to the ground, surmounted by a solar topee. As the lamplight struck it, this technicoloured object could be identified as what, I believe, is called a Hawaiian shirt. Within it there soon became evident a sturdy, dumpy human form, and following him another, less technicoloured, but similar.

'May we introduce ourselves—Rev and Mrs Wilks of Kansas City? Might we possibly occupy your veranda for the night?'

The Rev and Mrs Wilks too, in a different way, had excellent manners. They had undoubtedly opened far too many church bazaars and mission sales ever to be at a loss. They were perfectly equipped with bed and bedding so that their need for the veranda was easily met.

'Might we ask what brings you to India?' enquired the economist.

'Missionaries, sir, both Mrs Wilks and myself, missionaries in Assam.'

'What is your Church?'

'Church of the Seventh Day Adventists.'

'Ah.'

'Have you seen much of the rest of India outside Assam?'

'No, sir—been in Assam six years now and so far seen nothing outside of it—so Mrs Wilks and I thought we owed it to ourselves to do a little sightseeing.'

'Ah. Have you seen this temple yet?'

'No, sir, too dark when we arrived. Have to wait till the morning.'

'Ah.'

'Have you heard about the statues?'

'No, sir.'

'Ah.'

That seemed to conclude the conversation for the night. We moved to our respective couches, leaving the Seventh Day Adventists attached to pneumatic mattresses, and blowing strongly.

We were a little concerned with the possible shock which the temple might inflict upon the Wilks. But at 6 a.m. the next morning when we got up, ahead of the heat, they had already gone. All that was left of them were two little pneumatic mattresses under two beautifully arranged little mosquito-nets—the perfectly tidy camp of two perfectly good children.

As we walked over to the temple the young Frenchman said: 'I was at Yale for a year.' 'Oh: a pity,' said the eminent Harvard economist. The young Frenchman, with the faintest smile, came back to the subject of our immediate environment.

'Please tell me, what are Seventh Day Adventists?—is not that a very fanatical sect?' The economist confirmed his suspicion.

The young Frenchman shook his head, as one who discovers that he has been inadvertently travelling with wild and dangerous beings.

When we reached the temple we at first saw no sign of the Adventists. But as we climbed again upon it, revisiting musicians, lovers, horses, beasts, dancers, snake king and snake queen, the Sun God himself, and all its other innumerable inhabitants, we saw far below, and far away from the temple, two small bright objects. It was the Adventists, and they were busy with some activity. We soon saw that they were setting up an enormous and cumbersome kind of camera. They were training this apparatus, at long range, upon the temple, much as a cautious commander sets up his biggest cannon before an enemy fortress. If this was indeed for them the temple of Mammon, they were evidently approaching it with due circumspection and in accordance with all the rules of war.

Descending again we read the admirable notice, describing the temple, set up by the Department of Archaeology of the Government of India. It speaks of the 'exuberance' of the sculptures; the word, though tinged with a meiosis left behind, no doubt, by the British, is well chosen. The notice also informed us that the temple had probably been built '*circa* 1255 A.D.' This is disputed by some authorities: Mr Malk Raj Anand, for example, tells me that he considers that it is ninth or tenth century. In any case it was roughly coeval with the Gothic. Men were decorating these façades when other men, in Western Europe, were covering the great West fronts of the Cathedrals, with a statuary no less profuse, no less exquisite, but opposite in theme.

The world is not, after all, a particularly small place. The variety of the opinions which men have held, and still hold, is very considerable. For instance the court of King Narasimha of Orissa, the life of which the statues of the temple portray, must have been a particularly relaxed sort of place. Round the temple stood a major commercial port, trading with all the world through a habour long since silted up. While we in the west were crusading, extirpating heresies, sinning, repenting, agonising over our doctrines and our desires, men and women a good deal more civilised were here calmly exploring their somatic possibilities. Unfortunately it is impossible to say how well or ill a society thus

M

orientated would have fared in the long run. Soon after the flowering which produced this temple, Orissa began to be devastated by wave after wave of Muslim invasion, until it was reduced to the backwardness and destitution out of which it is only now attempting to emerge.

A third time we climbed the great hull of the temple to gaze once more, not only at the statues, but also at the ocean's line of surf, booming distantly upon the Coromandel beaches. And now we saw again the Adventists, their preliminary photographic bombardment apparently completed, cautiously circling the perimeter of the temple. As we watched we saw that they were gradually approaching it. When we had descended for the last time from those battlements of love, they were examining some of its outworks. I walked towards them. Somewhat hurriedly, it seemed to me, they walked away. I concluded that they were at least as embarrassed at the prospect of a discussion of the temple as we had been, the night before, at the prospect of introducing them to it. But now I felt that this was a pity. Now I would have liked to hear what they thought of it all. Perhaps we had done them an injustice; perhaps they were far more sophisticated and tolerant than we had supposed. Perhaps Seventh Day Adventists can take the Black Pagoda of Konarak in their stride. But perhaps not.

'I will ask them all about it in the bus going back,' the young Frenchman remarked with a jolly grin. And I think he really meant to. 'Typically Yale,' said the eminent Harvard economist. 'Always a touch of the cheerful playboy about them.' The resulting conversation, as those strangely assorted passengers bumped over the Orissa by-roads, may have been remarkable.

In the middle of the morning, and so this time in the middle of the heat, we too bounced away over the cart track towards the metalled road inland. We went to Puri, the holy city of the temple of Jugernauth. Like other holy cities of other faiths it did not prove an attractive place. It contains indeed a White Pagoda, comparable in size and importance to the Black Pagoda of Konarak. Moreover the White Pagoda of Puri may, for all I know, exhibit on its façades statuary and carving as important as those of Konarak. But the Puri temple is still operational, with the worship of

Jugernauth in full swing (though shorn now of its more spectacular features, such as the immolation of worshippers beneath the
wheels of the car in which the God takes an annual outing down
the main street). For these reasons the non-Hindu is not allowed
to pass the outer surrounding walls of the temple and cannot get
near enough to form an idea of its sculpture.

We turned away from the holy, beggar-ridden, fever-hot centre
of Puri, and discovered on its outskirts a quite first rate seaside
hotel. From it one may, and does, bathe delightfully in the surf
as it pounds upon the Coromandel sands.

(1956)

Part IV

People

The Webbs

MOST people would be inclined to say that the Webbs exerted more intellectual influence upon the British Labour Movement than anyone else has ever done. There was the influence of their books; and then there was the influence of their lives. Both were profound.

Their greatest book was one of their earliest: *The History of Trade Unionism* (1894). After more than half a century this remains a basic work of sociology. And in a way too it illustrates how their books and their lives were really one. For the manner in which the Webbs went about this first major task of 'their partnership', as Beatrice was to call it, set the noble pattern of their lives. They investigated the trade unions—the basic, indeed in the eighteen-eighties, almost the sole, organisation of the wage earners.

For the successful formation of the post-Chartist British trade unions was, as everybody can see now, one of the decisive events of modern history. These obscure molecular activities of the British wage earners, drab and prosaic compared with the revolutionary spirit of Chartism; feeble and precarious compared with the power of trade unionism today—these activities which had been thought below the dignity of social investigation —altered the course of history, and that not only in Britain.

Thus in investigating the 'new unionism', as it was called at the time, this brilliantly good-looking young woman, born into the highest ranks of the new class of captains of industry, and this strange, odd, awkward young civil servant from the lower middle class, united to accomplish one of the first major pieces of genuinely scientific field-work in sociology. They set out to discover how the British wage earners were organising themselves into stable and powerful association. Travelling indefatigably about the country, investigating the origins, the congresses, the disputes, the doctrines, the rule books of what were at that time obscure and unpopular organisations, they brought into the light of consciousness what was to prove one of the decisive social processes of modern times.

The establishment of trade unionism was one of the two decisive events which have modified the supposedly unalterable laws of capitalist development. The other decisive development was the establishment of political democracy under universal franchise; and, as the Webbs' book showed, these two events were linked together at a hundred points. It was out of and through the struggle of the trade unions, emancipated by the Cross Acts, struck down again by the courts, forming, in challenge and response, the Labour Representation Committee, and so the Labour Party, that the British wage earners won their political as well as their industrial influence. It was these two interlocked developments which falsified Marx's prediction that the fate of wage earners in a capitalist society must be 'ever-increasing misery'. And that has changed everything. But all this was far from obvious when the Webbs sat down to write *The History of Trade Unionism*. It was an act of faith to see that the obscure doings of rude men in Lancashire and Durham, or in the East End of London, were going to change the world. Yet by their exertions and their example, change the world they have.

It is curious to recall that Lenin translated the Webbs' book into Russian during one of his Siberian exiles. He evidently considered it of immense importance. But what did he think of its intensely cautious pragmatism, of the refusal of the Webbs to raise virtually any theoretical structure upon the immense factual groundwork of the book?

But let us turn to their lives. In the next period, in the Edwardian Age, in the nineteen-hundreds, it was the lives rather than the books of the Webbs which counted. From the turn of the century to 1914 they were the heart and core of the Fabian Society. In that brilliant, quarrelsome, extraordinary body, with Wells, Shaw, Leo Amery, and the young G. D. H. Cole, all brilliantly disputatious, the Webbs formed a central ballast and basis.

In the nineteen-hundreds, it is interesting to remember, the Webbs were by no means irrevocably committed to the nascent

Labour Party. It was part of their Fabian philosophy of permeation that they were as willing to work towards socialism through the Liberal, or even the Conservative Parties, if those parties could be cajoled or persuaded into serving their purposes. It was not until what they regarded as the breakdown of the old social system in the First World War—it was not until after 1914—that Sidney became a practical political leader of the Labour Party as well as a Fabian theorist. In 1918, at the end of the war, he and Henderson played a decisive part in re-forming the Labour Party as a national party with individual membership, whilst yet retaining its original character of the 'Labour Representation Committee' of the trade unions. And it was then that Sidney drafted Clause 4 of the Constitution which has been so much in the news in the last few years, that Clause which defines the common ownership of the *means* of production as a necessary basis for a reasonable and equitable distribution of the *fruits* of production.

Soon after this the Webbs produced what is to my mind their second best book, after *The History of Trade Unionism*. This is *The Decay of Capitalist Civilisation* (1923). They were convinced as early as the beginning of the nineteen-twenties, that capitalism, not merely as an economic but also as a social system, would never recover from its *felo de se* in the First World War. And this short book contains by far their sharpest—if you will by far their most left-wing—critique of the society which surrounded them. Its earlier companion volume, *A Constitution for a Socialist Commonwealth in Great Britain*, is frankly unreadable. It reveals the negative side, the limitations, of this great man and woman. There is a startling formalism, and a rigidly pedestrian spirit, about this attempt to foresee how socialism might be organised in Britain, a formalism which ignored many things which would, in fact, profoundly modify the real development of society.

It was at this period of their lives that I first met the Webbs. It was in 1923 and I had just joined the Labour Party. They asked me to dine at their house on Millbank. I remember Beatrice peering at me quizzically and asking: 'Now, on which side of us are you young people coming up now? We notice' (the "we" was always royal) 'that first a generation of young socialists comes up well to the left of us and then the next generation comes up well to the right of us. Now where are you, Mr Strachey?' My answer in those days ought to have been that I did not know where I was. But it was true that the Webbs remained massively placed at the centre of British socialism.

By the nineteen-twenties, Sidney was launched on his active political career. He was a member of the Labour Party Executive and he took office as President of the Board of Trade in the 1924 Labour Government. But his real test as a practical politician came five years later in the second Labour Government of 1929. In that Government he was Secretary of State for Dominion and Colonial Affairs. He was an industrious and competent departmental Minister.

But now another of the limitations of the Webbs came disastrously to the fore. Events, in their remorseless way, began to reveal the fact that both Sidney and Beatrice were great sociologists but by no means great economists. Their powers of economic analysis, as distinct from description, were severely limited. Sidney, no doubt, was a well-trained economist who knew extremely well economics up to and including Marshall. But somehow the subject had gone dead in his mind. He did not really believe that there was anything much new to say or think or do about economics.

Therefore when the catastrophe of the great slump struck the second Labour Government like a cyclone; when unemployment, which that Government had been elected to cure, or at any rate to combat, rose tidally to engulf it, the Webbs had nothing to offer. I was a young Labour M.P. at the time, and I, and other more important people than myself, tried desperately to make them and our other leaders face the issue. Keynes, it is true, had not then worked out the theoretical basis for the maintenance of full employment. Nevertheless, he had got the rough outline of how to set about the thing well in his mind. We young people in the Labour Movement were in touch with him and we were convinced that whether he was right or wrong, an attempt to combat unemployment on some sort of Keynsian lines was the one hope for the Government. Such an attempt might very likely fail, but it was certain that if it were not even made the Government would go down, not only to defeat but to discredit.

As I remember it, the Webbs did not so much actively disagree with the Keynsian analysis and prescription; it was rather that they were not really interested in it one way or the other. It was the inequalities, wastes, and injustices of the capitalist system which had produced their socialism. Both theoretically and practically, unemployment was to them essentially a passing phase of the trade cycle rather than the centre of the picture. So the two leading theorists of the Labour Party failed even to see the necessity of making an attempt to find a way out along Keynsian lines.

On the other hand, when the crash came in 1931, as come it duly did, the Webbs' reaction was in the end far-reaching. For some time they seemed numbed by the political catastrophe; but, in the end, they came near to what was in effect the orthodox Marxist conclusion. By an extraordinary but logical process these arch-reformists, the very authors of that watchword of the British Labour Movement 'the inevitability of gradualness', came, at the very end of their lives, to despair of the possibility of reforming the capitalist system. To them, just as to myself, in the nineteen-thirties, it looked as if the decay of capitalist civilisation had become irrevocable. We failed to see the extraordinary fact that Keynes's diagnosis and remedy, combined with the obstinate strength, industrial and political, of the wage earners, and combined, too, with the terrific jolt which the Second World War was to give to British society, would create a far more favourable opportunity for reformism in the latter part of the twentieth century than had ever existed before.

I never knew the Webbs well but I did occasionally go down to Liphook and see them during this period. I remember them telling me on one occasion that Keynes had been there the weekend before and that he was heartbroken by the fact that *The General Theory*, some time after its publication, had apparently fallen completely flat; that the economists were ignoring it; that nobody would pay any attention to it. I could not help noticing that Beatrice, at any rate, evidently thought that the book's apparent failure was inevitable; that it was a last despairing attempt to find a reformist way out which did not exist.

It was not that the Webbs had become communists. They still did not grasp, and were not really interested in, the whole massive body of Marxist theory; but they had despaired of reformism.

Their reaction was to go to Russia and to write that extraordinary and, to be frank, preposterous book, *Soviet Communism, a New Civilisation*, published in 1935.

I vividly remember the impression which it made on me, at the time. I was then much nearer to the communists than the Webbs ever became; but even I was staggered by the book's utter lack of any critical analysis of Russian society. It was not that the Webbs had seen Stalin's Russia as it was and had come to the conclusion that, nevertheless, since capitalism seemed to be dying, the Soviet system had to be accepted, with all its horrors, as the only remaining way out for human civilisation. That was a tenable proposition. But that was not the Webbs' reaction. Their huge, two-volume work gave the impression of taking Soviet society utterly at its face value. Their extraordinary formalism came out above all in their account of the political side of Soviet society. They described it as if it were in reality what it was on paper. Their formalism showed in their extraordinary belief that if a constitution said that democratic elections were to take place, that meant that they actually did take place. But there was also a fixed determination to see in Soviet Russia the hope of the world. They would not despair; therefore they had to have some repository for their hope. And they found it, not as many of the rest of us did, by concluding that the nightmarish features of Stalin's Russia had to be accepted as the inevitable birth pangs of a new civilisation: they found it by firmly shutting their eyes to the existence of any such features. Of course, they were old people by now.

It would be wholly wrong, however, to end this talk on a note of depreciation. The mistakes of a man and woman such as the Webbs are incidental and drop away in the tide of history. Their constructive achievements alone remain. It was said of a general in the last war: 'To say that he made mistakes is merely to say that he made war.' In the same way we may say of the Webbs: 'To say that they made mistakes is merely to say that they made social history.' Their theory deeply influenced what has become the major left-wing party in a virtually two-party system. The Labour Party might have been a very different thing without the life and theory of the Webbs.

Thus every British wage earner is profoundly in debt to the

Webbs. They are concretely and financially in debt to them: for whether they know it or not, and whether they vote Labour or Conservative, the standard of life which the British wage earners now enjoy was in some measure built up by the lives of this man and woman. The strange partnership of this prosaic, ugly, able little man, with a woman in her own way intensely romantic, laid down many of the lines of action by which the wage earners have won full status in British society.

Third Programme (1960)

Trotsky

It was George Orwell in *1984* who first asserted that forgery on the scale of world history could be a worse crime than murder. And there is something in it. In the perspective of history it may be that the crimes of the Stalin epoch in Russia which will stand out will not be the violence, the famines, the tyrannies, the murders. After all, such things as these have happened before—time after time in human history. The only genuinely *original* crime of the Stalinist epoch was the attempt systematically to falsify the historical record. Of course the Stalinists did not carry the thing to the lengths which Orwell imagined. But Orwell's nightmare was only an exaggeration of what Stalin actually did.

Nor is it a mere highbrow whim to say that there is a sense in which this crime is worse than murder. For it is the murder of a whole people's sense of reality. It is only by means of the historical record that a nation—that mankind itself, for that matter—can even attempt to keep in touch with social reality. It is only by means of studying what did happen that we can ever hope to achieve a rational social purpose. For a government to blot out whole vital incidents in a people's recent past, and then to write in forged records of what did *not* happen, is a truly ghastly crime. For that matter, it is a ghastly crime not only against a nation but against individuals. Most people, it is true, would much rather have their reputations murdered than be murdered themselves! But it may be that even this is not true of the great actors in history. For to murder the reputation of one of these is to murder the immortal part of him.

I have been reading a book called *A Prophet Unarmed*,* which is the second volume of Mr Isaac Deutscher's great life of Trotsky. Like the first volume, it is a splendid book. It adds to qualities of high academic scholarship an irreplaceable sense

* Oxford 38s.

of participation in the events which it describes. For Mr Deutscher, as a young man, was a member of the Polish Communist Party and saw at least some of these things at close quarters. His book bears out an aphorism which Trotsky himself wrote in the fragmentary diary which he kept in his last years of exile in the nineteen-thirties. 'Only a participant can be a profound observer.' But in addition to all this, the book is of high importance because it restores—this is Mr Deutscher's own word —the reputation of this great and extraordinary man, Leon Trotsky: and it does so not only with loving care but also with strict impartiality.

No one, I suppose, outside official Russian circles, would deny that Trotsky was a great man. The part he played in human history was so important that only historical forgery on the Stalinist scale could possibly deny him that epithet. But I suppose that many British readers will come to the book demanding to be told by Mr Deutscher whether Trotsky was a good or an evil man. Such readers may be disappointed. Mr Deutscher's whole approach is the very antithesis to the 'good man—bad man' approach. Yet after reading both this volume and the preceding one they will, I think, come to understand the way in which Mr Deutscher looks at things. He evidently feels that it would have been un-adult continually to pass moral judgments on the tragic events of the Russian revolution and its aftermath. He tells the story largely without moral comment but with complete comprehension of the ethical outlook of such a man as Trotsky.

On the whole, I think this approach is justified. In many respects Trotsky's errors were intellectual rather than moral. He was one of the most brilliant men of our century; but, as this record shows, he was very often brilliantly wrong. The gods endowed him with almost every gift except two: wisdom and self-criticism. On the purely intellectual side, he had a certain lack of scepticism about the absolute validity of ideas, his own and other people's. And then there was this tragic incapacity for self-criticism. A startling example of it is afforded by an incident which took place long after the period covered by this book. Again it comes from Trotsky's fragmentary diary of the nineteen-thirties. On one page he gives a terse and indeed harsh justification for his part of the responsibility for having, not only the

Tsar, but the whole of the Tsar's family, shot. On another page he writes with passionate indignation about the outrage of Stalin's persecution not only of himself but of his helpless family left behind in Russia. It may be objected that the two cases are not identical. The Trotskys were not a dynasty: the Romanovs were. But still. . . . Only a man with curiously blind spots in his make-up could have left those pages close together in the diary.

Mr Deutscher's present book deals, however, with a different period in Trotsky's life: the period from 1921 to 1929; the period of his long-drawn-out fall from power. The political issues are of high and continuing importance. What emerges above all is that during the nineteen-twenties Trotsky proposed roughly the same economic programme, namely sharply intensified industrialisation, and heavy pressure on the richer peasants, which Stalin carried out in the nineteen-thirties. Trotsky proposed to carry through this Draconian programme, of what he called 'primitive socialist accumulation' without Stalin's terrible methods. But was Trotsky sincere in his protestations of relative mildness and libertarianism? If he had come to supreme power, would he have behaved any better than Stalin did? The answer, I should guess, is that Trotsky would not have shrunk from something approaching, at any rate, Stalin's ruthlessness with the kulaks. But he would, I think, have shrunk from Stalin's total destruction of any shred of democracy and liberty of opinion within the Bolshevik party itself.

All this, as Mr Deutscher says, inevitably raises the general question: what would have happened if Trotsky and not Stalin had won, as, at the start of their duel, seemed highly probable? Mr Deutscher warns us that it is idle to speculate on such historical might-have-beens. But I cannot help feeling that it would have been something better than what has happened. At any rate it could hardly have been worse.

For the real tragedy of the Russian Revolution is subtle as well as profound. In a sense it is the tragedy of success, not the tragedy of failure. Stalin's methods of 'primitive socialist accumulation' succeeded. The kulaks were destroyed. The Russian land was collectivised. The peasants were bled white for the sake of rapid industrialisation. And what is the final result of this success? It is the Russia of today. And the cruel fact is that the Russia of today, while undoubtedly a strong and in many respects a fine country, is not particularly either better or worse than other countries at its stage of development. It is an illusion to think that it is a country differing in any decisive way from other recently developed countries in the world. Contrary to what most people suppose, even the speed of development has been ordinary. Russia has been industrialised in about forty years. This is about the time it usually takes a country to achieve the primary and always painful steps of industrialisation. It is true that Stalin has proved that the thing can be done without recourse to private profit and by means of centralised, state-directed, industry. But he has also proved that this method is more rather than less painful. Primary accumulation of capital by this new method proved in the Russian case at least as physically, morally, and intellectually costly as the older method. And at the end of the process, the results of each method seem to be similar. By each method you get a developed industrial country, sure to grow richer and richer. If it is industrialised by the socialist method it will have some advantages but also some disadvantages. You may achieve a more sustained rate of growth: but on the other hand you will be apt to have an inferior mechanism of consumers' choice. You will get a grossly inferior political system, but on the other hand many advantages for military purposes. And so on and so forth. Judged by Russian performance in eastern Europe, you will not even get a country whose external relations are any different or any better.

Thus we come to the bleak conclusion that the Stalinist methods were horrible, and their results commonplace. If Trotsky had come to power in the nineteen-twenties instead of Stalin, I think it probable he would have failed. He was too civilised a man to have resorted to the extremities of Stalinism. But would not such a failure have been preferable to Stalin's form of success? As the French mystic, Simone Weil, wrote: 'It is better to fail than to succeed in doing harm.' What a trick history has played on all those who sympathised with the Bolshevik party of the nineteen-twenties! 'History is more cunning than any of us': and it was Lenin himself who said that.

All this may seem to suggest that Mr Deutscher has written a

N

political thesis rather than a biography. That would be entirely wrong. This is the life story of a tragic human being. Trotsky, in one of his aspects, was the link between the romantic revolutionary of the past and the Marxist social scientist. What is appealing in the man is that throughout his rise and fall he really cared for the triumph of his ideas. He struggled, of course, for personal power, but the record shows that he genuinely wanted power in order to carry out his programme. There is a world of difference between such a man and Stalin. And it is the very stuff of tragedy to follow Deutscher's narrative of how the pure power seeker such as Stalin almost always destroys the man who is not single-minded about power but cares also about the purpose for which power should be used.

So although Mr Deutscher's book can be read simply as one of the great biographies of our time, yet I come back to the view that its ultimate importance lies in the political lessons latent in it. Mr Deutscher has something very important to say about this. He writes that Trotsky was

'. . . the representative figure of pre-Stalinist communism and the precursor of post-Stalinist communism. Yet I do not imagine that the future of communism lies in Trotskyism. I am inclined to think that the historic development is transcending both Stalinism and Trotskyism and is tending towards something broader than either of them. But each of them will probably be 'transcended' in a different manner. What the Soviet Union and communism take over from Stalinism is mainly its practical achievement; in other respects, as regards methods of government and political action, ideas and 'moral climate' the legacy of the Stalin era is worse than empty; the sooner it is disposed of the better. But precisely in these respects Trotsky has still much to offer; and the political development can hardly transcend him otherwise than by observing all that is vital in his thought and applying it to realities which are far more advanced, varied, and complex than those he knew.'

It will be fascinating to see whether this forecast of Mr Deutscher's is fulfilled. As Russia develops, will not educated people insist on being allowed to read both Trotsky's own writings and also such books as this, containing the true history of his struggle for inner party democracy? Mr Deutscher thinks that the only conclusion that they can come to is that Trotsky was deluding himself when he thought that democracy within the Communist Party could be preserved while all freedom of expression and association was denied to other political parties. In a striking phrase he says that the Bolsheviks could not give themselves both a monopoly of power and a monopoly of freedom. Yet it may be that as a transitional stage some degree of what is called 'inner party democracy' can be restored before there is any possibility of the freedom of rival political parties. But I would entirely agree that such 'inner party democracy' would again be stifled unless it led on to a wider freedom of expression and association for all.

What new worlds the educated classes—one can use no other word—in Russia will discover or rediscover when they get access to such books as this, to Trotsky's own writing, to Pasternak and to so much else in both their own literature and in the literature of the West. Moreover, I think Mr Deutscher is right in saying that this great enlightenment cannot be much longer delayed. Already the censorship is half-hearted compared with what it was in Stalin's time. But you cannot *half* blot out a nation's recent past, or *half* prevent its access to foreign literature. Once even the minor tolerations of the Khrushchev régime have been established, there will be no preventing the Russians from learning the truth sooner rather than later. And then, I am convinced, we shall see extraordinary things.

Third Programme (1959)

Laski

I WORKED with Harold Laski closely in the five years before the war: this was for us and for Victor Gollancz the period of the Left Book Club. The discussion and choice of the books; the constant public meetings at which we spoke together; the articles which we contributed to the *Left News*, constituted an intellectual collaboration. It was at this period that I got to know at first hand Harold Laski's remarkable mental powers. There was that alarming speed of reading, a page at a time; there was the photographic memory, any quotation from any authority instantly at command; there was that copious, indefatigable output of books, articles and speeches; there was that deep hold over the imaginations and affections of the rank-and-file members of the Local Labour Parties.

Under the shock of his death I, for one, find myself suddenly reversing one judgment I had made of his work. The very dazzling variety and copiousness of his intellectual output had always seemed to me Laski's chief weakness. It was always easy enough to point out the unresolved themes that ran through his books and articles and speeches. The deepest layer of his mind undoubtedly rested upon the main nineteenth century, Manchester, radical, rationalist, Benthamite tradition. But he had extrapolated that tradition further and further to the Left—further than any other English thinker, except perhaps J. A. Hobson in that one book *Imperialism*—until it touched, overlapped, and both collided and intermingled with Marxism. The result could not be consistency. But the pain and shock of his death makes one realise that this was certainly his main strength: that it was just this that gave him his hold over the mind of a whole generation of the British Labour Movement. After all, the contradictions were in our minds too—in a sense they were in the objective situation itself as it had developed historically in this country. Laski performed an immense service for us by making these contradictions conscious and articulate; for he gave us thereby at least one prerequisite for solving them. No one of his time and place could have done much more. To have struggled so long and to have done this much was, we now see, something which overshadowed the contradictions.

Quotations from my books are now in fashion, so I will give one more from *The Coming Struggle For Power* and apply it to Laski.

'. . . He who supposes that an Englishman of the present day can find his way either to intellectual certainty or political consistency, without doubts, hesitations and errors, shows little appreciation of the gravity or complexity of the present situation.'

It was, I have no doubt, just because Laski made so incredibly articulate those doubts, hesitations and errors that he gained and kept his enormous hold over the minds and hearts of the members of the Local Labour Parties. Certainly that hold, on the part of this physically childlike scholar, who never ran for a public office, but who for many years could be elected to the National Executive of the Labour Party at the top of the list of the constituency Labour Parties; who was thus elected all through the Left Book Club period when his views were sharply opposed, on the main issue of the day, to those of most of the other leaders of the Labour Party, and to the views of a majority of those who elected him—certainly that hold was the most remarkable feature of Laski's public life.

Somehow or other the members of the Local Labour Parties realised that what Laski was doing was to build up a climate of opinion which would make possible what has been attempted, and in part accomplished, in the past five years. If we have built a working, planned economy, and based upon it a Welfare State, with a considerable re-distribution of income, and have done so while not only maintaining but immensely revivifying British democracy and liberty, we have been enabled to do so by the mental climate which Laski did so much to create.

Do not let us doubt the significance of the contemporary achievement of the British Labour Movement, if—'repeat if', as they say in the official telegrams—this achievement can be secured, consolidated and extended. There are plenty of very influential persons in this country who are determined to stick at nothing to undo that achievement, or, if they cannot undo it, to undermine it, or at least to prevent, almost at all costs, its extension. For, in the long run the Labour achievement cannot be secured unless it is extended. Nevertheless, if the British Labour Movement can 'make good' what it has built in the last five years, the long-run effects on the world will be, in my humble opinion, almost immeasurable.

For in that event British Labour would have proved in practice that it is possible by democratic means:

1. To bring the naturally monopolistic basic industries into public ownership;

2. To run a planned economic system with, so far at least, a very considerable degree of freedom from the oscillations of the world market;

3. To re-distribute the national income to a very appreciable extent.

If, I repeat, these three achievements can be preserved, secured and, above all, extended, they will come to amount to the breaking of the arbitrary power of monopoly capital in one fairly large nation-state.

Now the great issue in the world today turns on whether or not it is possible to make such economic changes as these by democratic means. That in fact is the issue around which a very large part of Laski's writings revolve. For experience shows that, unless these economic changes can be made, a modern industrial society runs amuck in alternate war and stagnation. But if these indispensable economic modifications can be made by democratic means, then the central dilemma of our epoch can be resolved.

Democracy, in the simple essential sense of representative and responsible government, emerges as the solvent of our times. Democracy, if it can be preserved, emerges as that solvent precisely because it is incompatible in the long run with the arbitrary economic power of monopoly capital.

As early as the seventeenth century practical British politicians knew that if the democratic process were established and preserved, it must lead in the long run to a re-distribution of income. Laski was fond of a quotation from the Clarke papers (my colleague, the Minister of Health is equally fond of it). It describes how in 1647 Cromwell and Ireton were arguing (with Rainborough) against a manhood suffrage for their new Commonwealth. For, said these perspicacious squires, if you have a manhood suffrage, 'it may happen that the majority' may make just those economic changes which the squires did not want 'by law, not in a confusion'. Therefore, the squires said firmly, there must be no political democracy in their new Commonwealth. For political democracy would mean in the long run a levelling economic policy carried out by due process of law.

In Cromwell's and Ireton's day such a process of economic change and re-distribution, however ethically just, was unnecessary. In fact it is no doubt true that the economy of the seventeenth century worked better without it, and that in that sense it would have been historically premature. But in our day an appreciable re-distribution of income with its concomitant economic changes, such as to public ownership of the basic industries and control over the export of money and capital and the import of goods, have become prerequisites for the functioning of the economic system.

In the last five years the British Labour Movement has made at least an important beginning at doing the indispensable job of our times by democratic means. I do not think it is any exaggeration to say that if—but of course it is still a big if—British Labour can consolidate and extend its achievement, we shall have shown the world the way out.

Moreover, we now know that this is the only way out. The experience of the last quarter of a century has shown us that there is no other way out. True, if communities do not succeed in making their necessary economic adjustments by means of the democratic process, they sooner or later carry out their inevitable economic modifications by means of a dictatorship either of the Right or of the Left. But these dictatorships although they can be, in certain circumstances and in certain respects, fairly successful in the economic sphere, represent, we now know, no possible way out for the world. For the abolition of democracy in a modern State has in each contemporary instance entailed such frightful disasters and abuses that the attempted cure has been worse than the disease.

These, it seems to me, are the central issues with which Harold
Laski struggled. It is not to criticise him, it is to pay him the
highest tribute, to say that he could state, but not solve, them.
No man can solve them. They can only be solved in practice by
the political action of the people themselves. But that action can
be immensely assisted by the work of men such as Laski. For they,
by making the issues articulate, help to bring us all to political
maturity in time; and in all major political issues time is of the
essence of the contract between us and our fate.

Laski's whole life's effort was of this kind. What members of
the Local Labour Parties felt and honoured in him was his
unresting grapple with the central issue of our times—the issue of
the preservation of political democracy through the strains and
stresses of a period of rapid and inevitable change in the economic
structure. And these men and women of our Movement were wise
and patient to approve as a virtue in him the fact that in so doing
he often turned back and forth on his own argument, seeking
for the way out. May we not apply to Laski, in the political sphere,
Auden's measured but tender lines on Freud?

> *If often he was wrong and at times absurd*
> *To us he is more than a person*
> *Now but a whole climate of opinion.*

Laski has at last worn himself right out. But he has by no
means left his opponents masters of the field. When we consider
the post-war work of the British Labour Movement, we can
strike the same balance between Laski and his opponents as
Auden struck, in a line of the same poem, between the dead
Freud and his opponents—'They are still alive, but in a world he
changed.'

(1950)

John Kenneth Galbraith

I. THE BOOK

PROFESSOR GALBRAITH has written a searching, relentless, down-to-earth critique of American society in its economic aspects.* And he has written it from a completely American standpoint. The whole European controversy of socialism and anti-socialism is simply by-passed. If the book has an ancestry it is from Veblen, the one wholly original American economist and sociologist. Indeed in mood and method the book is decidedly Veblenesque, for it is often harsh, brash, and with something homespun, in the very best sense of that word, in its texture. But of course Professor Galbraith has an incomparably higher technique of economic analysis at his finger tips than Veblen could command.

The book is in essence a study, at once massive and intricate, of what happens to a society which chooses personal self-enrichment as its national goal or ideal. (Whether or not its author would agree with this characterisation I do not know, for he nowhere puts the matter like this: but that, as I hope this review will establish, is what it comes to.) His first proposition is that Americans, much more than any other people, have set up *the production of things* as their true object of worship. That which promotes production is good, that which hampers it is bad. But (though here Professor Galbraith is, in my opinion, insufficiently specific) the production to be thus worshipped must be of a particular sort. Because (I suggest) personal enrichment is the national ideal, it must be production for profit. It is the profit, Galbraith shows, given off like some precious vapour from the act of production, rather than that act itself, which is the national objective. The emergence of profit alone sanctifies the act of production; whether or not any particular

* See *The Affluent Society*, by John Kenneth Galbraith (Hamish Hamilton 21s).

activity will yield a profit is the unique criterion of its desirability.

Consequences of the utmost importance flow from the adoption
of this national ideal. On the positive side, to engage in all acts of
production which will yield a profit becomes a categorical imperative. In what Professor Galbraith calls 'the conventional
wisdom', this is justified by the explanation that what it is most
profitable to produce will be at the same time what best satisfies
a human want. Professor Galbraith agrees (here sketching some
of the history of economic thought) that, in the epoch of scarcity,
so to some extent it was. The criterion of profitability had a
relation, discernible if never exact, to the satisfaction of primary
human needs. It could be argued at least that if only the distribution of the national income were not too inequitable the criterion
of profitability would serve the essential purpose of allotting the
resources of the community in such a way as best to satisfy the
needs of the population. In 'the affluent society' it is no longer so.
And here Professor Galbraith introduces what is perhaps his
most important concept, 'the Dependence Effect'. The dependence effect is, in the main, simply advertising. But it is advertising
raised to the American level of intensity, in which some $11
billion a year—an appreciable part of the gross national product—
is spent on it. Such advertising has ceased to be a useful, if noisy,
accompaniment of the production and marketing of goods. Such
advertising has become an independent force. *It has become
nothing less than the prior production of the wants which the subsequent production of the goods is to satisfy.*

When this happens, advertising—in the widest sense of the
word—becomes a prime mover of the whole economic system.
When a society becomes so affluent that, far from its wants and
needs crying out of themselves for satisfaction, it becomes necessary to devote a very real part of the national effort to fabricating
them artificially, everything in both the theory and practice of
economics has been overturned. When the majority of all families
have already had not only their primary needs, but their desires
for television sets, for automobiles, for refrigerators, and the full
catalogue of 'consumer durables' satisfied: when it becomes im-
peratively necessary (in order to continue to produce at a profit)
to convince them that they need *another* television receiver,

another refrigerator and not only another, but a much longer, larger and more glittering automobile, the whole *rationale* of production for profit begins to totter. At that point the needs of men, the satisfaction of which is the sole rational object of economic activity have, like the fibres of our clothing, become man-made or synthetic: they have become secondary and derivative from the productive process itself. And with that the whole process has become circular. For any justification of capitalism to hold water, the consumer and his wants must be assumed to be sovereign. But where is that sovereignty if the consumer's wants must first be elaborately and expensively manufactured for him as a condition of manufacturing the goods to satisfy those wants? The consumer and his wants have become the mere puppets of the categorical imperative to produce at a profit. And if we ask the question why should we produce at a profit if not to satisfy natural human wants, the answer of the conventional wisdom will be that the distillation of profit is the aim and object of human activity, the primacy of which it is impious to question. When a capitalist society has reached the American degree of affluence, the manufacture of wants must at all costs be kept one step ahead of the manufacture of the goods to satisfy those wants. The image of the caged squirrel turning its wheel with every busy step it takes inevitably occurs to Professor Galbraith. The worship of production for profit now that it no longer serves the satisfaction of natural wants, has become an idolatry: how can such a thing for long provide a satisfying national purpose for adult minds?

This, however, is only the first of the consequences of taking personal self-enrichment as the national goal. It is an essential part of the system of production for profit, or capitalism, that men should only draw an income as payment for work. Therefore, in order to receive incomes, they must be kept continuously at work. If the production of goods—for which the need has had to be laboriously synthesised in advance—falters, the incomes of the producers are immediately cut off. The American family with its stock of television sets, refrigerators, automobiles, and all the rest is suddenly left without an income to buy necessities. If the effort to make such families buy one more automobile, with still larger tail fins, one more refrigerator, and one more television set ever fails, some at least of them will be abruptly cast down into a state in which they can hardly buy bread, clothing, or shelter. For their incomes—currently running at the average rate from wages alone of $85 a week—will abruptly stop. And Professor Galbraith traces the full consequences of the inherent instability which such an arrangement involves. He describes how, as an accompaniment of the advertising man's synthesising of wants, the vendor of hire-purchase has involved such families in heavy weekly payments for their last round of television sets, refrigerators, and automobiles. So the abrupt cutting off of their main wage incomes may, in the extreme case, leave them, in spite of unemployment benefit, with almost nothing to live on. (Professor Galbraith proposes the commonsense remedy of breaking the nexus between employment and income by paying unemployment benefit at almost the full wage levels whenever mass unemployment exists.)

Again, the functioning of the economy depends upon the uninterrupted investment of gigantic sums for the creation of new plant for the manufacture of a still ampler supply of television sets, automobiles, refrigerators, and the rest. If suspicion once crosses the thresholds of the board rooms that enough plant already exists to supply the American people with such things, the system must stall. Therefore, the productive system must not only be run flat out but must continually expand if a proportion of the American wage earners are not periodically to be thrown down from their affluence into the destitution of unemployment. The production of more and more things which are, in that quantity, so useless in themselves that nearly as much effort must be devoted to synthesising a need for them as for actually producing them, cannot be interrupted, upon pain of inflicting destitution upon a substantial section of their producers. The instability thus caused by the maintenance of a rigid nexus between the distribution of income and the production of things which can be sold at a profit, once a society has passed a certain degree of affluence, need hardly be emphasised. Nevertheless, Professor Galbraith does emphasise it by a searching analysis of the inevitability of inflation if an attempt is made to run such an economy continually at capacity and so to provide incomes to all its wage earners. He shows, too, that once the unpleasant effects of inflation have been felt for some time, action will inevitably be taken to check the expansion of the economy and that this can only be effective in so far as it ruthlessly deprives some millions of wage earners of their incomes. And in fact this very thing was occurring in 1958 between the completion of Professor Galbraith's book and its publication.

But personal enrichment as a national ideal has another consequence in addition to inherent instability. Not only must everything and anything be produced which will yield a profit, however little unsynthesised need there is for it, but nothing, or at least the lowest minimum, of those things the production of which will *not* yield a profit must be produced. This negative side of the worship of production for profit results in a condition which Professor Galbraith calls 'social unbalance'. (This is his second principal concept.) For it so happens that some of the most urgent of the real needs of an affluent society cannot, in practice, be satisfied by production for profit. These are broadly the needs which cannot be satisfied by the sale of goods or services to individuals, but must be catered for, if at all, by the provision of a public service. They range all the way from such *terre-à-terre*, but not unimportant services as refuse collection, street cleaning, town planning and satisfactory housing for the less well off wage earners to such life and death matters as the maintenance of law and order, education, and, finally, defence.

In a series of striking chapters, Professor Galbraith shows that twentieth-century America, by far the richest society which the world has ever known, is stinting itself to an almost insane degree of some or all of these public services. Nor is the reason far to seek. Because their provision cannot be left to private profit-seeking entrepreneurs who will themselves provide (or borrow) the necessary resources in the expectation that they will in due course be recouped manyfold, these services must be provided out of public funds raised by taxation. But in the ideology of a society which has taken personal enrichment as its goal, this has come to mean that their provision is not counted as a form of production at all. On the contrary they are regarded as grievous burdens upon the community, the size of which must be minimised almost at all cost if they are not to break the back of the economy. Municipal services, city planning, streets and roads (without which the automobiles, incidentally, cannot be either parked or run), schools, and more arms are not thought of as 'produced' but as something the community has to 'pay for'. And yet, all unknown to the public, the economists of all political persuasions add together roads and automobiles, schools and refrigerators, arms and television sets, to reach their total of the gross national product, which no one challenges as the measure of the income of the nation.

The consequences of the illusion that only that which is produced for profit constitutes wealth—that all the rest is burden and grief—would be comic if they were not so grave. Here is America, the Croesus of the nations, so rich that she diverts an appreciable part of her resources to an ever more frantic attempt to make people want things for which they have little rational use, half starving herself of essential public services. The American public have been persuaded that they cannot afford to have their garbage adequately collected, their cities properly cleaned, their slums cleared, or even enough parking places and roads built to enable them to use their third or fourth automobile. This is inconvenient and silly rather than tragic. Far more serious for the future of the Republic is the fact that the American people have been led to deny themselves anything approaching an adequate educational system for a community as rich as they are. Professor Galbraith shows that the scope and level of American education today might just be appropriate for a community still struggling with primary poverty and the early uphill tasks of industrialisation. We get a picture of cramped, inadequate, overcrowded, and under-staffed schools, unable to provide the children of the great American cities with facilities for either the work or the play which are the alternatives, for many a vigorous boy or girl, to those street activities which lead to the vast American problem of delinquency. And even in the fields of higher education, in which the quantity is indeed, by the standards of most other countries, very large, he describes a quality of instruction below that provided in many a much poorer country.

Professor Galbraith says a little as to what education at its highest, education as the development of the human being for his or her own sake, and needing no further justification, might do in so rich a community as America. But he bases most of his argument on the simpler proposition that even from the narrow objective of maximising production itself, this neglect of education is fantastically shortsighted. He explains that in the advance of modern technology the human being, the scientists, the engineer, the technician of every grade is becoming much more important than new plant. And yet in the American system, since the new plant is produced for the private profit of its builder, and the new scientist, engineer, or technician is produced at the public charge, the more that is spent on the former the richer, it is supposed, the community will become, but the less that is provided for the latter, the smaller, it is frugally concluded, will be the supposed 'burden' on production. Yet the education of future producers is almost certainly a much more fruitful form of investment, even on the narrowest calculus of production, than the construction of additional plant.

Finally, we come to the most curious effect of the illusion that all production which is not directly for private profit is not production at all. This is the effect upon defence. Now, nothing is more rooted in the lore of the 'left wing' criticism of capitalism than that defence is the one field in which a capitalist government will never stint its public expenditure. Yet present-day American experience bears out this dictum—which I have made a dozen times myself—but partially. The capacity of events in the twentieth century to outstrip our current comprehension of them and to render 'the conventional wisdom', either in its classical capitalist or its left-wing form, almost comically wrong, has become very great. In the economic field itself, the Marxist prediction of ever-increasing misery has turned out to be the reverse of the truth. It is ever-increasing affluence which is in America becoming increasingly incompatible with an unmodified capitalism. And, so curiously does history tease the prophets, that in the field of defence, a similar, if by no means so absolute, a reversal has taken place. It has not turned out to be the wicked armament contractor, avid for dividends from cannon, who rules the roost in the most advanced capitalisms. It has been, on the contrary, the American business man, fanatically determined on business as usual, and regarding defence expenditure, since it has to be paid for out of taxation, as a most unpleasant necessity, who has become the representative figure. True, dominant American opinion has not nearly the same degree of hostility to public expenditure upon defence as it has upon public expenditure upon education and the social services. Up to a point contemporary America, with a defence expenditure of nearly $40 billion, or between 10 per cent and 12 per cent of her gross national product, confirms the traditional radical view that this is the one field in which public expenditure is respectable. Nevertheless, Professor Galbraith points out that *on the hypothesis upon which the American Government is working* (he is careful to point out that he considers it a false hypothesis), namely the hypothesis of an implacable and irremediable conflict between America and the Communist world, this is certainly an inadequate expenditure. It is an expenditure which was proved inadequate in the autumn of 1957 when the soaring Russian sputniks revealed to a horrified America that even in some aspects of nuclear warfare the Russians were already ahead of them. More importantly, perhaps, if less dramatically, it was a rate of defence expenditure which had clearly left America with painfully exiguous conventional forces with which to counter Communist moves in various parts of the world, without resorting to the mutual suicide of nuclear war.

Nor is there any doubt as to the reason why the 'business man's administration' of President Eisenhower felt it necessary to cut American defence spending. The President announced the conclusion of his economic sages that there was a mystic figure of some $38 billion which American defence spending could not exceed without gravely damaging the American economy. And yet he did so at a moment when it was necessary somehow to persuade as many American families as possible that they needed still another or newer automobile, with still longer tail fins, in order to keep that economy going. Sir Winston Churchill, at an early stage of the British rearmament programme, said that 'we arm to parley'. In 1958 the most powerful nation on earth seemed to be getting herself into a position in which she would neither parley nor arm—at least on the scale which would have been necessary to support her intransigent policy. So remarkable are the effects of a fanatical adherence to personal self-enrichment as the goal of life.

These are the main concepts of Galbraith's book. There is one further concept which he discusses but only cursorily. And this inadequacy leads on to what is, in my view, the one false conclusion of the book. This further concept is that of equality. Professor Galbraith devotes a chapter to the issue and in the course of it says a number of interesting and important things. He contends, no doubt correctly, that a sort of informal truce has been arranged between American conservatives and liberals on the question of the redistribution of the national income. An appreciable redistribution in the equalitarian direction was effected under the New Deal and in the course of the war of 1940/45. (Professor Galbraith gives the figures.) Very broadly this new pattern of distribution has now been accepted as a norm. The liberals may here and there, but very feebly, try to improve on it: the conservatives, a good deal less feebly, may try to edge back towards the old unequal pattern. But in the main both sides accept the new status quo. And they do so for two weighty reasons. First, both sides are simply afraid of re-opening the fierce social struggles of the thirties, which went quite a measurable distance towards destroying that national unity which Americans, not necessarily irrationally in their conditions, value almost above anything else. Second, on the basis of the rate of expansion of the American national income annually achieved (until a year or two ago) there was far more to be gained by *both* the rich and the poor uniting to produce more than by fighting each other over a static total. Thus the sleeping dogs of social conflict have been prudently let lie.

No doubt this is all true and important. But the trouble is that Professor Galbraith does not seem to see the consequences for the rest of his argument of his own (implicit) acceptance of the present pattern of distribution of the national income. Yet surely his whole argument as to the minimal marginal utility of producing still more automobiles, refrigerators, television receivers, et al., is only valid, *given the present distribution of the national income.* He tells us that the median income of all American families was in 1956 just under $4,000 a year—say £1,000 to £1,100 a year in our purchasing power. That is marvellously high. It is quite true that for the millions of American families well above this median income, an additional automobile, etc.,

o

probably has a marginal utility approximating to zero. But
surely this is by no means true of the millions of American
families with incomes well below the median? An American family
with an income of, say, $2,500 a year or less, is by no means
affluent—(and there must be, on the figures, an awful lot of them
even apart from the 'poverty patches' in the Appalachians and
elsewhere which Galbraith rightly regards as special cases). A
better automobile, a refrigerator, a television receiver has a by no
means zero marginal utility for them. Therefore Galbraith's
argument against concentrating America's effort on the further
production of saleable consumer goods is only correct *on the
hypothesis that the present distribution of the national income is
taken as a constant.* Shift that distribution in the direction of
further equality, and an increased production even of saleable
consumer durables will become rational again. After all, the
American distribution of the national income is still by no means
equalitarian. Galbraith gives the figures in some detail on p. 66
of his book. He shows for example that the highest 10 per cent
of American incomes are twenty-seven times higher than the
lowest 10 per cent. And that over 16 per cent of all American
families had less than $2,000 a year (say £11 a week in British
purchasing power).

This consideration seems to me to modify, but not to destroy,
much of Galbraith's thesis. After all, it may still be correct to
say that the best use for unused American productive capacity
would be to provide more education, sanitation, housing, etc.,
more, in general, of the services of the public sector, even for the
worst off 16 per cent of Americans rather than more automobiles,
refrigerators, television sets, etc. Again, it remains true that to re-
open the social conflict by suggesting a more equitable distribution
of the national income is an uninviting prospect, from which it is
not necessarily craven to shrink. Yet curiously enough, Galbraith has himself proved, though unintentionally, that a more
equitable distribution is indispensable if there is to be a rational
case for increasing production, at any rate outside the provision
of public services. As a matter of fact, and whether we like it or
not, the dispute over the distribution of the national income is
bound to be re-opened now that 'the conventional wisdom'
appears to have stopped the growth of the gross national product,

as the only way by which the pundits could conceive of stopping inflation. It is, as Galbraith notes, when everybody is getting more cake, and then alone, that people will stop disputing about how big a slice they are to get.

A second omission rather than error of the book is that Galbraith says nothing of government-sponsored foreign lending to the undeveloped world as a method of employing America's productive power to satisfy genuine human needs. Galbraith is, of course, a strong and devoted advocate of such a policy. One must presume that he simply considered that the subject lay outside the scope of his book.

But to note that Galbraith has made what seem to me mistakes and omissions is merely to say he has made a book. The marvel is that he has packed so much original horse sense between his covers.

Finally, we come to Galbraith's remedies. These are sketched rather than elaborated. For as he rightly says, *destructive* criticism and analysis, and the more astringent the better, is what America needs today: she is surfeited with cloying 'constructiveness'. Still Galbraith makes clear the direction in which his thought is moving. It is, I repeat, to cut or at least loosen the nexus between the performance of a job and the receipt of an income. By means of establishing far higher—though varying—levels of unemployment insurance and other social services, and by means of far higher spending on the provision of public services, he would ensure every American family a good basic income, irrespective of the vagaries of the trade cycle. And paradoxically, in doing so he would, doubtless, greatly diminish the intensity of that cycle. In fact as I read his pages a strange thought crossed my mind. What Galbraith was really after was the provision of something uncommonly like old Major Douglass's 'national dividend': and it is none the worse for that. Major Douglass's analysis was defective, but his broad conclusion is, *for a society which has reached the American degree of affluence,* unexceptionable. After all, now that one major human community really has reached affluence, why not make at least a tentative start with the application of the simple Christian principle of distribution according to need? It would even prove to be extremely beneficial to the economy. As the late Mr George Bernard Shaw remarked: 'Decidedly, whether you think Jesus was God or not, you must admit that he was a first-rate political economist.'

Finally, let us note thankfully that Professor Galbraith's book is as much an American product as the silly tail fins on her latest and shiniest cars. And for my part I have no doubt that it is a great book. It is a major work of sociology rather than of economics. But in its own field it will stand being mentioned in the same breath with the one or two books which have made history in our period. Indeed the contrast between it and Keynes' *General Theory* is striking. Keynes' book was a technical treatise expressly addressed to his brother economists. Galbraith's work is extremely readable for any educated man or woman. On the other hand, in style and presentation, where Keynes used the rapier, Galbraith wields a club. But the blunter instrument can accomplish as much execution. In fact, let me take my courage in both hands and predict that twenty years after its publication, *The Affluent Society* will be exercising an influence comparable, though of a very different kind, to that exercised by *The General Theory* today.

(1958).

II. THE MAN

I am proud of that last sentence in my 1958 review of the English edition of *The Affluent Society*, in the 'spotting a winner' sense. True I may prove to have got the timing wrong. We still do not know what the book's reputation will be twenty years after its publication. But after four years it is undeniable that its influence, though quite different, is of the same order of magnitude as that of *The General Theory*. The very title has become the almost universally accepted name for the present state of things in the advanced Western societies. People who have never read the book, or who have not understood a word of it, or who have carefully distorted its thought to suit themselves, all talk in terms of 'The Affluent Society'. This is fame.

It may be interesting to carry the contrast between *The Affluent Society* and *The General Theory* over into the field of a contrast between their respective authors. No enterprise could, no doubt, more infuriate Galbraith's professional colleagues. His reputation with them moves inversely to the extent of his world-wide influence. For the laity to mention him in the same breath with Keynes will be thought illiterate. Well, let the professionals recollect how *The General Theory* itself was reviewed. Pigou himself wrote that 'we have seen an artist shooting arrows at the moon'. Keynes was (very temporarily) broken-hearted at the cold incomprehension of his colleagues. (See p. 187 above.)

However, it is true that *The Affluent Society*, and Galbraith's whole cast of mind, could hardly be more different to *The General Theory* and the mind of Keynes. Keynes as a matter of fact had worked out the whole outlook embodied in *The General Theory*, and the practical political programme which issues from that outlook, before and apart from the theoretical structure of his great book. It is in *Economic Possibilities For Our Grandchildren* (*Essays in Persuasion*, 1931) for example. What he set out to do in *The General Theory* was to *prove* the validity of the new outlook to his fellow economists (he says so in the Preface). For this purpose he deliberately made the book technical, erudite, exact, with plenty of equations. And, in the end, the main body of his colleagues came to agree that he had proved his point: that Say's Law was dethroned and economics had entered a new period.

But *do* the equations in fact prove Keynes' thesis? It is a shockingly irreverent question. I have always had my suspicions of these equations, partly because even I can understand them. When I first read the book I laboriously wrote out what appeared to me to be their meanings in words. And the words appeared to me to make excellent sense, but to be paraphrases of the passages in the book which, usually, either preceded or followed the equations. In a word the equations seemed to be merely shorthand versions of the arguments which Keynes was using in the body of his text.

So I wondered if *either* the equations *or* the text proved that Keynes was right, in the sense that it was certain that if governments did what he proposed the result which he promised would follow. I felt that it was probable that they did not. What the book did do was to provide a rational and persuasive argument for trying out certain 'reformist' policies for the remedy of the then intolerable consequences of capitalism. I, for one, concluded that it was a thousand times worth while to try out the remedies and see if they worked. Accordingly, at the very end of the thirties, I wrote a book called *A Programme for Progress* which, to the dismay of my then fellow Marxists, far from being the stock Marxist denunciation of Keynes, is a programme for the application of his ideas by a British Labour Government.

Now, twenty-five years later, Keynes' fundamental ideas have, in my opinion, been proved: but not by the equations and technicalities in *The General Theory*. They have been proved by the event. More or less generally in the highly developed non-communist world they have been, to a greater or lesser extent, applied by governments; and the predicted results have tended to follow. That is proof, and the only proof which there can ever be in this plaguing field of the social sciences.

What Galbraith has done in *The Affluent Society* is to leave out the equations: and not merely the equations themselves but the whole almost fantastically sophisticated apparatus of contemporary mathematical economics, upon which whole schools of economists have ridden away, far out of sight of the laity. Galbraith cannot have supposed that it would be a popular move in academic circles; nor was it. For his colleagues the main concepts of *The Affluent Society*—the dependence effect, the social imbalance, the desirability of loosening the nexus between incomes received and work done for the mass of the population—are mere speculations, since they are unsupported by 'the apparatus'. And so no doubt they are: but then so are the conclusions —if any—arrived at by means of the other economists' labyrinths of equations. Their conclusions and his can only be proved or disproved by being applied. Theory is a guide to action, no less and no more.

In effect, then, Galbraith turns his back upon the main stream of contemporary economics. He turns his face towards sociology—or more precisely towards the original form of economics, to 'political economy'. He is a political economist in the full eighteenth-century sense of the term. *The Affluent Society* is a Smithean book, and like Smith himself, its author would have been suited by a chair of 'moral philosophy'.

But, as it has turned out, no chair has proved very suitable to Galbraith's preposterously elongated form—he measures 6 ft. 7 in. He is the least 'chairborne' of fighters for the causes in which he believes; he has always been in the front line. The cause he fights for is the cause of American liberalism. And what a fight he puts up!

It must be admitted, of course, that he has a most marvellous time doing it. Over the last few years there has hardly been a government in the undeveloped world which he has not advised. He has held learned disputations with the high priests in Moscow and Leningrad. We British, even, have seen quite a lot of him as he swished through on his way out or back, eastbound or westbound on his circumnavigations. All this at least he has in common with his fellow economists. They all do it. Kaldor and Balogh and Joan Robinson and Lewis and Little from Britain—and, of course, whole fleets of them from America. They are what astronomers were to the fifteenth century, sacred cows licensed to roam through the Chancelleries and the Ministries of the world, reproving, approving, admonishing, suggesting. It must be tremendous fun.

It would be very wrong, however, to suggest that Galbraith's fight for what he believes in has always been easy or without risk. On the contrary in America let it be remembered, liberalism is still a fighting faith—a faith which for that matter has had to fight for its existence within the last ten years. And in the course of this struggle with the McCarthyite reaction, in the broadest sense of that term, Galbraith has displayed two of his finest qualities. One is courage: moral and intellectual courage of the first order; not so common a thing as might be supposed. And the second is benevolence. Moreover his is now a well tested benevolence. At very considerable risk to his own reputation and to his own political success, to which he is not indifferent, he has stood by many a man and woman who was being prosecuted for association with communism. As a matter of fact just because Galbraith is, and has always been, deeply (and in my view culpably) un-interested in communism, he has been able to go, and has gone, to great lengths in defending men and women who have had far more stormy pasts than himself. There is a sturdy, broad-shouldered quality in the man's outlook upon both economics and upon life which can hardly be too much appreciated.

A man cannot have all the gifts. And what Galbraith lacks is something which Keynes had to a greater degree than any economist before or since: the aesthetic sense. Not that Galbraith is a poor or undistinguished writer; the force, wit and verve of *The Affluent Society* puts most of the flaccid pages, not merely of contemporary works of economics, but of what are laughingly called works of literature, to shame. But there is seldom that extraordinary addition of art—of art in Pasternak's sense of the word*: of art which 'if there is a particle of it in any work which includes other things as well turns out to be heart and soul of the work'—of that something which in Keynes suddenly pierces us like a dagger.

Galbraith is now American Ambassador at New Delhi, in my—and his—estimation one of the key positions in the world. Our generation of citizens of the world is very lucky to have him.

(1961)

* See page 51 above.

Victor Gollancz

PUBLISHER and Author: Capitalist and Socialist: man of the world and latter day saint: Jew and Christian: rationalist and theologian: rebel and traditionalist.

'A man so various . . .?' But the great, sensible thing about Victor Gollancz is that nine times out of ten he has kept both his jest *and* his estate. And as for that list of opposites, well, of course, they can be called fatal inconsistencies, or the richness of a many-sided nature, according to whether you like the fellow or not. Those who are fond of V.G. will continue to say to the scoffers: 'Let him without contradictions first cast a stone at him.' Anyhow, this generous, emotional, greedy, intelligent, gorgeous and sometimes absurd, *man* is worth a hundred of the neat little *petits-maîtres* of this world.

But it must be admitted that, for the purposes of brief biography, Victor is so many-sided that, like Mistress Quickly, a man does not know where to have him. His life has had several very distinct phases. For example, there was his first great experiment in redemption through education at Repton in the First World War, of which he has himself written brilliantly in his vast autobiography. From it too the world learns in the utmost detail of his latest phase, the phase since the Second World War, the phase of international philanthropy, theology, authorship and sainthood.

On the whole, beatification has sat lightly upon him. He is far too intelligent to fail to see the humorous side of the dilemmas into which the latter day saint must hourly be thrust. But, then, one knows so few saints that the impulse to tease one is irresistible! And the teasing has a basis. For Victor is the least self-conscious of men: not the least self-critical, of course. On the contrary, his autobiography is marked, and perhaps marred, by an extreme sense of his own failings, his own errors, his own sins. True to the traditions of Hebrew Prophets and Rabbis to which he belongs, not only by race but profoundly by temperament, his cry is one of lamentation for both himself and for the world. But he is one of the least self-conscious of men in the simple and direct sense of that term: in the sense that he is sometimes even less aware, perhaps, than the rest of us of the real impulses, the real motives, which actuate him.

How odd, for instance, in *Timothy II* to find him protesting, even though with Christian humility, against a critic's charge of egotism and exhibitionism, and defending himself by saying that he tried to wriggle out of discussing his 'boyhood sexualities', but knew that he 'mustn't and couldn't' hide them! What better definition of exhibitionism could one find? Of course he is an exhibitionist and proud of it; how few of us have so much to reveal! The saints were never squeamish about their sins and sorrows. And neither is V.G. No mediaeval mystic counted the lice on his body with more satisfaction than Gollancz apologises for his own self-indulgences. He says so much in the confessional that the priest can't get in a word sideways. His gusto for life and his intense interest in himself and his own soul, his compassion, his horror of violence, his phobias and weaknesses, his boasts, humiliations and his aspirations—these pour out in his autobiography in a torrent which to some people is merely embarrassing but which others are ready to compare with those of St Augustine. It is at least as truthful as Rousseau's *Confessions*.

The new Victor, storming heaven for signs of God's grace, is not really so different as he thinks from the old unredeemed V.G. He is the same bundle of contradictions; still a rogue elephant among publishers and an idealist, saved by the gift of divine discontent. Just as today he is not prepared to find comfort in the easy discovery of a conventional God, so in the thirties he was a tireless dynamo, not content merely to publish some Left books, but ready to seize on a nation-wide response to found a Club whose object was nothing less than the prevention of the Second World War. Then, as now, he was a preacher seeking not only his own salvation but insistent on carrying us all into the fold with him. But his present phase is the direct result of the conflict of the thirties; of Marxism; of the anti-Fascist Front; of Stalin and the great purges; of the Nazi-Soviet pact and the great

Communist disillusionment. It was not after all the war, horribly
though he dreaded it, that ended that phase of V.G.'s career. It
was that, like many others, he suffered intellectual and spiritual
shipwreck, was drowned in the raging waters of our epoch, duly
died, and was reborn with a new message for his fellow-men.

It is one individual story in the trial of a generation. But it was
a trial not before fallible Courts of Law. It was trial by events;
trial by one event above all; trial by the fact that, before the middle
of the twentieth century, Communism under Stalin had become
something which Western men and women could not support.
They simply could not. It was not a question of some careful
addition and subtraction sum as to the ultimate amount of good
or ill which might be done by the establishment of a socialised
economy by Stalin's methods; it was an ungovernable revulsion
from, and repudiation of, the great secular faith and society of our
times.

It is impossible to over-estimate the convulsions in the minds
and hearts of an important number of Western men and women
which this event caused. It was by no means necessary to have
joined the Communist Party, or even to have come close to it, in
order to have suffered this convulsion. It was only necessary to
have been a Socialist. The shipwreck affected men like Gollancz
who were always spiritually remote from Communism and Russia.
Such men were affected to the very depths of their beings by the
fact that Communism and Russia had by 1940 become, beyond
the last lingering possibilities of doubt or denial, causes which it
was, almost physically, impossible to support.

It is true that the bankruptcy of the Communist ideal in the
West was not the sole cause, by any means, of the subjective crises
of the mid-twentieth century. There was plenty more besides!
There was renewed world war: there were the Nazis: there was
the Spanish defeat: there was the general social regression of the
West. But for Socialists at least it was not these horrors, in and
by themselves, that took men beyond their breaking point. For
these horrors were not in their camp; or rather they did not
start in their camp. No doubt it was the cumulative effect of
everything combined, and in a different proportion for each case;
but for Socialists what did the psychic damage were the horrors
in their own camp. For they forced the rupture in those basic

identifications which had been made by much wider circles than Communists and fellow-travellers.

Thus it may be possible, and necessary, for a man to be an apostate from a faith he has never embraced. And the apostate is never scatheless. Just as after a major war one sees '*les mutilés de guerre*' dragging themselves through the streets of a stricken country, so now the mutilated of the catastrophe of the Communist ideal in the West can be seen making their way across the face of Europe and the Americas. Such psychic mutilations are not indeed irreparable. There is a plastic surgery of the spirit by means of which men put themselves together again. But, of course, in so doing they become different. One very natural method, much used by men who were actual members of the Communist party, is to become what may be called counter-Communists, on Koestler-Chambers lines. Another popular method of reconstruction is provided by the Catholic church. Gollancz, probably because he was never near the Communist stereotype, has never been near these reconstructions either. Instead he is increasingly taking the road out of the day-to-dayishness of things: he is taking the traditional road of the Orient, and for that matter of the mystical part of the Western Christian tradition.

Does this mean that all the work of his middle period has proved to have been uselessness and illusion? It is not so, nor would he say it was so. In the perspective of twenty years, it is interesting to look back upon the effort—a considerable one—of the Left Book Club in particular. The Club was formed to prevent Hitler being allowed to start the Second World War, and to popularise Marxism in Britain. It succeeded in doing neither. But there was never a better case of failing to do what you intended, and yet succeeding in doing something quite different, but in the long run perhaps hardly less important. For what the Left Book Club actually did do was to play a considerable part in making possible the Labour victory in 1945. Nor was its influence by any means confined to Britain. It is curious today to find in unlikely places, high and low, East and West, amongst law-makers and law-breakers, minds which were sparked by the Left Book Club.

It is, of course, far too early to say by how much that achievement has deflected the march of world events. But that anything which contributed appreciably to the emancipation of India, the redistribution of income in Britain, and the first constitutional socialisation of the basic industries of a major state, had *some* effect, is a contention open to dispute by the Great Red Pedants alone. For these events may yet be found to have been the beginning, however halting, of the real forward movement along the line which is alone possible for the workers of the Western world.

If so, Gollancz's middle period, of which the Left Book Club was, of course, only one part, will have been fruitful indeed. Before these fruits are gathered, he may have departed from amongst us into the wilderness, there to set us a pattern for our imitation. If so, his interest in the results to which the work of his middle period have contributed, will be less than ours. Not that Gollancz has ceased to be a Socialist; but his attention shifts from Socialism towards salvation—from the Third Symphony to the C Sharp Minor Quartet. That has been his way of putting himself together again.

(1954)

Walther Rathenau, Dr. Schacht and The German Tragedy

THE history of every great nation is tragic: but the history of Germany is more tragic than any other. She developed into the last stage of capitalism ahead of any other nation: and then she gave that type of economy an almost inconceivably horrible form. In the history of Germany during the first half of the twentieth century we are confronted with what occurs if the attempt to provide a democratic environment for the last stage of capitalism fails: if the democratic forces do not set up those central controls which have become indispensable: if the levers of power are grasped by the hands of criminals, who are half the agents, and half the masters, of the owners of capital.

The possibility of the last stage of German capitalism developing in a democratic political environment, and so taking on a relatively beneficial form, appeared for a brief period, and then was blighted. It was incarnated in the life and death of one man, Walther Rathenau. His career, his doctrines, and above all his death, acted out, as it were, the alternative social forms which the last stage can take. He was the incarnation or avatar of the better possibility: in his actions and his writings he strove for it: but his fate pointed inexorably towards the dark alternative.*

Walther Rathenau

Walther Rathenau was born into the topmost circles of German big business. His father, Emil Rathenau, had begun life as a typical small, competitive, independent owner-manager capitalist, with his own little North Berlin iron foundry: a figure from the economic textbooks of the last century. And then, in middle life,

*It was Lord Boothby who, many years ago, first called my attention to the significance of the life and death of Walther Rathenau.

Emil Rathenau was caught up by the surge of technical development of the eighteen-seventies and eighties. At the 1881 Paris
exhibition he bought the European rights for Edison's patents in
the incandescent electric lamp. In a few years he became the
leading figure in the German electrical industry; he founded
the AEG—the German General Electric Company. By the first
decade of the twentieth century he had become one of the new
type of capitalists. For he was both the director of the vast AEG,
and had also interlocked that firm with a dozen others, including
the leading banks of Germany. And even this was only the
beginning. German industry, this late comer to the gargantuan
feast of world capitalism: German industry which had still been, in
the eighteen-sixties, the industry of a half feudal country—often
employing Emil Rathenau's iron foundry, for instance, on making
the scenery for Meyerbeer's operas—was now rushing forward
into its last stage with a velocity far greater than British industry,
and at least as great as American. And Emil Rathenau had a son.

This second Rathenau, Walther, was thirty-three years old at
the turn of the century. Though born into the industrial purple,
he had been compelled, in the fierce commercial tradition of
his family, to spend his early manhood in making good on his
own as a business man. And it was not until he had, after severe
struggles, made a success of a small enterprise that he was, in
1899, invited to join the Board of AEG. The new director must
have seemed an apparition indeed to his colleagues. To say that
he was an intellectual is an under-statement which amounts
almost to misrepresentation. He was an intellectual in a sense,
and to an extent which perhaps only a German, and a German
Jew at that, can possibly be. Rathenau himself described his
joining the Board of AEG as follows: 'In 1899 after I had spent
seven years in the little manufacturing town of Bitterfeld, the
undertaking began to prosper. I decided to retire from industry
in order to devote myself to literature.' (And he already was a
considerable *littérateur*, a metaphysician and an author!) 'But,' he
continues, 'the AEG invited me to join the Board of Directors and
take over the department for constructing power stations. . . . I
built a number of stations—e.g., in Manchester, Amsterdam,
Buenos Aires and Baku . . . in 1902 I joined the management of
one of our big Banks. . . .' By 1909, instead of having devoted

himself to literature, Walther Rathenau was associated with eighty-four large German concerns, either as a member of the Supervisory Board or as Managing Director, and with twenty-one foreign enterprises.

Nevertheless, all this was only one side of his activities. He had at the same time become a considerable figure in German Court society, and to some extent in German public life, and he had begun to write books and to express views on social and economic questions. In order to try to give a contemporary British or American reader an idea of his position, it would be necessary to imagine that Keynes, at the height of his career, had been, in addition to the author of his books, a figure in the most influential governing circles, had been Chairman of the ICI and the Midland Bank, and had been on the Board of most of the other principal British enterprises.*

In 1909 Rathenau wrote these fateful words: 'Three hundred men, all acquainted with each other, control the economic destiny of the Continent.' In one sentence he outlined the profile of capitalism in its last stage. It was a sentence that was not to be forgiven him in big business and official circles. For the folk-lore of the system still required the preservation of the myth of a self-regulating, fully competitive system on the old model. And here was one of the oligarchs himself announcing that in fact the system was now centralised in, and controlled by, the hands of a knot of super-directors! But worse was to follow. Rathenau not only dared to describe the system as it was. He began to suggest what ought to be done to change it. In a series of books and papers he began to advocate a political programme to which the nearest analogy would perhaps be provided by a mixture of the British Labour Party's 1945 programme and the American New Deal of the nineteen-thirties. There were to be a redistribution of income by high, progressive, direct taxation, including in-heritance taxes so high as virtually to prevent the passing on of wealth from one generation to another, the nationalisation of natural monopolies, and various measures for the 're-organisation', i.e., further centralisation, with some State control, of industry—a little on American NRA lines.

* The main sources used are Count Harry Kessler's biography, *Walther Rathenau* (Gerald Howe, 1929) and Rathenau's own works.

Such a programme is unmistakably akin, also, to the conclusions which emerge from the body of economic theory which
Keynes was to elucidate thirty-five years later. But that is far
from saying that Rathenau's books were in the least like Keynes'.
With little of Keynes' insight into economic theory, Rathenau
made a typically German, typically metaphysical approach. His
earlier works were, on the face of them, as much philosophical
and even mystical, as political or economic. One of them was
called *The Mechanism of the Mind*. In a sense they were far
more radical than Keynes', in that they envisaged, more or less
clearly, what a Socialist would call a classless society. But they
did so in an almost wholly Utopian way, by discussing what was
good in the abstract and should, at some unspecified date in the
future, and in some wholly unspecified manner, come into existence.

Rathenau and the War Economy

The outbreak of the First World War saw Rathenau still only a
supremely successful millionaire oligarch of big business, who,
unaccountably and irritatingly enough, had these strange fancies
about the future. True he dabbled in politics by writing articles
criticising the narrowness and shallowness of the Kaiser's
Government from the point of view of a liberal patriot who
earnestly desired his country's welfare under its present régime.
No one took that very seriously. But Rathenau had far too
intelligent a mind not to be shaken to the core by the cataclysm
of 1914. In the early months of the war it was found that the
German Government, and the German General Staff in particular, which had planned the strictly military side of the war in the
utmost detail, had given scarcely any attention at all to the
planning of the economic and industrial basis upon which all
their military power depended. In particular they had omitted
to notice that the war machine uses up raw materials at an
astronomical rate. Literally within a few days, they saw that they
would be soon running short of one after another of the fundamental raw materials of industry. In panic they sent for Rathenau.
On August 9th, 1914, he was given a desk in the War Office as

P

director of the 'War Raw Materials Department', and told to provide the German war machine with what it needed. His difficulties were extreme. He was subjected to a degree of non-co-operation on the part of the rest of the War Office which rose to a point at which, during one night, a partition was secretly built across the long room at one end of which he and his department worked, so that there might be a Ghetto-wall between the officers, gentlemen and Aryans of the War Office proper and the dirty Jew who was doing something squalid about industry at the other end of the room. Yet this organiser of genius, almost single-handed, conquered the effects of the British blockade, and somehow conjured the raw materials indispensable for the whole German war effort out of the air. (In the case of the most acute shortage of all, nitrogen, that is literally what he did; for, after requisitioning every ton of existing stock, he got going the new Haber-Bosch process of extracting nitrogen from the atmosphere just in time to prevent the German armies running completely out of ammunition on both the Eastern and the Western fronts.) Rathenau was a patriotic German working for his country: but never did work of genius have more terrible results both for his country and for himself. For Germany, he uselessly prolonged the war for nearly four years without changing its issue; and as for himself, his countrymen thanked him with a bullet.

Rathenau's war work, in fact, went a good deal farther than the organisation of the supply of raw materials. Arising inevitably out of the necessities of that work, he soon found himself setting up bodies which he called 'War Industrial Companies', which handled and allocated the scarce raw materials. Anyone familiar with the consequences of the war-time organisation of industry in any major combatant country in either world war will appreciate that it was not long before the whole of German industry was tightly organised upon a planned, state-controlled, instead of a competitive, basis.

By the middle of the war Rathenau had done this job and had either resigned, or been made to resign, from the Government service. He was free to write books on the lessons of war organisation for the post-war world. These war-time books of his (especially *In Days to Come* and *The New Economy*) are far more political and concrete than his earlier works had been. True he

still formulates his goal in a way that sounds fantastically metaphysical to Anglo-Saxon ears. That goal is 'the overcoming of
mechanisation through a realm of the soul'. Imagination boggles
at the idea of any British or American big business man talking
like that! But what he meant by this high-flown phrase was, he
made clear enough, a non-commercial, much more equalitarian,
planned economy—in a word, a socialist and classless society
such as has always been the goal of every school of socialist
thought. Nevertheless Rathenau's whole approach remained in
one decisive respect fundamentally non-socialist and indeed anti-
socialist. Even in these later books there was no hint of the social
agency by which the mighty changes which he advocated and
predicted were to come about. He is full of sincere pity and
remorse for the lot of the working class. But the workers remain
for him people who must be helped, uplifted, planned for—
patronised. The conception that it may be the workers themselves
together with the mass of the population, who are the real people
who will effect the social transformation which he desires, never
enters his head, or, if it does do so for a moment, it is dismissed
as a crude illusion of the socialists. In a word, he stayed strictly
within the compass of his governing-class world even when he was
advocating its total transformation.

The Isolation of Rathenau

The effect of such an advocacy by a man in Rathenau's position
can be imagined. This time his books sold by the tens of thousands
and were passionately discussed. But in the governing and middle
class worlds they merely infuriated their readers. All the normal
reactions provoked by the spectacle of the millionaire radical
came into play. That this super-tycoon, this trust and cartel
manipulator, this king of capitalists, this Jew, should now start
lecturing people about how to set up Utopia—it was too much!
Moreover, big business for the first time had a startled suspicion
that Walther Rathenau actually meant some, at any rate, of the
things which he said! It began to use its giant powers against him.

On the other hand, he himself ensured that there should be no
rapprochement with the world of German labour. He was totally

out of sympathy with, and ignorant of, socialism in any form. He was not only a millionaire of millionaires, but he was in some, although not all, respects a snob. He was that strangest and saddest thing in a man of his people, a race snob, worshipping pathetically at the shrine of the blond, Aryan Prussian. Finally, he never lost an opportunity for displaying his hatred and contempt of Marxism. And this last was a far more important factor than it would have been in Britain and America. For the German socialists were rigidly orthodox Marxists, albeit of the most conservative and frozen type.* Moreover they contained several leaders like Kautsky and Hilferding who, whatever their faults, were men of deep erudition and wide culture; they cannot have escaped the impression that Rathenau was painfully re-discovering for himself some of the commonplaces of Marxist theory, while stridently rejecting other and equally important Marxist tenets, such as the central and indispensable role of the wage earners in the struggle for social change.

Rathenau and the Patriots

The net result was total isolation. By 1918 he was one of the most discussed, but one of the most distrusted, men in all Germany. And then, at the moment of the collapse of the régime which he had come to criticise so severely, he committed an act which seemed finally to sunder him from the new forces to which he might have given so much. And yet it was a simple and sensible act. In the autumn of 1918, it will be recalled, Ludendorff (for whom Rathenau had had a typically discreditable *faiblesse*) and the General Staff, seeing that victory was now out of the question, lost their heads and proposed what amounted to, and in fact became, Germany's unconditional surrender. The blond overlords of Germany, the super-nationalists, the super-patriots, showed themselves to be lacking in elementary courage and elementary good sense. For, it is now clear, an offer to negotiate a peace which admitted defeat but not surrender, followed if necessary by a stubborn German defensive effort in

* I know of no record of any attempt by Rathenau and Edward Bernstein, the revisionist, to meet.

the West, for which Germany had substantial resources, freed by the collapse of Russia, could very likely have forced a negotiated peace on the Allies.

Rathenau, on October 7th, seeing this simple fact, and being above all else a German patriot, called for a *levée en masse* and an all-out effort to defend the fatherland from invasion in case a German offer to negotiate, instead of surrender, was refused. The Generals would have none of it—they feared the very sound of that word *masse*. And the workers, strained almost beyond endurance, and now told by the military leaders themselves that all was lost, saw in Rathenau only a man who wanted to prolong the war. Thus, when there actually occurred that revolution which could alone make the application of ideas such as his possible, the people who made it regarded him with even greater suspicion and dislike than the reactionaries! It was a perfect example of the folly of the intellectual in politics: or rather of the intellectual with the wrong training. For Rathenau's error was not that he had too much insight into the social process, but that he had too little. In particular his insight was hopelessly one-sided. His immense business experience and his splendid mind allowed him to see the mechanics of the economy almost perfectly. He understood excellently what ought to be done to make the last stage of German capitalism work by means of progressively modifying its nature. But the psychology—which is to say the politics—of the social process was a closed book to him. The dullest drudges of either the Nationalist or the Social Democratic parties instinctively understood better than he the way in which the minds of people would reflect the realities about them. The hack politicians knew from hard-won experience how the crises of our times come into the consciousness of men, and how alone, therefore, they can be appealed to, and perhaps led *towards*, at least, constructive action.

The extraordinary thing is, indeed, not that Rathenau ruined himself politically, but that, for a fleeting and tragic moment, he recovered his position, held office and power, and paid for so doing with his life. The German revolution was a sufficiently long-drawn-out, chaotic and at the same time constitutional process for any man of Rathenau's consummate ability to have more than one opportunity. By 1920 the first phase of the revolution was over. An uneasy equilibrium between the social forces had established itself. The Kapp Putsch of the open reactionaries was defeated in March of that year. On the other hand, the impetus of the revolution had been largely dissipated. Men of middle views began to form the governments. In this situation a friend of his, Dr Werth, became first Finance Minister and then Chancellor, and began to use Rathenau. In 1921 Werth made him Minister for Reconstruction. This was the proper post for him, and if he could have occupied it for some time, and if, but only if, he could have found a way of collaborating with German Labour, it is possible to believe that he might have modified the further development of the German last stage economy in the democratic direction. It was not to be. In the first place, within six months of his joining the government the Democratic Party, of which Rathenau was, rather nominally, a member, happened to withdraw (quite temporarily) its members from the Cabinet because the Allies gave part of Upper Silesia to Poland. Superficially this enforced resignation did not seriously interrupt Rathenau's career. For within a few months more, in January, 1922, he was back in the Cabinet as Foreign Secretary.

Rapallo and Russia

But this accidental change of post may have been decisive. For it took him from the economic and industrial sphere in which he had expert knowledge to the sphere of Foreign Affairs. He was one of the few Germans in a ruling position intelligent and courageous enough to see as early as this that German capitalism had at that time absolutely no alternative but co-operation, on almost any terms, with the West—while, of course, seeking any counter-weight it could possibly find in the East. But this necessity was soon to become obvious. And this was the, in retrospect commonplace, Foreign Policy which Rathenau pursued. It took him to the great Genoa Conference and to the signing of the Rapallo treaty with the Russians. It is this last act for which, oddly enough, he became chiefly famous, or, in conservative circles, infamous. In fact, the signing of a treaty with the Russians at that particular time and place, and in that particular form, may or may not have been a wise move on the part of the hard-pressed German Government. But that *some* German Government, of that period would in *some* way or another play the gambit of seeking support from Russia as a last resort, and in order to bring the West to reason, can be seen in retrospect to have been something obvious and inevitable. If Rathenau had not happened to do so, some other Foreign Secretary would have. There was really nothing distinctive or personal about it.

So much the greater is the irony that it was this act that led him to his death. Contact with the Bolshevists was in fact the one possible way of asserting some German independence before the all-powerful West. But because that contact was made by Rathenau it was represented as the final proof that he was the author of a 'Jewish-Bolshevik-internationalist-capitalist' plot—indeed that he was the author of that 'plot' which was to haunt the imaginations of those blond Aryans whom Rathenau so admired for the next twenty-five years; of that 'plot' obsession which in the end drove the German people to the most awful collective dementia suffered by any nation in human history.

Rathenau had been back from the Genoa Conference only a few weeks when a young ex-naval officer named Kern shot him to death as he was driving to the Foreign Office. Kern was that very type of young German for whom this Jewish intellectual had been unable all his life to repress his infatuation. Rathenau was betrayed by what was false within. In the end it was his inability to break with the old Germany, and identify himself with the new, which was struggling unavailingly to be born, which undid him.

If Rathenau had lived

Rathenau's career was one of the great might-have-beens of history. It is not that his ideas were particularly profound—politically they were often extremely naïve. But he was perhaps the first man to sense one of the possible lines of development which a society in the last stage of capitalism can take. What in fact his ideas really amounted to was the attempt to give a democratic character to the *central economic authority* which, his enormous business experience convinced him, had now become indispensable. He understood—none better—he had been an arch-builder of cartels and mergers himself—that the old automatic self-regulating mechanism of capitalism in its competitive stage was fast disappearing. He realised that *some* form of control from the centre was indispensable. The real question at issue was to be—should or should not that new central control be responsible to the people? And he sincerely wished that it should be.

Whether, if he had lived, he could have significantly contributed to guiding German development along these lines is, of course, another matter. He might well have had the opportunity to do so. In the latter part of the nineteen-twenties the Weimar Republic made a real and, at first, not unsuccessful effort to cast German last-stage capitalism into a democratic mould. The period of 'rationalisation' combined with Stresemann's foreign policy of 'fulfilment' was one in which Rathenau would have been eminently at home. And it may be that if Rathenau had been a Minister in these periods he would have found ways of building up a less fragile and precarious economy than was in fact erected.

But for him to have done so two conditions would have had to have been fulfilled. First he would have had to find his way to collaboration with the German Labour movement. And this would not have been easy for him. In this respect Rathenau resembled Keynes. He never even attempted to cross the river which runs between the world of big business and government, and the world of Labour. Moreover that river was far wider and deeper in Germany than in Britain: although even in Britain it was (and to some extent still is) deep enough, even if it is often invisible. It proved far easier for brilliant men of the world of capital to put forward even the most daring ideas within their own world than to take one step towards the world of Labour.

And the second thing which Rathenau would have had to do would have been to evolve a technique by means of which a last-stage capitalism in a democratic political setting could have been made reasonably stable. For nothing is now more obvious than that no democratic society can long withstand economic instability of the degree which struck Germany in 1929. Whether Rathenau could have evolved such a technique of economic

stability on behalf of German Democracy is a question which can
never be answered. His difficulties would have been immense.
Germany's economic position was very weak, even in 1929.
Keynes had not discovered his new body of theory. Both of the
recent democratic attempts at economic stabilisation and control,
namely the American New Deal and the British post-Second
World War programme, were far in the future.

It is thus impossible to believe that Rathenau, or anyone else,
at the end of the nineteen-twenties, could have succeeded in fully
shielding democratic Germany from the effects of the great slump.
But this is not to say that his influence, if he had been near the
centre of power in those years, might not have been decisive. For,
as we shall see immediately, the actual leaders of German democracy pursued a policy of insane economic pedantry, a policy
exactly calculated to intensify to the uttermost degree the
catastrophic consequences of the world slump. And even then
the Nazis only conquered by a hair's breadth! Thus there exists
a possibility that a man of Rathenau's incomparable industrial
experience, resourcefulness and contrivance, would have succeeded at least in mitigating the effects of the slump sufficiently
to have preserved the German democratic environment. Even the
fact that he seems to have known little economic theory would
probably have proved an advantage. For it was the rigid, doctrin-
aire, fanatical adherence of Dr Bruenning and his economic
advisers to pre-Keynsian theory which was, above all, their
undoing.

The Breakdown of Weimar

Such speculations serve only this purpose. They illustrate the
suggestion that Walther Rathenau in his life and death incarnated
the initial attempt to establish a democratic environment for the
last stage of German capitalism. If that attempt had succeeded, the
history of the world would have been different indeed. The
dynamic of German industry might have been harnessed, by the
action of powerful counter-capitalist forces, to raising the
standard of life of the German people. And then, as the contradiction between its nature and such a purpose became too

great, German capitalism might have been steadily modified
(although not, of course, without profound political struggles)
until it ceased to be a predominantly capitalist system at all.
After all, such a development seemed at one time by no means
inconceivable, even to such an observer as Frederick Engels in
his last years. For the German wage earners possessed by far the
most solid and effective organisations, in both the industrial and
the political fields, of any of the wage earners of the major
capitalisms.

The history of German capitalism has, however, known no
such happy endings. In the event Rathenau was murdered and
the Weimar Republic broke down; and it broke down, above all,
because it never learned how to manage its economic system.
Then at length, and far more terrible and disastrous even than
these failures, there appeared the appalling phenomenon of
success under anti-democratic auspices. The Nazi servants of
Hell found a way to make an economy in the last stage of capitalism
work only too effectively. And they used the vast powers so
generated to shatter themselves and the world.

For a time after Rathenau's murder it looked as if the democratic institutions which had been established by the revolution
had, after all, taken root in German soil. It is true that for two
more years they were subjected to frightful strains and stresses.
German democracy in 1922 and 1923 went through the staggering
experience of seeing a currency inflation carried to its logical
conclusion: German money, that is to say, actually did become,
at one moment, virtually valueless and this highly developed,
complex and still rich society was left without any effective
medium of exchange. The fact that anything like this was allowed
to happen was a sign of the immaturity and incompetence of the
democratic authority. Serious inflation was no doubt inevitable
in the circumstances and with the limited degree of existing
experience in the overall control of a last-stage capitalism. Nevertheless any really determined Government could and should have
done in 1921 or 1922 what was in fact done in late 1923 and early
1924 to stabilise the currency. For what was above all necessary
was to overcome the resistance of that section of big business
which was making immense profits out of the situation. It was
pitiful that the German Social Democrats and Democrats who

controlled the Government did not produce a man who could do the job. For at the last moment, in 1923/24, the job was done *for them* by a man who was far from being one of their number. It was done by Dr Hjalmar Schacht, who became Reich Currency Controller in the autumn of 1923 and subsequently President of the Reichbank. This was the first appearance upon the page of history of a figure who, as we shall see, was destined to play what was in some respects the most baleful role of all. Nevertheless, for the time being, in the mid-twenties, it appeared that German Democracy had, in spite of everything, won through. True it had not itself mastered the inflation, but it had in the end hired Dr Schacht to do so for it. Moreover the other fearful strain to which it was exposed, namely the violent ill-will of the powers which had defeated Germany in the First World War, culminating in the French occupation of the Ruhr, no doubt cut both ways. It created, of course, terrible difficulties: but, on the other hand, it provided a convincing alibi for the German democratic government's own failures, both over the inflation and over much else.

Rationalisation and Oligopoly

At any rate, from 1924 to 1929 a period of marked recovery and economic reconstruction set in. This was the period of 'rationalisation'. Rationalisation was essentially a name for the process of carrying much further than it had yet gone anywhere else, the process of increasing the size and diminishing the number of the units of economic life. Attention was often at the time focused upon the technical aspect of rationalisation; and it is true that important new capital investments greatly improved the productivity of much of German industry. But, side by side with this technical process, the network of interacting trusts, associations and cartels, to which Rathenau had pointed in 1917, was carried many stages further. This was 'oligopoly', as we should now call it, with a vengeance. Indeed, in many spheres of the German economy it definitely went further than the pattern of oligopoly as we know it in America and Britain today, and became outright monopoly in one form or another. The essential result, as we shall see immediately, was that prices ceased to move of themselves and came under the control of the oligarchs. And that was the end of real competition over a wide field of German industry.

When in 1929 the slump struck Germany this new feature of the economy greatly contributed, in the absence of any overall, central control, to her undoing. For, of course, the industrial oligarchs who could (partly) control *their* prices did not drop them when all the other still freely competitive prices around them began to tumble. Between December, 1930, and December, 1932, for example, the free prices of raw materials and semi-manufactured goods dropped (1926 = 100) from 68.3 to 45.7, while the 'cartel prices' dropped only from 97.1 to 83.7. One can imagine the social and economic consequences which such figures reflect. They mean, of course, that, while all the remaining small businesses were being ruined, the cartels were for a time surviving pretty well. Here was lop-sidedness with a vengeance. Here is the record of the process by which the whole surplus of the community is sucked up into fewer and fewer hands. But in this case the lop-sidedness went so far that in the end the cartels themselves were ruined, for they had nobody solvent left to trade with. By ruining all their competitors they had in the end ruined themselves.

' Uneven Development '

This process was only one aspect of that 'uneven development' which was itself the general and underlying factor producing the German, and for that matter the world-wide, collapse of 1929. There were special weaknesses in German capitalism which amply account for the especially catastrophic character which the slump there assumed. How catastrophic it was, is now perhaps in danger of being forgotten. Even two or three figures can illustrate the steepness of the descent. They are taken, as were the above figures on prices, from *The Economic Recovery of Germany, 1933/1938*, by C. W. Guillebaud (Macmillan). The German national income fell from 76.0 milliard Reichmarks in 1929 to 45.2 milliard Reichmarks in 1932. The receipts of German agriculture fell from 10.0 milliard Reichmarks in 1928 to 6.5 milliard Reichmarks in 1932. Finally unemployment had risen by 1932 to some 7 millions! (Out of a labour force of wage earners of under 20 millions.) All in all it is often calculated that the real standard of life of the German people was cut in half during those three years!

It is, surely, a measure of the continuing unwillingness of many observers to acknowledge the economic motivation of great events, that they look further for an explanation of the collapse of German democracy. Naturally all sorts of historical and psychological factors played a part in, and gave a particularly national and local colouration to, the catastrophe. 'Hitler', we used to be told, 'was born at Versailles'. That may be. But the fact remains that he would have remained a mere monstrous curiosity, on the lunatic fringe of German politics, if German democracy had succeeded in fulfilling the first and most elementary duty of any government, namely to feed and employ its people. All sorts of other reasons can be advanced for the fall of the Weimar Republic: they are not so much false as otiose. How *could* any system survive which was unable or unwilling to prevent such miseries as are reflected in the above quoted figures from descending upon its people?

For now, in the first years of the nineteen-thirties, German democracy allowed *deflation* to run its full course to its catastrophic logical conclusion, just as nearly ten years earlier these same democrats had allowed *inflation* to run its full course! The very conception of the overall control of the economy seems to have been absent from the minds of these impotent men! Was it, however, that German democracy was *unable*, or was it that it was *unwilling*, to prevent the social catastrophe of deflation from being played right out to its logical conclusion? No doubt it was both. On the one hand, the necessity of, and the technique for, the central control of a now inherently unstable last-stage capitalism had not been recognised or discovered. And, on the other hand, there was, on the part of orthodox economic opinion, which had the ear of the German Government, a fanatical determination not to interfere with the, supposedly, natural and beneficial working out of the (largely non-existent) competitive process. This suicidal economic pedantry was itself, in part, the

expression of the fact that 'leaving things to work themselves
out', although it produced ruin and agony for the German
people, was calculated in the long run to bring vast *relative*
benefits to the great trusts, who it was felt would alone survive
the deluge.

Be that as it may, on two separate occasions the Bruenning
Government deliberately and drastically accelerated the process
of deflation. In 1930 all official salaries were reduced by 6 per
cent: the tax on wages and salaries was increased from 1 per cent
to 5 per cent: the sugar tax was doubled: the rate of the turnover
tax increased from .75 per cent to 2.0 per cent: and unemployment benefits were slashed. But even this was only the first dose!
In December, 1931, all wages subject to collective agreements
were cut by 10 per cent. Cartel prices, rents, railway fares and
municipal services were also cut by 10 per cent, and official
salaries were cut by another 15 per cent! The effects of all this
can be imagined. Coming on top of a heavy drop in demand for
German exports, which the world slump was in any case im-
posing, this drastic reduction in home purchasing power went
fully halfway towards bringing the economy to a total standstill.
Just as the German inflation of the early nineteen-twenties is
likely to remain the great inflation of all time, so the German
deflation of the late nineteen-twenties will remain, with one
possible exception, the great deflation of all time. Those disastrous Germans did nothing by halves!

It may be said that the Bruenning Government, in all the
circumstances of that time and place, had no alternative but to
carry the deflationary process through, cost what it might. It is
not true. We now *know* that it is not true, for the anti-democratic
governments which overthrew Bruenning found that there was an
alternative course, and by adopting it rapidly carried the economy
back to full activity. There was an alternative. But what is true is
that, in order to avoid the murder of German democracy by
deflation, the Bruenning Government would have had to adopt
drastic and far-reaching controls over the economy—controls,
above all, over the foreign transactions of its citizens. As it was,
the leaders of German democracy, besotted as only Germans can
besot themselves with a theory, drove on to doomsday. The
economic doctrines to which they madly clung had been more

or less applicable to capitalism in its earlier competitive form, but had become almost meaningless when applied to a capitalism far advanced in its last stage. And so the German democrats perished miserably.

Illusions as to the Nazis

The tortured German people were amazingly faithful to a democracy which was refusing to allow them to gain their livelihood. Even in 1932 the central mass of the wage earners, and a part of the peasants and middle classes, were still supporting the democratic parties. It was not enough. The Communists had gained sufficient strength fatally to divide the strength of the wage earners, and the Nazis had gained almost, though not quite, half of the electorate as a whole. There is no need to retell the sordid story of the final deals between Hitler and German big business, the General Staff, and the landowners, which brought the Nazis to power. As all the world knows, by the summer of 1933 every element of German representative democracy had been destroyed.

It is agonising, even now, to recall the illusions which every section of democratic opinion, and still more Communist and Marxist opinion, entertained as to the economic possibilities open to the new Nazi Government.* It was taught as an article of faith, above all by the Communists, that it was by definition impossible for any government, such as the Nazis, which would not expropriate the capitalists, to alleviate, far less to cure, mass unemployment. It was this article of faith which alone explains, although it does not justify, the manifest complacency with which the Communists regarded the Nazis' accession to power. This complacency led them, it will be recalled, to proclaim almost up to the last that the democratic parties were their main antagonists, and to allow them to take part in *ad hoc* joint activities side by side with the Nazis, as in the Berlin transport strike. For, of course, it is a fact that, if it had proved true that the

---

* Illusions fully shared by myself at that time; but illusions which I had already shed by 1939, vide my last pre-war book, *A Programme for Progress* (Gollancz, 1940).

Nazis possessed no effective remedies for the paralysis of the German economy, then they would not have proved formidable. If after the Nazis had come to power mass unemployment had persisted at anything even approaching the seven million level, the revulsion of feeling against them would no doubt have been seismic. In that case the Communist calculation that 'we shall come next' might have proved correct. Thus in the case of the Communists also it was a mad adherence to dogma which was their undoing. In common with all Marxists they had seen that the developments of the last stage were making capitalism far more unstable and lop-sided, nationally and internationally, than ever before. But they utterly failed to notice that a strong central authority could, *actually without undue difficulty*, control those tendencies, harness the system, and drive it in any desired direction!

Yet so it proved. With horror, anti-Fascist opinion began in the mid nineteen-thirties to realise the inescapable fact that the Nazis were succeeding in re-animating the German economy. For some time it was possible to explain away the supremely distasteful figures. It was possible to say that the trade cycle was now in its ascending phase internationally. It was possible to try to overlook the fact that, while mass unemployment was only alleviated in Britain and America, it had actually disappeared in Germany. It was possible to go on predicting that this or that novel economic control imposed by the Nazis must inevitably 'bring the whole crazy edifice crashing to the ground'. It was possible for a long time. But heads buried ever deeper in the sand become less and less in touch with reality. I recollect, for example, the incredulity and sense of outrage with which the work from which most of the figures given in this essay are taken, was received. Mr Guillebaud's *The Economic Recovery of Germany, 1933/1938*, is well worth re-reading today. I cannot say that I think that the sense of outrage was altogether misplaced. It still seems to me a scandal that this well known British economist could, in 1938, publish a full review of the Nazi economy without including, almost literally, a single word of condemnation of the supremely criminal methods, purposes, and ideology which that economy was being made to subserve. But if a sense of outrage at Mr Guillebaud's omissions was not misplaced, incredulity of his facts and figures most emphatically was.

The success story of the Nazi economy which he had to tell was only too true. By 1937 the seven million unemployed had almost all been reabsorbed into the productive life of the nation: full employment had been achieved. Industrial production, at 1928 prices, was 33.7 milliard Reichmarks in 1928, fell to 19.6 milliard Reichmarks in 1932 and rose to 40 milliard Reichmarks in 1937. The total returns on German agriculture had been raised by at least 30 per cent. True the standard of living had not risen as sensationally as these figures would in themselves suggest. It was far above the terrible level of 1932, but had not, it is usually estimated exceeded the best year of the democratic régime, 1928. This is borne out by the fact that, while the production of capital goods had more than trebled, the production of consumption goods had not quite doubled. And, as one would expect from such figures, profits had risen from 13.7 per cent to 16.0 per cent of the national income, while the real earnings of a wage earner who was lucky enough to be in employment in 1932, as well as in 1937, had only gone up on the average about 8.0 per cent. Nevertheless, when due allowance has been made for this worsening of the distribution of the national income, the massive gain in prosperity and security for the mass of the population is wholly undeniable.

The Nazi Measures

By what black magic, as it seemed to most contemporary observers, had the thing been done? As a matter of fact, the Nazis had merely applied, albeit with whole-hearted vigour, measures for the restoration of full employment which have now become a commonplace of almost all informed economic and political discussion. They had simply applied those obvious remedies of 're-flation' which follow naturally from Keynes' critique of the loss of inherent stability in latter-day capitalism. They had restored the balance of the system, by organising the scattered independent, mainly agricultural, producers into a counter-cartel, thus endowing them with bargaining-power: they had at the same

Q

time very slowly raised industrial real earnings from their 1932 level, which, it must be recollected, were, *for a still employed worker*, themselves high, since prices had fallen catastrophically, and they had applied specific measures of re-flation, mostly of the public works character: land drainage, motor roads, house building and repair, and, of course, rearmament. In a word, they had distributed money to people for doing various things, such as draining land, building roads, making guns, or, at one stage, simply for getting married! It did not really matter, *economically*, what they spent the money on. They spent it. In doing so they automatically incurred a large budgetary deficit (see below) which they easily financed by internal borrowing. This budget deficit measured roughly the amount of new money which they put into the system. There was no more to it than that.

The ' Balance of Payments ' crises

There was 'no more to it than that' so far as the internal structure of the German economy was concerned. But what of its external economic relations? In order to envisage the external problem we must take a slightly closer look at the character of Nazi financial policy. When the Nazis took power it was said by the Marxists that they could accomplish nothing because it was inherently impossible to 'overcome the contradiction of capitalism'. On the other hand, orthodox, pre-Keynsian capitalist opinion proclaimed that they would be helpless because 'Germany was bankrupt'. In so far as people meant by this dictum that the *internal* German financial mechanism had largely broken down— that there was 'no money' to finance new enterprises—they were, of course, guilty of a primitive type of economic thinking—on a distinctly fetishistic level. The Nazis made short work of such arguments by simply issuing a sufficient quantity of government credit in the form of 'bills' which the contractors for their public works could discount with the banking system, and so pay their wages and other costs. This was, in effect, simply an indirect way of printing the necessary money. And, as the wheels of the economy had ground to a halt for lack of money to spend in people's hands, it was the very thing to do.

The figures illustrating the means by which the Nazis 'spent their way out of the slump' are, in essence, simple. Between 1932 and 1938 the German Government increased its annual expenditure of all kinds over fourfold, namely from 6.7 billion Reichmarks to 31.5 billion Reichmarks (of which 24 billion Reichmarks was, by 1938, on armaments). But how could a bankrupt government, inheriting a bankrupt country, with a frightful budget deficit, possibly pay for such expenditures? 'Where did the money come from?' The answer is that by 1938 taxation (of all kinds) was bringing in 19.7 billion Reichmarks, leaving only 11.8 billion Reichmarks to be financed by internal borrowing. This was perfectly manageable. In a word, the mere fact of having gone ahead and spent had resulted, as it always must, in the money paid out flowing back (if the money is not allowed to go out of the country), in one way or another, into the government's hands. The reality is not the circulation of the money, but the decision to spend, to act, to build. (For details of these figures see *A Programme for Progress*, p. 266.)

Thus no *internal* financial obstacles in fact existed to German recovery. All that was necessary was a determined Government with a will to act and the nerve to spend. The orthodox financier's pedantries could be, and were, brushed aside. But in so far as the economists were referring to Germany's *external* economic relations, they were pointing to a real problem. Since Germany was far from self-sufficient, but had, on the contrary, to import substantial quantities of raw materials and food, she was severely handicapped by such facts as that in 1932 she had virtually no reserves of foreign exchange or gold, that the world owed her nothing, and that she owed the world a great deal. This, in effect, meant that Germany had to earn by exports on current account all, and more than all, which she spent on essential imports. All this has a familiar sound to British ears in the nineteen-fifties. But in fact Germany's balance of payments problem in the nineteen-thirties was much the more acute. Repeatedly between 1933 and 1939 the Nazis found that they were importing more than they could pay for, that they were not exporting enough, and that their last reserves were running out. Balance of payments crises succeeded each other in rapid succession.

The Nazis learn the Trick !

At first sight this issue seems to resolve itself into one of finding some method by means of which a controlled last-stage capitalism can put aside enough of its annual product for export to pay for necessary imports. Even this, however, is not a simple business for an economy which has only imperfect and indirect control over what is produced and where it is sold. In the last resort there may be no effective way of making manufacturers cultivate the export market except by cutting down their home market. But this means reducing the effective demand of the home population by deflation, and if such deflation is carried an inch too far, it may put the economy into the vicious circle of depression.

Moreover, the mere provision of sufficient exports to pay the bills of the country's necessary imports is far from being the whole problem. On the contrary, there are many other purposes for which the citizens of a capitalist country pay out money to foreigners as well as buying imports from them. They may wish to send their money abroad because, on balance, they think it will be safer and more 'productive' (i.e., it will earn more profit) there than at home. This, if it becomes a strong impulse, is called 'a flight of capital'. Or again, they make take the view that the exchange rate of their country's money with foreign money is going to go down. In this case, if they change their money into foreign money betimes, they will make a profit or avoid a loss. This is speculation on the foreign exchanges. Either means that some of the reserves of gold or foreign exchange which have been so painfully earned by means of exports is spent without buying any imports at all. And as these movements of money 'on capital account', or for speculative purposes, are by nature of unlimited extent, they can totally wreck any controlled last-stage capitalism in a few months or weeks, by denuding it of its reserves and so making it impossible to import. This is an inevitable consequence of the ownership of liquid capital remaining in the hands of private persons.

How did the Nazis deal with this life and death issue? They acted (under, as we shall see, expert guidance) with both ingenuity and vigour. They, of course, instantly established a system of exchange control by means of which it was made

illegal to send money out of the country without the permission
of the Government. Without this they would have been bank-
rupted, in the specific sense of being unable to pay for their indispensable imports of food and raw materials, in a few months. For,
although much capitalist opinion was far more favourable to
them than it ever is to a democratic government which is attempting to operate a controlled last-stage economy, Jewish capital was
naturally passionately anxious to fly, and this alone would have
been quite enough to destroy them. They faced, however, still another difficulty. German democracy had borrowed very large
sums from abroad. This had been partly inevitable, in the sense
that it was the only way of meeting the unmanageably high
Reparations payments on which the victors of the First World
War had tried to insist. Some of the borrowed money had been
well spent on increasing German productivity. But some of it
had been badly and extravagantly spent on unproductive public
works for which, in the twenties, Germany ought certainly not to
have used money borrowed from abroad. Moreover, by the thirties
the world-wide deflation had greatly increased the real burden
of this foreign debt, since the value of money had sharply risen.

It was obvious that Germany could not pay the stipulated
services of these accumulated foreign debts. Again under the
aforementioned expert guidance, the Nazi Government dealt
with them skilfully. Not all the skill in the world, however, would
have availed if the Nazis had not encountered creditors who were
remarkably complacent in the matter of seeing their debts
written down and even written off. The explanation of this
complacency is, of course, political. The foreign creditors of
Germany were at heart far more friendly to the right wing,
dictatorial Nazi Government than they had ever been to German
democracy. Hitler was their champion against Communism. For
that, not only his atrocities, but even his debts, were forgiven him.
The indulgence of property owners cannot go farther.

Exchange Control

But even all this was not enough to solve Germany's balance of
payments problem in the thirties. Because of the political shock,

which, after the horrors of the inflation of the nineteen-twenties, it might have caused, the Nazis were unwilling to devalue the mark, when their level of costs and prices got out of line, as it did, with the world level. Accordingly Dr Schacht devised for them an extremely intricate system of special export marks (Aski marks as they were called) by means of which, in effect, premiums on exports were given. (At the same time this system helped to ensure that the foreign exchange earned by exports really was spent on essential imports.) Moreover vigorous efforts were made to save imports by means of increasing home food production and the production of substitute, synthetic, raw materials. On the whole these efforts were successful. Germany was chronically short of foreign exchange, and at intervals there were crises in which she was threatened with running out altogether. But she never did run out: and the Government never lost control of the movement of money out of the country on capital account.

This ability to control the *foreign* transactions of its citizens is the acid test for any government, whether democratic or dictatorial (except perhaps the American) which is attempting to control a last-stage capitalism. Unless such a government can do this it will never even have the chance to apply its other measures for redressing the lop-sidedness of the economy or for re-animating it. Instead it will be sucked into the maelstrom of the totally unregulated world market and lose all control. For a time, of course, if the world market happens to be in its expanding phase, all may go well. But that will simply be luck; control of its own economy means, above all, control of the relations of that economy with the outside world.

But how, the reader may well be asking, did it come about that the Nazis showed such remarkable economic skill? Hitler and his associates always prided themselves on their total ignorance of economics. How was it that where all the learned men of Weimar so egregiously failed, they succeeded?

In part, no doubt, it was just *because* of their economic illiteracy that the Nazis could do what seemed the impossible to all their predecessors. For their ignorance freed them from the body of nineteenth-century economic theory, grown ludicrously inapplicable to last-stage capitalism, which hung like a millstone round the necks of the Weimar Republicans. But sheer ignorance alone would not have been enough. Ignorance could, and did, remove their inhibitions, but it could not have given them the remarkable expertise in the control and management of a last-stage capitalism which the Nazi Government exhibited in its first six years.

The explanation is provided by a man. It was Dr Hjalmar Schacht who did the job. Schacht possessed both a complete freedom from, and contempt of, the *laissez-faire* pedantries and inhibitions of the democrats, and a high degree of expertise in the conscious management of a contemporary capitalist economy. Schacht was the quintessential 'practical man': the technocrat of finance and administration: the man who makes things go—without knowing or caring whether they are going to heaven or to hell. We may accuse Keynes of failing to see his own theories and acts in the context of history. Schacht, on the other hand, never even troubled to develop a body of economic theory of any kind. He just knew from experience that capitalism was no longer self-equilibrating, and he was supremely confident that he was the man to control it. Nor did he care on whose behalf he did the controlling.

Dr Schacht the Second Avatar

We noted above that it was Schacht who took over the control of the currency, and later the whole financial machine, on behalf of the German democrats in 1923. And he stopped the inflation for them. By 1930, however, Schacht could see that German democracy was riding for a fall. He opposed the rake's progress by which every emergency was met by still larger borrowing from abroad, for he realised that this process could not possibly go on in face of the world slump, which had already begun. In 1930 he resigned from the Presidency of the Reichbank. Nor, perhaps, can he be blamed for having done so; for there was little sign that German democracy was willing even to contemplate the drastic measures of control which would have been necessary to save it.

It was not Dr Schacht's resignation from the service of German democracy for which he is to blame. The stain which will for ever

discolour his name is that he put his vast abilities at the service
of the Nazis. Hitler reappointed him President of the Reichbank
and later Minister for Economic Affairs. From then on till his
quarrel with the Nazi Government immediately before the war,
he was at the controls. It was, above all, his ability and his work
which made possible the immense economic successes of the
Nazis which have been described. In the 320 pages of self-justification which Schacht published in 1948 (*Account Settled*,
Weidenfeld and Nicolson) he cannot help emphasising the immense success of his measures. He cannot help pointing out the
immense reinforcement of the Nazi régime which his conquest
of unemployment and general restoration of prosperity brought
about. And yet all this is incongruously interlarded in his text
with denunciations of Hitler, the Nazis and all their works.

' A Practical Man '

And yet it would be wrong to suggest that Schacht was himself
a Nazi.* He was something more subtly dangerous: he was the
mechanistically practical man. His own general outlook, as it
emerges from his book, is that of any ordinary German big
business executive of his day: nationalist; intensely property
conscious; conventional; philistine. It was only in his quite
exceptional degree of insight into the sort of things which had to
be done in order to run a last-stage capitalism that he differed
from many another banker or business man of his circle. In the
event, and again like the rest of his friends—the bankers, the
Ruhr barons, the Generals—he was quite willing to put himself
at the disposal of the Nazis. But it was *his* services which proved
decisive. Unless he had enabled them to conquer unemployment,
and to do so without sacrificing the internal or the external
stability of the economy, the Nazis could not have survived. It
was, above all, Schacht who saved them. All his denunciations
of Hitler, all his detailed account of the part which, he tells us,

---

* It is immensely characteristic of Dr Schacht that he is still alive. As these lines
are being written he is still in the banking business. When almost every other
major actor in the ghastly scenes of the German tragedy has been assassinated,
hanged, shot, or committed suicide, or simply died, Dr Schacht lives on.

he took in the plot to arrest Hitler in September, 1938, and in the subsequent plots to murder Hitler during the war, cannot make us for one moment forget that it was Schacht who made possible the success of Hitler's régime. He tells us that he did it, not for the Nazis, but for the sake of the German people. But, even accepting for a moment his declarations that he all along loathed and despised the Nazis, he evidently never considered what would be the effect of restoring prosperity to Germany under *such auspices and for such purposes.* Too 'practical' a man to have any interest in the final goal or purpose of policy, he ignored the fact that success on behalf of the Nazis was a ten times greater crime even than failure on behalf of the democrats. The aphorism of the twentieth-century French mystic Simone Weil, 'It is better to fail than to succeed in doing harm', would have meant nothing to him. And so the supreme tragedy occurred. The fabulous Rathenau, the learned Hilferding, the pious Bruenning, all failed to manage things on behalf of German democracy even sufficiently well to provide a livelihood for the German people. And then Schacht, this typically unthinking figure of big business, succeeded in the same task on behalf of Hitler. His success on behalf of such a master and in such a cause has half destroyed the world.

Even now we perhaps underrate the immense power which its *economic* success conferred on the Nazi régime. It made inevitable a collaboration with the Nazi régime on the part of the mass of the German people. They collaborated because the Nazis had made it possible for them to work and live, while the German democrats had left them to starve and rot. No crimes, no horrors, no abominations could turn a people, which had experienced what the German people had experienced between 1914 and 1933, from a régime which had restored to them jobs, wages and security. Nor must we suppose that the memory of this contrast has yet disappeared. I recently asked a young German girl of the working class, now in England, who had been an adolescent when the Nazi régime fell, what she thought of Hitler. She thought a moment and then replied with the utmost simplicity, 'Oh, he was a man who looked after the people.' She was not a Nazi; she had had no part or lot in the crimes of the régime. Its anti-semitism, its race-hatreds, its war-lust and all the rest of it seem to have passed her by, without either attracting or repelling her. The *one* impression which the Nazis had made upon her was that they had provided a stable and secure economy in which the German people could work and live. But that impression was indelible. Such was the work of Schacht.

Was Rearmament Inevitable ?

It remains to examine the character of the economy which Schacht and the Nazis succeeded in constructing. A series of interrelated issues confronts us. First, was rearmament, as is so often asserted, an integral and indispensable part of the Nazi conquest of unemployment? Second, was war itself in turn the inevitable consequence of such rearmament? Third, was the type of economy which the Nazis built a variant of last-stage capitalism, or was it, as is sometimes asserted, not a capitalist society at all? Let us deal with these points in turn.

The question of whether a last-stage capitalism which has fallen into slump can in practice be re-animated by a rearmament programme alone is a complex issue, part economic, part political, part psychological. Schacht, in his self-justification, naturally argues that there was no need for the object of Nazi state expenditure to be guns; they could just as well have built more autobahns, more houses, more equipment for German industry, etc., etc. This, he implies, is what they did do at first and while his influence prevailed; it was only when he lost favour that all-out rearmament set in; and then, far from it proving an asset, it began disastrously to overburden the economy.

There is truth in this argument, if the problem is looked at from a strictly and narrowly economic standpoint. Armaments are economically merely one type of public works, and a million pounds, marks or dollars spent on guns might be expected to have neither more nor less effect on the economy than a million pounds, marks or dollars spent on draining land, making roads, building houses, or what you will. Moreover, as we have seen, public works as a whole are themselves only one method, and that by no means the most important or effective, of re-animating or re-dressing an economy. A budgetary deficit produced simply by remitting taxation on the mass of the population, social services financed by the taxation of the rich, the reinforcement of the bargaining power of the farmers by their state-effected cartelisation, and of the wage earners by protecting the Trade Unions, are all more important measures. All these measures *could*, in principle, have been taken in Germany in the nineteen-thirties. True, some of them, such as protecting the Trade Unions, were not politically available to the Nazis. But others, such as bolstering the bargaining power of the farmers, were actually used by them.

This takes us to the limits of a narrowly economic consideration of the matter. Clearly, however, some methods of re-animation are *politically* impossible for a democratic government, and others are *politically* impossible for a dictatorship. The Nazis could not have strengthened the Trade Unions instead of destroying them. The fact that Trade Union strength had been destroyed reconciled the German capitalists to full employment. Otherwise they would probably have felt that full employment would have too seriously strengthened the wage earners' bargaining power. But without Trade Union strength there was little prospect of the distribution of income becoming such as would allow of the consumption of the final product of the German economy, producing for peaceful purposes at full blast. Therefore some destination other than useful consumption for that final product had to be found. And armaments were the obvious answer.

On balance, therefore, it is probably true to say that, while there was no logical economic *necessity* for rearmament, yet *such* a government as the Nazis would in practice almost inevitably turn to it as their main method of restoring full employment. And, in fact, they did so.

We can now ask the further question: Could the Nazis have refrained from going to war, when by the late thirties they had created a prosperous and heavily-armed Germany? The answer must be again that *economically* they could have. It would have been quite possible, economically, to carry on the Nazi system indefinitely. The 1937 or 1938 levels of armament expenditure could, for instance, have been held constant, ever new types of weapons being substituted for old, while the increase in productivity was allowed to raise the standard of life. The thing could have been done. But can we really imagine the Nazi Government doing it? The answer must surely be that we cannot. The whole ideology of Nazism was designed to make, and did make, such a stabilisation impossible. It was an ideology of conquest. Nor were economic attractions, as distinct from necessities, lacking for such conquests. While the economy *could*, no doubt, have been carried on on the 1939 basis and within the 1939 frontiers, it could, the Nazis felt, be carried on far more *profitably* by enlarging those frontiers.

Was it Capitalism ?

In this matter, then, we should be particularly careful to avoid talking in terms of absolutes, inevitabilities, and 'laws'. On the one hand, it is not true that a controlled last-stage capitalism *must* embark on a policy of conquest and war. But, on the other hand, it certainly *may* do so and there may be very great conveniences and attractions for it in so doing. Indeed, its natural 'set' will be in that direction, and it will take powerful non-capitalist forces to divert its development into other channels.

And this in turn brings us to the third question, namely: was the fully developed Nazi economy a version of last-stage capitalism, or was it some form of non-capitalistic system? The answer cannot be in doubt. The Nazi system was the contemporary example of last-stage capitalism in its dictatorial or totalitarian form. This, or some variant of this, is what happens if the counter-pressures of democracy are finally removed from a highly developed last-stage capitalism.

In the Nazi example the resolution of social forces which the régime represented drove with unexampled singleness of purpose towards conquest and war. As we have seen, the Nazis, with Schacht's help, succeeded in running the German economy at full speed again: but they did so by heading it direct for war. The very internal changes, efficient and beneficent as they would have been in other hands, all tended, in theirs, in the direction of the abyss. In applying overall controls, in instituting a realistic financial policy, even in such things as organising the farmers, they drained the competitive element ever more completely out of the economy, and this 'took the brakes off', as it were.

By smashing the bargaining power of the wage earners, they left nothing to balance the overwhelming pre-eminence of the great trusts and cartels. For a time, perhaps, their own state power, based upon their support amongst the masses of the German people, exerted some counter-pressure. But, especially towards the end, in the war years themselves, the great German trusts seem to have come very near to the horrifying logical conclusion of the process of capitalist monopoly. Existing in, not a counter-balancing democratic environment, but in the environment of a totalitarian régime and a war of conquest, the vast organisations of the German economy began to take on a truly nightmarish character. They began to carry on their relations with other firms, and more especially with other *foreign* firms, not at all by the methods of commercial competition, but instead by the methods of conquest and military annexation. And even within Germany the great trusts, in their Hitlerite incarnations, seem, towards the end, to have been more and more ceasing to operate by means of the purchase of 'labour-power' from free wage earners, and to have been increasingly adopting a recruiting programme of direct enslavement.

What this meant in actual practice may be studied in the accounts of the last phase of the Nazi economy. For example, a recent American book entitled *Generals in Grey Suits*, by Josiah E. Dubois (The Bodley Head), gives a memorable description of this last phase taken from evidence presented at the Nuremberg trials. The lamentable degree to which this work has been sensationalised should not blind us to the evidence which it adduces to show that after each one of Hitler's European conquests the greatest of all the German combines, I.G. Farben, forcibly 'bought', at knock-down prices, the chemical industry of the conquered state, and added it to its already prodigious industrial empire.

Far more sinister still is the account given of the organisation by I.G. Farben of vast new synthetic petrol and synthetic rubber plants, as convenient adjuncts to the most ghastly of all the Nazi murder camps—of Auschwitz itself. It appears that the gentlemen of the I.G. 'Vorstand', or Management Board, tiring of the process of attracting workers to their plants by offering them wages, saw in the Jews, the Poles, the Socialists, the Czechs, the Communists, the French, and the other victims of the Nazis, a limitless supply of slaves to be had at cost price. Not content with setting up their new plants conveniently adjacent to Auschwitz and its ovens, they organised a camp of their own called Mono-witz, as a sort of annexe to the other establishment. Moreover, they appear to have conducted this private concentration camp of their own with a savagery not only equal to, but exceeding that of the Nazi Government. In fact, they drew down on themselves the shocked protests of the SS themselves for working their labour to death with an uneconomical rapidity!

This, of course, simply means that the eternal characteristics of slavery, wherever it has existed, from Peru to Georgia, had reappeared in the Germany of the nineteen-forties. Moreover, it means that a last-stage capitalism, working in a dictatorial political environment, tends to become a slave state. It becomes so as soon as competition disappears from the crucial labour market also. For then the employers—transformed into slave owners—attempt to wring by force the entire surplus out of finally power-less workers. In such a system 'the labour problem' is reduced to one simple question: At what speed is it most economical to work your labourers to death? This important issue was earnestly debated between Roman Senators on their Latifundia two thousands years ago, by the squirearchy of the old South, in the last century, and between the gentlemen of the I.G. Farben's Vorstand and the SS in our own day. Such is the end towards which latter-day capitalism, in a dictatorial environment and bereft of all democratic countervailing forces, inevitably drives.

A Footnote

In the event the Nazi example of last-stage capitalism in a dictatorial environment drove, not to world enslavement, its intended destination, but to its own destruction and Germany's. But Germany's destruction proved temporary. Horribly maimed, with her Eastern provinces amputated and re-peopled with Slavs, bisected by the world-frontier between communism and capitalism, Germany and German capitalism, it is staggering to relate, has now fully risen from the dead. The extraordinary vigour of her people, combined with the passionate desire of the American Government, in particular, to revive West German capitalism, plus the almost incredible degree to which Russian methods have made any form of Communism stink in the nostrils of the German people—these factors, taken together, have produced that extraordinary phenomenon, that Lazarus capitalism, the Federal German Republic.

It is still too early, however, to do more than note the existence of this remarkable phenomenon. We do not yet know what its nature or development will be. But it is, inevitably, with mixed feelings that the other peoples of Western Europe greet this *revenant*. About its vigour, its rapidly growing wealth, and finally its intensely *capitalist* character, there can be no doubt. For the moment the German economy has in some respects returned to the earlier and more competitive phase of capitalism. The sheer extent of the physical destruction, as well as the de-cartelisation measures imposed by the occupying powers, have helped this return. Again the German Federal Republic is at present a democracy, under any realistic definition of contemporary democracy. Its government, that is to say, is responsible to a parliament freely elected by universal suffrage. The character or tendency of that government could undoubtedly be changed by the German voters giving their votes to parties other than those which they have so far, in a majority, supported. And, equally important, West Germany again possesses a stable, massive and genuinely independent Trade Union movement.

In a word, the scene is again set for the attempt to establish a democratically controlled central authority for the regulation of German last-stage capitalism. For one thing is certain. Some strong, central regulating authority will again become necessary. German capitalism will not run itself. It is certainly not self-equilibrating, even if it is now somewhat more competitive than it was. As soon as the first rush of reconstruction is over the familiar problems will reappear. Then will come the testing time. Can or will the reconstructed German democracy of the Federal Republic succeed where Weimar failed? There is no insuperable economic obstacle to its doing so. We now know that a last-stage capitalism can be regulated and controlled. Sufficiently resolute democratic governments can do the job, although it can only be done, in the end, by so complete a remodelling of the economy that the word 'capitalist' ceases to be genuinely applicable to it. But can or will West Germany produce such governments?

(1958)

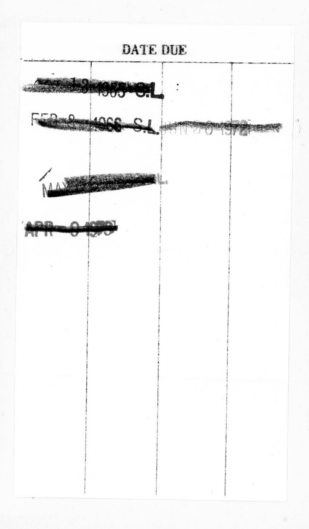

DATE DUE

JAN 1 3 1965 C.L.

FEB 8 1966 S.I. JUN 2 6 1972

MAY

APR 9 1970